D1087691

The Literary Imagination

The Literary Imagination

Studies in Dante, Chaucer, and Shakespeare

Derek Traversi

Newark: University of Delaware Press
London and Toronto: Associated University Presses

© 1982 by Associated University Presses, Inc.

Associated University Presses, Inc.
4 Cornwall Drive
East Brunswick, N.J. 08816

Associated University Presses Ltd
27 Chancery Lane
London WC2A 1NF, England

Associated University Presses
Toronto M5E 1A7, Canada

Library of Congress Cataloging in Publication Data

Traversi, Derek Antona, 1912–
    The literary imagination.

    Includes bibliographical references and index.
    1. English literature—History and criticism—
Addresses, essays, lectures.   2. Dante Alighieri,
1265–1321. Purgatorio—Addresses, essays, lectures.
3. Chaucer, Geoffrey, d. 1400. Canterbury tales—
Addresses, essays, lectures.   4. Shakespeare,
William, 1564–1616—Criticism and interpretation—
Addresses, essays, lectures.   I. Title.
PR161.T7   1983   820'.9   81-50650
ISBN 0-87413-198-7   AACR2

Contents

AUTHOR'S NOTE

Four of the essays that make up this book—those on Dante and Chaucer—appear for the first time in print. The three Shakespearean studies expand and reconsider ideas already advanced, in part, in my *Approach to Shakespeare* (New York: Doubleday), published in its latest form in 1968. Any critic's perception of great works of literature is bound, if it is to remain valid, to develop and change with the passage of time, and it is my hope that there is enough that is new in what I have written to justify their publication at this time.

In quoting from the work of the authors studied, the following editions have been used: Dante Alighieri, *The Divine Comedy,* trans. Charles S. Singleton, Bollingen Series (Princeton, N.J.: Princeton University Press, 1970–75); Geoffrey Chaucer, *Works,* ed. F. N. Robinson, 2d ed. (Boston: Houghton Mifflin Co., 1957); William Shakespeare, *The Complete Works,* ed. Alfred Harbage, Pelican text, revised (Baltimore, Md.: Penguin Books, 1969).

The Literary Imagination

1

The Theme of Poetry in Dante's *Purgatorio*

THE early cantos of the *Purgatorio* are marked by one of the most significant and humanly appealing transitions in Dante's poem. One comes to them, if one reads them as the poet intended, with the long journey through Hell present as a vivid memory in the mind. It has been a long and relentlessly downward journey toward the center of ultimate darkness, where Satan draws to himself and feels converging upon his ice-bound person the forces of negation that press downward, following their own law of deadening inertia, upon the material core of the created universe. It has also been a journey marked by the increasing absence of communication: the souls in the ten "pouches" of the *Malabolge* (the eighth and penultimate of the nine circles of which Hell is composed) are inexorably separated from all contact with one another in their respective compartments, and those in the ultimate ditch of *Cocyto* are fixed with varying degrees of grotesquerie and horror in the isolating ice fanned by Lucifer's batlike wings in the twilight world—"less than night and less than day" (*Inf.* 31. 10)—in which the ultimate death of the spirit is consummated in absolute negation and hatred.

Among the human manifestations that have died at the bottom of the infernal pit is poetry, including—we must understand—that of the poet-traveler himself. The successive stages of the infernal journey have been marked to an

11

ever-increasing degree by what one might call a deliberately created anti-poetry: a verse marked by the use of powerfully "unpoetical" images, clashing and dissonant sounds and harsh rhymes, with an increasing concentration on the ugly, the deformed, and the grotesque as appropriate reflections of the infernal reality. It is only after we have lived these experiences with the traveler of the poem, sharing imaginatively the successive stages of his alienation and mortification—for the Dante who "swooned," humanly if misguidedly, in pity for Francesca's story (canto 5) is also the Dante who treats Bocca (canto 32) and Fra Alberigo (canto 33) with cruel, if "just" inhumanity—that we can respond to the full meaning of the poet's cry of relief as he enters on a new stage of his work: "Ma qui la morta poesì resurga" ("But here let dead poetry rise again" *Purg.* 1. 7). As a creative manifestation of human life, poetry could not exist where life itself was submitted to denial. Now the time has come to reaffirm its place in the living order of things; and since Purgatory, unlike Hell, is a state where logic prevails, where things hang together and are sustained in their approximation to the reality that embraces and sustains them all, the process of its recovery will correspond to the stages of the traveler's advance toward the right, the *natural* ordering of his human experience.

The process has about it, then, a logic that governs its successive stages and answers to the presence of a structuring principle that distinguishes Purgatory from Hell. It is important to have this logic in mind as we read, and to respond to each stage in its development by recognizing its meaning for our own experience. After nine cantos of ante- or pre-Purgatory, which contain some of the most delicate and appealing episodes of the entire poem, we follow the two poet-travelers as they ascend the seven terraces of the Mount on which the human spirit is purged of the burden of sin (cantos 10 to 27), and finally enter the Earthly Paradise with a Dante who has recovered his freedom, who no longer requires the guidance of Virgil and is at last ready for the meeting with the transformed Beatrice, which has been foreseen from the beginning of the poem as the goal of his journey. The process recorded in the journey is one of justification, the "making just" of a soul that fulfills its potentiality by understanding its nature truly and by living in accordance with what it has come to understand. In the course of its progress toward this end, the soul comes to appreciate reality under many of its aspects—religious, political, amatory, and personal, to name a few of the most important—and to weave each of its component strands into a continually developing pattern. Poetry is one of these strands, both important in its own right and significant in relation to the rest; but because Dante *is* a poet, because he is coming to see in his work the justification for a life that has consisted largely of failure and disappointment,[1] it can reasonably be presented as crucial in its relation to the greater whole.

The theme of poetry, then, more particularly in relation to Dante's own poetry, will play its part in the *Purgatorio* interwoven with other themes, which will progressively emerge as connected and mutually illuminating. In the first eight cantos—those dedicated to ante- or pre-Purgatory—the emphasis lies on the recovery, after the infernal experience, of distinctively human attributes—on relationship, friendship, love—and among these poetry has its part to play. It is significant that Dante's first exchange with a purgatorial soul (if we exclude the encounter with Cato, who guards the access to the Mount, but who is not permitted to climb it) is with a friend who is also an artist. In Hell, he has met souls to whom he was attached in life by bonds of admiration and friendship—we think, very notably, of his master Brunetto Latini in canto 15—but there the reality of the infernal condition stood between them, poignantly but irrevocably, as an impediment to full communication. Now, however, Dante meets a soul who comes forward to embrace him

> con sì grande affetto,
> che mosse me a far lo somigliante:

("with such great affection that he moved me to do the same": 2. 77–78.)

a soul who greets him with a smile (2. 82), "gently" (*soavemente:* 2. 85), and who refers to the "love" that united them on earth and which still moves him in his new condition:

> Così com'io t'amai
> nel mortal corpo, così t'amo sciolta.

("Even as I loved you in my mortal body, so do I love you freed from it": 2. 88–89.)

Dante, in response, salutes the shade of his friend, naming him with a superbly effective directness, "Casella mio" ("Casella mine": 2. 91): simple but deeply moving words, which require for their full appreciation the renewed memory of Hell, where such a salutation would be unthinkable.

Having affirmed in this way the continued force of their renewed human contact, and with the infernal experience still very alive in his mind, Dante addresses his newfound friend in words that refer directly to the artistic concerns which united them during their earthly lives:

> Se nuova legge non ti toglie
> memoria o uso a l'amoroso canto
> che mi solea quetar tutte mia voglie,
> di ciò ti piaccia consolare alquanto
> l'anima mia, che, con la sua persona
> venendo qui, è affannata tanto!

("If a new law does not take from you memory or practice of the songs of love that used to quiet in me all my longings, may it please you to comfort my soul somewhat, which coming hither with its body is so wearied": 2. 106–11.)

Dante's words are variously relevant to the present state of the journey. He expresses himself in awareness of what it has meant to bear the physical burden of his mortality to this point: in awareness also of the moral cost that the journey through Hell has imposed upon him and of the need to receive relief ("consolation") from the experience he has undergone. Equally, however, he is aware, in the presence of Cato, that a "new law," appropriate to the resurrected condition that he is now entering, may require him to renounce "memory or practice" of the "songs" that he once wrote under the inspiration of what he called "love": songs the writing of which used to "quiet" all his "longings," but which may now—inasmuch as they may have rested upon what he is now being brought to see as an inadequate, or incomplete conception of "love"— become obstacles to his further progress.

The recognition of the need to move onward, to accept renunciation as a necessary condition of continued life, is present at this point and affects the poet's sense of his meeting with his friend and fellow artist, but a very real part of his human nature clings to the remembered past and is given in Casella's reply, which consists in his singing of a musical setting, composed by himself, to one of Dante's own lyrics:

> "Amor che ne la mente mi ragiona"
>   cominciò elli allor sì dolcemente,
>   che la dolcezza ancor dentro mi suona.
> ("'Love that discourses in my mind,' he then began so sweetly that the sweetness still within me sounds": 2. 112–14.)

Dante's poem was a song inspired—as all poetry, and indeed every creative effort is—by love: a love that stirs to emotion, but that is also capable of intellectual apprehension, of moving the mind by reason. The two aspects, of spontaneous feeling and rational understanding respectively, are rather complementary than mutually exclusive.

The purgatorial process will be largely devoted to achieving this right relationship, which finally will be made manifest at the summit of the Mount; but, meanwhile, the effect on the band of listening souls is such as to make them listen, "rapt and attentive . . . as content as if nothing else touched the mind of any" (2. 116–18). The reaction is exquisitely touching, a recall to that tender humanity which is now reborn after its extinction in Hell; but the law of the new order—the law of life properly understood—requires of those who have willingly accepted it that they move on in mindfulness of their further destination. To live, in purgatorial terms, is to recognize incompleteness: and so Cato brusquely interrupts this communion in art and urges those who have joined it to the further fulfillment of their destinies:

> Correte al monte a spogliarvi lo scoglio
> ch'esser non lascia a voi Dio manifesto.
> ("Haste to the mountain to strip off the slough that lets
> not God be manifest to you": 2. 122–23.)

For all its beauty, which has been so movingly celebrated, poetry must not become an occasion for delayed fulfillment. To understand it fully requires an onward progress, an integration into a continually developing understanding of its relation to the rest of life. Only in the light of this understanding can poetry itself become something more than an unreal refuge: only so will the poet himself realize his work in the fullness of his potential.

The next reference to poetry, in canto 7, concerns the exchange between Virgil and the Provençal poet Sordello. It is marked once more by the gentle humanity that so movingly prevails in this part of the poem. Sordello is stationed "apart," watching the passage of the two poets, "a guisa di leon quando si posa" ("after the fashion of a couching lion": 6. 66): but when Virgil approaches him with a request to point out the way for their further ascent, the first words of "the gentle leader" ("il dolce duca": 6.

71: the tone of the references to Virgil is subtly shifting, becoming closer and more intimate in the new surroundings) are a reference to his own city of Mantua, which prompts from Sordello the outburst of emotion implied in his response:

> O Mantoano, io son Sordello
>   de la tua terra,
> ("O Mantuan, I am Sordello of your city": 6. 74–75.)

and leads to an affectionate embrace between the poets.

The episode, however, is something more than a repetition of Dante's own meeting with Casella. Virgil and Sordello, as shades, are able to carry out their embrace, whereas Dante, as a living and corporeal presence, has been prevented from achieving his. The full sense of this new meeting, in which Dante is only a spectator, begins to emerge when Sordello challenges his interlocutor to name himself and receives a reply that points to the essential pathos of Virgil's condition:

> Io son Virgilio; e per null' altro rio
> lo ciel perdei che per non aver fé.
> ("I am Virgil, and for no other fault did I lose Heaven than for not having faith": 7. 7–8)

Sordello's immediate response is a gesture of reverence that is full of meaning in relation to the deeper sense of the poem: a gesture in feudal terms, as of the vassal to his lord, whom he approaches in humility and "embraces . . . where the inferior embraces" (7. 15): kneeling, in other words, and clasping him round the knees. The sense of the gesture in relation to the conception of the poem is apparent. The lesser poet, who is a Christian and therefore capable of salvation, salutes the greater in recognition of his inferiority: this is the first declaration of a theme that will in due course be carried to its fulfillment in the meeting with Statius.[2] Poetry, it seems, is not enough to ensure salvation, and reliance upon it beyond a certain point can become an obstacle to fulfillment: but meanwhile two poets, separated in their earthly lives by time and belief but united by their origin in a single city, offer by their recognition of a common "civility" an example to a world that stands in desperate need of it. The long apostrophe, in canto 6, to "Italy enslaved" (6. 76–151) is not an irrelevant digression but is essential to the developing theme. The poet, like other men, is a "citizen" and needs to justify his nature as such and to incorporate this justification into his work. The special concern, which the nature of his art imposes upon him, for the language that is the instrument of his craft, involves a responsibility that can only be fulfilled in recognition of the public implications of his work. In this way, one more theme is in the process of being woven into the complete design at which the poet is aiming.

It is only, however, when we pass from ante-Purgatory to the Mount proper that the themes of art and poetry can begin to receive logical development in relation to the larger design. Ante-Purgatory has been, justly and necessarily, a place of waiting: the souls at the foot of the Mount are neither capable nor desirous of ascending until they are granted the possibility of doing so. The ascent itself is another matter. The fact that it is an ascent implies a progress, a purposeful passage from one terrace to another, and the sense of a destination. The journey to the summit takes three days and is divided up by three nights, during which upward movement is impossible. The three nights are matched by three dreams—one to correspond to each night—in a sequence that traces the progress by which the various faculties of the soul are integrated and in which what is originally human disorder becomes the order of God. In the course of this progress the various themes of the poem are brought together until the poet, standing at the entrance to the Earthly Paradise and aware of his representative human significance, finds himself in the position vacated by Adam as a result of his sin, restored to a proper understanding of his freedom and to a true sense of his human possibilities.

At the time of the first dream, in canto 9, this state is far from being achieved. It is true that the dream reflects the process by which Lucy, representing "illuminating grace," brings the sleeping poet to the foot of the Mount and to the beginning of the process of purgation—something that Virgil, as representative of unaided human reason, was unable to accomplish. The dream has therefore a positive significance in its true aspect; but it has, as experienced by the poet, a fevered, almost erotic quality that differentiates it from the two visions to follow. Its associations are notably tragic, relating to the story of Philomela (9. 14–15), who was raped by Tereus, the husband of her sister Procne, and changed into a bird: there is also a reference (9. 34) to Achilles, who was taken to the island of Scyros by his mother to save him from the Trojan War, but who was taken from there by the Greeks and eventually slain. Dante, in his dream, sees himself (9. 23) in the position of Ganymede, the boy whom Jove desired in the form of an eagle and took up to Olympus as his cupbearer. The dream, in fact, represents a kind of rape, and there is a violent, disquieting note about Dante's account of it. The eagle's descent is "terrible as lightning" (9. 29) and it comes to "rape" ("rapisse": 9. 30) the sleeping poet, raising him to the sphere of fire in which aggressor and victim "burned together, and the imagined fire so scorched that perforce my sleep was broken" (9. 32–33). At the moment of his awakening Dante describes himself as turning "pale, like one who is chilled with terror":

> diventa' ismorto,
> come fa l'uom che, spaventato, agghiaccia.
> (9. 41–42)

The dream can be seen as having a number of allegorical significances, beyond that of the "gracious" intervention required to set the traveler at the foot of his climb. The eagle is the symbol of empire, and will appear as such in the *Paradiso*.[3] It can also stand for "poetic inspiration"; but what is stressed either way is Dante's impression of personal helplessness, the sense of being emotionally—and indeed physically—assaulted, taken out of himself. It is notable that when he wakes from his dream, Virgil shows no sign of knowing anything about what has occurred. Virgil does know (9. 55) that the dream is the reflection of a favorable intervention by Lucy. The approach to the life of "grace" involves initially a taking of the soul *out* of itself, which is only made possible by a gratuitous intervention from without. This is the reality, of which the dream is a broken, fevered reflection; indeed, the relation of dream to reality, or the fulfillment of "nighttime," physical "dream" into "spiritual," daylight "reality," is significant at this point in the journey. The state of purgation is—as we have said—the turning of man's disorder into the order of God: and it would seem that both sets of terms—*disorder* and *order, night* and *day*—are present at this stage in the journey.

In the progression thus introduced by the first of Dante's dreams, the theme of art—or, more specifically, of poetry—constitutes one element among the many that require to be woven into the developing pattern. The process begins on the terrace devoted to Pride (canto 11) where Dante and Virgil meet exemplars of three different forms of that basic sin. Two of them are examples of the misrule and disorder that prevail in Italy and are therefore related to one of the main themes of the poem: the third, and from our present point of view the most important, is more directly connected with Dante's own art. After pride of birth, represented by Omberto Aldobrandeschi, who was murdered by the Sienese after the destruction of his power in 1259, and after pride of power, embodied in Provenzan Salvani, who was at the head of the Sienese government at the time of the battle of Montaperti (1260), when the Ghibelline forces defeated Florence and proposed to destroy the city,[4] the poet meets a certain Oderisi, greeted by Dante as "the honor of Gubbio and the honor of that art which in Paris is called 'illumination'" (11. 80–81). It is at this point that the theme of art, its meaning and place in life, its greatness and limitation, is explicitly introduced into the poem. It is a theme that touches Dante closely, and its introduction answers to the tendency, which prevails in Purgatory as it could not do in Hell, to see things as drawing together, throwing light progressively upon one another. This is a principal feature of this part of the poem, which becomes increasingly evident as the travelers approach the summit of the Mount, where the integration of the various themes will be, within the limits imposed by a humanity still bound by the temporal, complete.

Oderisi, in the lines just quoted, recognizes himself to be the master of a pupil who has surpassed him: Franco of Bologna, who introduced into Italy from Paris a new or more developed technique for illuminating, or illustrating manuscripts. Oderisi recognizes, not without a certain residue of human wistfulness, that his pupil has advanced further in his art than he was able to do. "Brother," he says, using the typical purgatorial form of salutation,

> più ridon le carte
> che pennellegia Franco Bolognese.
> ("'Brother,' he said, 'more smiling are the pages that Franco Bolognese paints'": 11. 82–83.)

"He has now all the honor," he goes on to say, "of which part is mine" (11. 84). The effect is to stress the speaker's sense of involvement in a common enterprise ("*part* of the honor is mine") and at the same time to underline the law of advancement that governs the arts, as indeed it does all forms of creative human endeavour, and which saves them from stagnation. During his life on earth Oderisi confesses that he was less generous (*cortese:* 11. 85) in his recognition of his pupil's excellence, impeded by

> lo gran disio
> de l'eccellenza ove mio core intese.

("the great desire for excellence whereon my heart was set": 11. 86–87)

This is a manifestation of pride, of a kind to which Dante himself was—and knew himself to be—intimately susceptible. The "fee" for it (11. 88) is paid on the first terrace of Purgatory, as part of the reshaping of "desire" to which the Mount is dedicated; and it requires for its overcoming a recognition of the gap that necessarily separates all human aspirations in time from the reality of the eternal:

> Oh vana gloria de l'umane posse!
> com' poco verde in su la cima dura,
> se non è giunta da l'etati grosse!

("O empty glory of human powers! how briefly lasts the green upon the top, if it is not followed by barbarous times!": 11. 91–93.)

What is involved here is something notably more interesting than a preacher's commonplace concerning the vanity of human wishes. Oderisi, from his new perspective in Purgatory, has come to understand not only that his pupil has taken their common art further than he himself could have done, but that this "moving beyond" answers to a necessary and salutory law, which prevails whenever human affairs and projects have not lapsed into a state of stagnation.

Where an age of "barbarism" does not follow it is right and indeed necessary that the pupil, building on the achievement of his master, should go beyond him. Oderisi goes on to illustrate this necessity by referring to the "revolution" in the art of painting that Dante had witnessed in Florence and that he sees as related to his own work in another medium:

> Credette Cimabue ne la pittura

> tener lo campo, e ora ha Giotto il grido,
> sì che la fama di colui è scura.

("Cimabue thought to hold the field in painting, and now Giotto has the cry, so that the other's fame is dim": 11. 94–96.)

As the fame of Cimabue (ca. 1240–1302), who was in his day an innovator in art, has been replaced by that attached to Giotto's (1266–1337) more "modern" way of painting, so—to come closer to Dante's own concerns—has it been in poetry. "The glory of our tongue" has been taken by "one Guido from the other" (11. 97), Guido Guinizelli of Bologna has been overtaken by Dante's own friend and rival Guido Cavalcanti, and—most significantly of all—

> forse è nato
> chi l'uno e l'altro caccerà del nido.

("he perchance is born that shall chase the one and the other from the nest": 11. 98–99.)

At this point, in effect, Dante is incorporating himself into the body of poetic tradition, seeing his own work as standing in relation to that of his predecessors, much as the art of Franco of Bologna stood with reference to that of Oderisi. Guido Guinizelli (d. 1276) we shall meet in person at a later stage of the ascent.[5] There Dante will recognize his merit as the author of a poem—*Al cor gentil ripara sempre amore* ("Love always comes to the gentle heart")—which he sees as a point of departure for all that followed. Here he is concerned to stress how the work of Guido Cavalcanti (ca. 1255–1300) has come, in the natural course of time, to outstrip that of his predecessor, resting creatively upon it: and how a "third"—Dante himself—may be building in turn upon the achievement of both to create his own unprecedented work.

The affirmation is evidently one that can be inspired by a form of pride: a pride to which Dante is, and recognizes himself to be, susceptible (he will refer later to his fear of being required to return, after his death, to the terrace of the proud)[6] and which needs to be restrained—as Oderisi, speaking from the viewpoint of Purgatory, now teaches him—by a proper, indeed a realistic sense of moral perspective in relation to the reality of the timeless:

> Che voce avrai tu più, se vecchia scindi
> da te la carne, che se fossi morto
> anzi che tu lasciassi il "pappo" e 'l "dindi,"
> pria che passin mill'anni? ch'è più corto
> spazio a l'etterno, ch'un muover di ciglia
> al cerchio che più tardi in cielo è torto.
>
> ("What greater fame will you have if you strip off your flesh when it is old than if you had died before giving up *pappo* and *dindi,* when a thousand years shall have passed, which is a shorter space compared to the eternal than the movement of the eyelids to that circle which is slowest turned in heaven?: 11: 103–8.)

What has been manifestly true for the representatives of family pride and political arrogance mentioned in this canto is also valid in the order of art. In artistic achievement, as in all human effort, death and life are interwoven, inescapable parts of a single reality: "he discolors it through whom it springs green from the ground" (11. 116–17). To recognize this is to find the necessary antidote to pride, and—in the long run—to see whatever significance one's own work may have in relation to laws that govern a reality larger than that of any individual effort: to fail to do so, by overstressing the importance and finality of one's own achievement, is—finally and logically—to render that achievement meaningless.

In all this Dante is evidently moved by a sense of personal involvement. His pride in his own achievement—which can on occasion border on an arrogant assertion of his own worth[7]—is balanced by his recognition of a greater truth in a way that does not exclude conflict. We begin to understand why this day's journey was preceded by the dream we have already considered and why this carries with it a sense of uneasy "desire" and fevered exaltation. On the terrace that purges the root sin of pride—the refusal of the soul to temper its desire by accepting its natural place in the order of things—Dante recognizes that Oderisi's words have struck home with a unique force of personal reference:

> E io a lui: "Tuo vero dir m'incora
> bona umiltà, e gran tumor m'appiani.
> ("And I to him, 'your true words fill my heart with good humility and abate in me a great swelling' ": 11. 118–19.)

These are words of acceptance: acceptance of "good humility," a proper recognition of the evident reality of things, of a truth that alone can make the poet's efforts significant in relation to the larger reality of which they form a part. They have abated "a great swelling," a tumor of ambitious and presumptuous thoughts that were in danger of turning into illusions capable of destroying the end they aimed at achieving. The balance of pride and humility, the arrogant assertion followed by its rebuke, is very characteristic of Dante and answers to one of the main emotional driving forces behind his poem.

After the meeting with Oderisi the theme of artistic achievement, of art in its relation to tradition, is submerged for a while by other concerns. The other manifestations of "perverted love"—envy and wrath—are no doubt relevant to Dante's poetic concerns, but this aspect does not surface directly on the terraces devoted to them. When the theme reappears, it is after the dream in canto 19 (1–33) that marks the second night passed by the poets on the mountain. The dream, which follows the long and thematically central discussion of free will and love that spans cantos 15 to 18, is designed to mark a turning point in the entire conception. It concerns the vision of a woman first perceived as "stammering, with eyes asquint and crooked on her feet" (19. 7–8), who is transformed under Dante's gaze until she appears to him "straight" and with "her pallid face even as love requires" (19. 14–15). The vision, in other words, is subjective in kind. Dante, as dreamer, confers beauty upon an object initially repulsive. The illusion, however, is broken by the intervention of "a lady holy and alert" (19. 26), who exposes the repellent reality and leaves the awakened poet ready to accept Virgil's invitation to resume the climb. The appearance of "the sweet Siren who leads mariners astray in mid-sea" (19. 19–20), who turned Ulysses, the adventurous traveler on uncharted seas of "experience,"[8] to her song,[9] is broken and the proper relationship between dream and reality, illusion and the reasonable truth of things restored. Dante, in terms of his journey, is ready to pass from the terraces devoted to essentially perverted forms of "love" to whose that call, not for final renunciation, but for incorporation into a more adequate understanding of the meaning and end of "desire."

The sense of this new development, inasmuch as it concerns our present theme, begins to emerge in the meeting of the poets with Statius (cantos 21 and 22). Here the situation first approached in Virgil's conversation with Sordello is resumed at a higher level of understanding. Dante accepts, at least for the purpose of his fiction, the medieval tradition which affirmed that the Roman died a Christian: he adds, for ends of his own, the recognition by Statius that it was the work of Virgil that not only inspired him to poetry (21. 94–99) but gave him the light that led him to salvation. The pathos of the situation is developed with rare immediacy in Statius's own words to his predecessor, words that refer to the "prophecy" of Christ's birth in Virgil's *Fourth Eclogue*[10] and are resonant with a sense of history fulfilled:

> Facesti come quei che va di notte,
>   che porta il lume dietro e sé non giova,
>   ma dopo sé fa le persone dotte.

("You were like one who goes by night and carries the light behind him and profits not himself, but makes those wise who follow him": 22. 67–69.)

"Per te poeta fui, per te cristiano" ("Through you I was a poet, through you a Christian": 22. 73). At this point, the theme of tradition, as developed by Oderisi, is being taken to a new and higher level of understanding. The meeting is between two poets, the lesser of whom (in terms of his art) is a Christian who has just been granted freedom to rise to the summit of the Mount, whereas the greater remains wistfully relegated to "eternal exile" (21. 18). In the order of poetry, which is also, in Dante's conception, the order of human civility, Statius recognizes the debt to his more illustrious predecessor and presses it to the point that makes of Virgil his "father," not only in poetry but in religious "truth": in the order of "grace," which reflects divine purposes beyond the scope of human reason, the need imposes itself to recognize the gap that separates human experience in time from the timeless reality of things, the order of a God who remains, in the phrase that will appear in the *Paradiso*, "in infinite excess"[11] of his creation.

That is the truth, to which human perception must conform if it is to remain meaningful; but there is tension of the most creative kind implied in Statius's attitude to his great predecessor, more especially in the affirmation (21. 100–102) that he would have consented to delay his progress toward salvation "by a sun" in order to have enjoyed the privilege of living on earth with his master in poetry. This is the situation that produces from the two poets, in the inexpressibly tender moment of recognition, some of the most humanly moving lines of the entire poem:

> Già s'inchinava ad abbracciar li piedi
>   al mio dottor, ma el li disse: "Frate,
>   non far, ché tu se' ombra e ombra vedi."
> Ed ei surgendo: "Or puoi la quantitate
>   comprender de l'amor ch'a te mi scalda,
>   quand'io dismento nostra vanitate,
> trattando l'ombre come cosa salda."

("Already he was stooping to embrace my teacher's feet;

but he said to him, 'Brother, do not so, for you are a shade and a shade you see.'

And he, rising, 'Now you may comprehend the measure of the love that burns in me for you, when I forget our emptiness and treat shades as solid things": 21. 130–36.)

At the end of the Statius episode, Dante tells us that the conversation between the two poets, which he depicts himself as following in the attitude of a reverent listener, "gave him understanding *(intelletto)* in making verse" (22. 129). This makes a suitable prelude to his meeting, in the next canto (23), with a friend of his youth, Forese Donati, with whom his association in Florence had been in part connected with matters of verse writing. Forese is on the terrace of the gluttonous, among those who "in hunger and in thirst regain their holiness" (23. 66). The encounter is an occasion for shared memories, and in these poetry has only a minor part to play; but when Dante refers feelingly to aspects of the past that have come to fill him with shame—

> "Se tu riduci a mente
> qual fosti meco, e qual io teco fui,
> ancor fia grave il memorar presente.
> ("If you bring back to mind what you have been with me and what I have been with you, the present memory will still be grievous": 23. 115–17)—

the reference is to verses exchanged between them, verses inferior in literary quality and scurrilous in kind, in which Dante had joked concerning Forese's gluttony and made ribald references to the wife whom his friend now calls "la vedovella mia, che molto amai" ("my widow, whom I loved so well": 23. ;92), in words that underline Dante's present sense of the sin committed against "love," which produced inferior poetry and which will shortly need to be purged in purgatorial fire.

The exchange with Forese, brief and reticent as it is, anticipates Dante's own acceptance of the need for per-

sonal purification, affecting indeed the man rather than
the poet, but involving the latter in the greater reality,
from the sins of the "flesh." Truly valid poetry can only be,
for Dante, the fruit of a valid life, and it is this that he is
seeking—both as individual and as a "figure" for humanity—in his ascent of the Mount. When the time finally
comes for him to face Beatrice,[12] it will be seen that she
accuses him bitterly of unfaithfulness, of the sinful following of misplaced desire.

Cantos 24 and 26, closely related to one another, return
more explicitly to the theme of Dante's own poetry in its
relation to that of his predecessors and contemporaries. In
this respect, they look back to and build upon statements
already put forward by Oderisi. Dante has been aware
from the start that his poetic undertaking is of the kind
that is liable to involve him to a dangerous degree in pride,
or presumption, a sin that has already affected his passage
through the first terrace and that needs to be further subjected in its various ramifications to the purgatorial process. The poet, moreover, is now coming to see the resolution to this personal problem in terms of his increased
understanding of the nature of tradition: the inheritance
of the past that has made him what he is and to which he is
now making his personal contribution by creating his
poem. Something of this was already implied in the meeting with Oderisi, who—as we saw—emphasized the onward movement of time, which affects poets as it affects all
men, and which imposes a realization of the insignificance,
or at least the necessary lack of finality, which conditions
all temporal achievement in relation to an ultimate and
"eternal" reality.

In canto 24, then, and in Dante's meeting with
Bonagiunta of Lucca, the poem returns to consider
further the nature of poetry as an expression of creative
love. The meeting with Forese had been concerned, in
part and in passing, with poetry—with verses once written
by Dante that he now wishes to forget. Bonagiunta, like
Forese, is vividly marked by the signs of the ordeal to

which their common sin has submitted them.[13] He is introduced as a versifier of the "old school," Dante's senior and representative of a conception of his art that can now be seen, from Dante's own perspective, as dated, outstripped. In greeting Dante, whose identity and mission have no doubt become clear to him from the preceding conversation with Forese, Bonagiunta refers to him as the creator of the "nuove rime"—the "new rhymes" (24. 49)—and expressly relates the new manner of writing to the *canzone, Donne ch'avete intelletto d'amore* ("Ladies that have intelligence of love": 24. 51), which Dante had placed in a central position in the *Vita Nuova*,[14] where it seems to develop themes foreshadowed in the concluding stanzas of Guido Guinizelli's *Al cor gentil ripara sempre amore,* and which he evidently regarded as the poem that, more than any other, made explicit the poetic "revolution" implied in the "new rhymes." Dante's reply to Bonagiunta amounts to a definition of the essential content of the "new" poetry. He says of himself,

> "I'mi son un che, quando
> Amor mi spira, noto, e a quel modo
> ch'e' ditta dentro vo significando."

("I am one who, when Love inspires me, takes note, and goes setting it forth after the fashion that he dictates within me": 24. 52–54.)

This is the inspiration of what Bonagiunta, in his reply, calls the *dolce stil nuovo,* "the sweet new style" (24. 57). The term is evidently applied in this context to Dante's own poetry, though it implies the growth from a common effort that he shares with certain of his contemporaries as well as his own outstandingly novel position among them. It is poetry that is distinguished from that of earlier writers, such as Bonagiunta himself—who recognizes (24. 55–56) that he and such earlier poets as the Notary[15] and Guittone d'Arezzo[16] were held back in their day by a lack of understanding (*il nodo,* "the knot": 24. 55) from following the new path—by its recognition that true poetry reflects real emotion and is achieved by those who keep close to the source of their inspiration. This source is declared to be *amore* on all its levels of meaning: for to be alive is to be creative and to be creative is to be "in love." The new conception of poetry rests, in short, upon a more adequate conception of "love": the understanding, which Dante's journey of "experience" has given him, that it is the nature of "desire" to look beyond itself, to seek fulfillment in relation to the loving purpose that, in the final words of the poem, "moves the sun and the other stars."[17]

From his new perspective, achieved in Purgatory, Bonagiunta accepts the reality of the revolution that those who followed him have brought to the understanding of poetry, just as Oderisi, the artist in illumination, had stressed acceptance of the law of change and succession as necessary in all human endeavor that aspired to remain creative, and as such subject to perpetual renewal. Bonagiunta's words to Dante beautifully combine this recognition with a note of human wistfulness:

> "Io veggio ben come le vostre penne
>   di retro al dittator sen vanno strette,
>   che de le nostre certo non avvenne;
> e qual più a gradire oltre si mette,
>   non vede più da l'uno a l'altro stilo';
>   e, quasi contentato, si tacette.

("'Clearly I see how your pens follow close after him who dictates, which certainly befell not with ours—and he who sets himself to seek farther can see no other difference between the one style and the other.' And, as if satisfied, he was silent": 24. 58–63.)

Already, in the exchange with Oderisi, the implication had been that Dante's own writing was the consummation of the preceding process. The plural reference to "your pens"[18] further indicates that Dante's own achievement, for all the uniqueness that he feels belongs to it, is built upon the work of those who went before him. It was also implied that this assertion might present itself to him as a temptation to pride, which could only be overcome by an acceptance of the idea of tradition as a continuing process: a process to which each member has something new to contribute (for it is only by building something new on older foundations that tradition remains alive), which will in turn—while the tradition continues to live—be superseded by the achievement of those who, in the future, will base their own contribution upon what has been achieved. Bonagiunta, not without a touch of human regret—"as if satisfied"—has come to accept the law of change that is an essential part of any living conception of tradition: and the implication is that Dante, in his turn, will have to learn to accept it too.

The lesson is both rendered explicit and carried further in canto 26, the last expressly devoted to poetry in the course of the traveler's ascent. By this time it is evident that Dante is involving himself, not only as man but as poet, in the purgatorial process. The two aspects, indeed, are seen to be inseparable. Poetry, like all motions of the spirit, needs to be justified, "made just," conforming to its essential nature as truly understood, and achieving in this way the freedom that is the fruit of this understanding. It needs to be "made just" in relation to the ultimate source of the love that it aspires to express and that confers upon it its meaning: and it is in part as poet that Dante will now, at the approaches to the summit of the Mount, be called upon to pass through the flame in which the sin of lust, or misplaced desire, is purged and the soul "justified." If the theme of poetry is "love," as has been declared, "lust" is one of the masks which conceal or deform that reality and which needs, as such, to be purified.

It is appropriate, accordingly, that the return to the theme of "poetry" should take place in relation to Dante's passage through the fire that at once burns and, by burning, purifies. It is appropriate also that this should be the final stage in his approach to the Earthly Paradise, where his poet-guide, Virgil, having fulfilled his mission, finally leaves him. The process of Dante's personal purification is seen at this point more clearly than ever to be inseparable from his achievement of a true understanding of his poetry as a manifestation of creative love. There are signs at the end of the previous canto that Dante means us to be aware that he is approaching a moment of peculiar significance, even of fear, in his journey: he expresses himself as afraid of falling into the fire (25. 116), and Virgil at the opening of canto 26 is careful to deliver an insistent warning by saying "often," "Watch, take heed" (26. 2, 3).[19] This fear in Dante is balanced by the more positive attitude of the souls, who are described as willing their suffering as a means to their onward progress: for, though some of them are moved to approach the newcomer to satisfy their curiosity, they are "always careful not to come out where they would not be burned" (26. 14–5). The tone, then, is one of tension, since great issues, in which the traveler is very personally involved, are at stake but the sense of mortal danger does not prevent him from greeting the souls he meets as "anime sicure/ d'aver, quando che sia, di pace stato" ("souls, certain of gaining, whensoever it may be, a state of peace": 26. 53–54), and from stressing his own faith (26. 58–60) in the providential nature of his passage.

The rest of the canto, for which all this is a preparation, is devoted to Dante's meeting with two of his predecessors in poetry. The first is Guido Guinizelli, whose *canzone, Al cor gentil ripara sempre amore,* he evidently regarded as the point of origin from which his own developed ideas on the nature of poetry had derived. Dante greets the soul of Guinizelli in words expressive of the joy felt by him

> quand' io odo nomar sé stesso il padre
> mio e de li altri miei miglior che mai
> rime d'amor usar dolci e leggiadre.

("when I hear name himself the father of me and of others my betters who ever used sweet and gracious rhymes of love": 26. 97–99.)

The expression at this point is delicately poised between reverence and a recognition of distance. The reverence is certainly there, movingly and unequivocally expressed. Dante greets Guido as his father in poetry, at the same time as, in the phrase which speaks of "sweet and graceful rhymes" of love, he distances the work of his predecessor, in the act of giving it its due, from his own endeavors: for the adjectives "sweet and graceful" applied to Guinizelli's verses evoke a form of writing that, intensely, almost nostalgically attractive as it is, stands at some distance from what is attempted with greater scope and more open universality of reference in the *Commedia*.

It is typical of the mood of the meeting that Dante describes himself as at once deeply, personally moved—

> sanza udire e dir pensoso andai
> lunga fiata rimirando lui,
>
> ("without hearing or speaking, I went pondering, gazing a long time at him": 26. 100–101.)

at the same time as, conscious of the reality of the fire between them (26. 102) and of the difference between his own physical shrinking and Guinizelli's willing, even joyful acceptance of pain, he recognizes the reality that separates them.

The lines that follow, in which the meeting of minds is consummated, bring home the sense of the encounter in relation to the poet's unfolding plan. Guido takes the initiative by recognizing Dante's achievement, news of which has reached him in his purgatorial situation:

> "Tu lasci tal vestigio,
> per quel ch'i' odo, in me, e tanto chiaro,
> che Letè nol può torre né far bigio.
>
> ("You leave, by that which I hear, traces so deep and clear in me that Lethe cannot take them away or make them dim": 26. 106–8.)

The praise is generous, given—as is now fitting—without

that shadow of human resentment at the thought of being overtaken that had colored the earlier words of Bonagiunta. The speaker senses in Dante's reverent attitude the presence of an intimate community (as of a son to his father), which moves him to inquire the reason for it:

> Ma se le tue parole or ver giuraro,
>   dimmi che è cagion per che dimostri
>   nel dire e nel guardar d'avermi caro."

("But if your words just now swore truth, tell me for what reason you show youself, by speech and look, to hold me dear": 26. 109–11.)

Dante's reply replaces the familiar "tu" with the more honorific "voi," as though to stress a relationship in which respect and gratitude, as well as love, play their part:

> E io a lui: "Li dolci detti vostri,
>   che, quanto durerà l'uso moderno,
>   faranno cari ancora i loro incostri."

("And I to him, 'Your sweet verses, which so long as modern use shall last, will make dear their very ink'": 26. 112–11.)

The exchange is central to the entire conception at this point, and its expression needs to be weighed with care. Dante's admiration for Guinizelli is given to his "sweet" lines, echoing the reference to "sweet and graceful rhymes of love" just above, and confirming the balance of admiration and distance there conveyed. Dante assures Guinizelli that the fame of his work will live for as long as the "modern use"—the writing of poetry in the "sweet" but "corruptible" and fluctuating vernacular—will last. The language in which both Guinizelli and Dante have chosen to write is, as he was acutely aware, subject to change when compared with the stability he associated with the tongue of Virgil.[20] The effect is both to join the two poets in a common, intensely felt but inevitably precarious endeavor and to reinforce the warning, already put forward by Oderisi and now confirmed in an appropriately purgatorial act of recognition, of the futility of pride and self-assertion in the face of the necessary evanescence of all forms of human expression.

Beyond this, the exchange between the poets finally unfolds the conception of "tradition" that all the references to poetry scattered, or significantly disposed through the canticle, are intended to affirm. By saluting his predecessor in such generous, expressly "filial" terms, Dante is giving recognition to the fact that his own "modern" work is built on the prior achievement of such as Guinizelli; while the latter, in his reply, recognizes that Dante's poetry is to be seen as the fulfillment, the consummation, of what existed potentially in his own work but never came there to full expression. The relationship between "father" and "son" in poetry has become central to the entire conception. To belong to a "tradition" is to be aware of building upon the foundations of the past, but—at the same time—to recognize the need to bring something new into being: something that, following the logic of the entire development, will in turn and in the fullness of time be superseded. What Dante has done is both to recognize the presence of the past in his present achievement and to justify, in the process of "placing" it, his own creative and fresh contribution. Where the sense of the past and the recognition of its relevance for the present are lacking, there can be no tradition, no sense of a continuing and developing creative effort of which each personal achievement can be no more than a part; but where the tradition does not renew itself, where it becomes no more than a matter of repeating dead forms, its own death is equally certain. To recognize the past in ourselves is a necessary part of being alive in the present, since we are, in a very real sense, the sum of our past experiences and those of the humanity to which we belong; but acceptance of the past as a continuing reality in our lives needs to be balanced at each moment, and as a condition of continuing to live, by a renunciation of it as final. The past can only be valid in human lives inasmuch as it is alive in the present and is continually projected towards a new and unpredictable future. Continuity and renunciation have come to be seen as necessary aspects of tradition, woven together in the light of the purgatorial experience.

Even this, however, cannot be quite the end of the story. Dante has become increasingly aware, as he has advanced on his journey, of the full implications of the statement that poetry is concerned with *Amor,* love. The subject of poetry is, by definition, love; for to love, or to be "in love," is to be creatively alive. Dante has developed this aspect of love, in its relation to poetry, in his words to Bonagiunta defining his own poetry and that of the contemporaries whose work he associated with his own; he has also recognized, generously, the presence of that inspiration in Guinizelli. Love, however, is in the Aristotelian terms that Dante chose to adopt for this part of the poem, a movement of desire: and it is desire that has to be purified, rendered adequate in relation to its end, by submission to the purgatorial process.[21] So much has been anticipated, in relation to poetic art, by the substitution of Virgil by the "Christian" Statius, in preparation for a new stage in the journey for which the pagan poet's guidance can no longer suffice. Virgil, though excluded from "grace" and about to make his exit from the poem, is yet the greater poet: this is important as one of the main sources of tension in the poem. For Virgil's greatness, real as it is, cannot finally be sufficient, just as "poetry," or "art," are not, and cannot be, ends in themselves. The recalled passion of Paolo and Francesca at the outset of the *Inferno* (canto 5) produced undoubted "poetry" and moved the poet-traveler to sympathy; but it ended in Hell. Even Virgil, with his more civil, universal view of his art, remains unalterably bound to his infernal status. At the point we have reached, we are required to join Dante in moving *beyond* poetry, in making an act of renunciation that, by a paradox vital to the conception, will become a source, even a condition, of fuller poetic achievement. The new poetry itself, to which Dante has dedicated his creative life, needs to be brought into the purifying process: and poetry itself, like the "love" that it expresses, is called upon to submit to the purifying fire.

First, however, Dante needs to take up one more aspect of the poetic tradition to which, as he now recognizes, he is creatively related: that thread of it that derives from Provençal, troubadour verse, and that, having contributed to his own achievement, calls now for incorporation into his design. Guinizelli departs (26. 134–35), but not before he has recognized that Dante has been granted the privilege of going beyond him (26. 127–29), and not without asking him for the benefit of that prayer in which the past and the present, the living and the dead, are joined in recognition of their respective parts in a common endeavor. Before leaving to reenter the flames, he refers Dante to one whom he calls, with the abandonment of pride or self-assertion that now belongs to his state, "miglior fabbro del parlar materno" ("a better craftsman of the mother tongue": 26. 117).

The poet so designated is Arnaut Daniel, master of the *trobar clus,* the most intricate and at times obscure manner of Provençal writing. He is saluted by Guinizelli, who presumably built on the foundations he provided for his craftsmanship in words. By dignifying this aspect of the poet's endeavor and by incorporating it into the process of purgation, Dante is adding another necessary element to his pattern. The words that the Provençal poet addresses to him in greeting are delivered in a spirit of elaborate and achieved courtliness; the aristocratic virtues, too, when purged of the elements of artifice and deception that commonly accompany them, are a reflection of positively human possibilities and, as such, worthy of incorporation into the creative order of life. Dante assures Arnaut that his "desire offers a place of welcome for his name" (26. 137–38), and he in reply begins to speak "liberamente" ("freely": 26. 139). Since the journey through Purgatory has been a movement towards freedom,[22] the adverb has an appropriate significance in relation to the whole. The words addressed by Arnaut to Dante, some of the most movingly personal in the poem, amount to an incorporation of the Provençal tradition as a necessary element to be fulfilled by being placed in a greater context:

> "Tan m'abellis vostre cortes deman,
>   qu'ieu no me puesc ni voill a vos cobrire.
> Ieu sui Arnaut, que plor e vau cantan;
>   consiros vei la passada folor,
>   e vei jausen lo joi qu'esper, denan.
> Ara vos prec, per aquella valor
>   que vos guida al som de l'escalina,
>   sovenha vos a temps de ma dolor!"

("So does your courteous request please me that I neither can nor would conceal myself from you. I am Arnaut, who weep and sing as I go; contritely I see my past folly, and joyously I see before me the joy that I await. Now I pray you, by that power which guides you to the summit of the stair, in due time be heedful of my pain": 26. 140–47.)

The exchange between the poets is couched in terms of "courtesy," as between feudal equals: the questions of precedence and succession, which played so large and necessary a part in the earlier encounters between poets, are now no longer relevant, have been taken up into an achieved state of gracious civility. Dante's question enhances, "beautifies" *(abellis)*, his colleague, who responds by the free, outgoing gift of self that amounts, in the purgatorial condition, to a recognition of the "bond" that unites human beings in a common state of "grace." Arnaut "weeps" for the "folly" of the past, which needs not to be forgotten but rather remembered and recognized together with the pain to which it has given rise. Only as remembered and recognized for what it has been will it become suitable material for renunciation: and only once the necessity of renunciation has been accepted will it be found to offer expanded possibilities of life. It is right, therefore, that Arnaut should "rejoice" in the possession of "hope": the quality that distinguishes Purgatory from Hell and that sees pain and renunciation not as inflicted penalties but as means to the achievement of an enhanced and "joyful" life. Conscious of the "goodness" (the *valor*, the "value") that constitutes the end of the journey and confers meaning upon it, Arnaut warns his mortal fellow-poet to consider these matters "in due time"—before it is too late, and since it is only in time that human choice is meaningful—and turns back, willingly, freely, and acceptingly, "into the fire that purifies them" (26. 148).

As Dante stands, then, with Statius and Virgil, close to the fulfillment of this stage in his journey, with the purgatorial terraces behind him and only the last trial by fire to be faced, he has incorporated into his poem the various elements that have gone into its making and that are now revealed in their full potentiality in the light of his achieved understanding of tradition. Nothing has been lost, everything has been "redeemed,"[23] given its place in the complete pattern at which his work has consistently aimed. It remains, in canto 27, to pass through the final test that separates the poets from access to the summit of the Mount and, with it, to the achievement of the traveler's restored humanity. Evening is falling as "l'angel di Dio lieto ci apparse" ("the angel of God appeared to us rejoicing": 27. 6), singing beyond the intervening flames the last of the Beatitudes—*Beati mundo corde* ("Blessed are the pure in heart")—"in voce assai piu che la nostra viva ("in a voice far more living than ours"). From now on the emphasis on life will be expansively present in the poetry. Dante, confronted with the fire, is urged by the angelic voice to prepare himself for the passage through it:

> "Più non si va, se pria non morde,
> anime sante, il foco: intrate in esso,
> e al cantar di là non siate sorde."

("No farther may you go, holy souls, if first the fire sting not; enter into it, and to the singing beyond be not deaf": 27. 10–12.)

The reality of the pain, of the biting of the fire, is stressed. It is a suffering not to be evaded but rather accepted in humility and in a sense of the joy of the end achieved. Dante, still conscious of his human flesh, mindful, as he puts it, of "human bodies once seen burned" (27. 18) strongly present in his imagination, is led on by a Virgil who addresses him, more directly than at any previous point in the poem, as "my son" and who reminds him that "here may be torment, but not death" (27. 21).

In this spirit Virgil urges Dante to try the effect of the fire by placing into it his own hand wrapped in his garment. The invitation is to a necessary confidence:

> Pon giù omai, pon giù ogne temenza;
>   volgiti in qua e vieni: entra sicuro!

("Put away now, put away all fear, turn hitherward, come, enter with confidence": 27. 31–32)

and when Dante remains humanly hesitant—"And I still adamant and against my conscience"—the thought of Beatrice is offered him, as to an unwilling child coaxed toward the achievement of his goal:

> Or vedi, figlio:
>   tra Beatrice e te è questo muro.

("Now see, son, between Beatrice and you is this wall": 27. 35–36.)

The encouragement is offered in an engaging tone of fatherly solicitude that expresses itself in an affectionate informality of language:

> "Come!
>   volenci star di qua?"; indi sorrise
>   come al fanciul si fa ch'è vinto al pome.

("'What? Do we desire to stay on this side?' then smiled as one does to a child that is won with an apple": 27. 44–45.)

At last Dante, persuaded by the thought of "the name

which ever springs in my mind" (27. 42), moves into the fire, with one poet, Virgil, before him and another, Statius, behind—perhaps to cover any lingering tendency in him to turn back. Virgil continues to encourage him with the thought of Beatrice, who is now so near—"Li occhi suoi già veder parmi" ("Already I seem to behold her eyes": 27. 54). The pain of the passage is real, felt with anguish by the poet, who tells us that "molten glass" would be cool in relation to it. It must be not only suffered but willingly accepted, before at the end of it the poets come "to where the ascent began" (27. 57), to the sound of the last angelic salutation—*Venite, benedicti Patris mei* ("Come, O ye blessed of my Father": 27. 58)—emerging from a light that so struck the poet's unaccustomed eyes "that it overcame me and I could not look on it" (27. 60).

Evening is falling, as the sun sets on a horizon the vast expanse of which is stressed—"le sue parti immense": "in all its vast range" (27. 70)—to remind us that the pilgrims now stand high, near the summit of the Mount. Dante further tells us that he saw the stars "di lor solere e piu chiare e maggiori" ("bigger and brighter than was their wont": 27. 90). This final stage in the ascent is marked by the third and last of the dreams that have served to structure the various stages of the purgatorial progress. After the fevered disorder of the first dream (canto 9) in which the poet suffered passively an experience for which he was unprepared and from which Virgil, as representative of reason, was excluded, and after the second (canto 19), in which the relationship of reason and desire, spiritual love and fleshly instinct, were seen in the process of being set into order, the final dream (canto 27) is of Leah, the wife of Jacob, who was interpreted as a symbol of the active life, as her sister Rachel was of the state of contemplation; the first state is to lead, as its natural fulfillment, to the second and higher condition. As Leah in the dream puts it, accepting her relationship to her sister: "lei lo vedere, e me l'ovrare appaga" ("she"—Rachel—"with seeing, I with doing am satisfied": 27. 108). These are the Old Testament "figures" that will find their completion in the New in Martha and Mary, the New Law as fulfillment of the Old. The dream concerns desire and its right ordering. It comes in the hour "when Cytherea" (Venus), who seems always burning with the fire of love, first shone on the mountain from the east" (27. 95–96). The "lady young and beautiful" (27. 97) who appears in the dream as Leah is an anticipation of the Matilda who will, in the next two cantos, lead the poet to the eyes of Beatrice. Once again, "everything in the poem connects and nothing is lost: one "love" leads into another, not to replace or annul it (except insofar as it is evil, hostile to the law of being that gives life to the universe and fulfillment to man's nature and his place within it), but to confer upon it a greater measure of life.

With the achievement of this status, the moment has come for something that has been anticipated since the beginning of the journey: the moment of Virgil's departure. His last words to Dante are a handing over of his protégé to his own devices, his own achieved freedom. The splendors of the dawn, "which rise the more welcome to pilgrims as, returning, they lodge less far from home" (27. 109–11), scatter the darkness on every side and restore the travelers to a wakefulness in which the sense of their arrival at their destination will become clear to them: as Virgil tells Dante,

> "Quel dolce pome che per tanti rami
> cercando va la cura de' mortali,
> oggi porrà in pace le tue fami."

("That sweet fruit which the care of mortals goes seeking on so many branches, this day shall give your hungerings peace": 27. 115–17.)

The "fruit" of mankind's search for happiness is described as an "apple" *(pome)*, with the effect, no doubt, of recalling the desire that led Eve (and Adam with her) to the loss of Paradise, for themselves and for the following humanity. Now, however, it is a "sweet fruit" that brings the gift of peace, the word that resounds through the *Commedia* as the object of mankind's search and that is now seen to be achieved through the right ordering of desire.

Dante is to be fulfilled in natural happiness, his hunger satisfied as was that of Adam in his God-given natural state before the Fall. In response to these words of encouragement, he feels his own desire increase, in preparation for what will soon become his paradisal flight:

> Tanto voler sopra voler mi venne
> de l'esser sù, ch'ad ogne passo poi
> al volo mi sentia crescer le penne.

("Such wish upon wish came to me to be above, that at every step thereafter I felt my feathers growing for the flight": 27. 121–23.)

The end of this stage in the journey—the first *end:* there will be a further journey for the simple reason that every human end is also, in time, to be seen as a beginning—is marked by Virgil's words, the last he will speak in the poem: words that constitute a solemn charge to the poet who began as his ward and whom he now addresses in words that are very like those spoken by a loving father who is conscious of having led his child as far as the light granted to him will take him, and who will now, with his loving approval, outstrip him. Virgil begins by summing up the sense of the journey they have undertaken together and by recognizing the limit they have reached:

> Tratto t'ho qui con ingegno e con arte;
> lo tuo piacere omai prendi per duce;
> fuor se' de l'erte vie, fuor se' de l'arte.

("I have brought you here with understanding and with art. Take henceforth your own pleasure for your guide. Forth you are from the steep ways, forth from the narrow": 27. 130–32.)

Virgil is justly proud of what he has achieved. He has brought his charge to where he stands by the exercise of the highest faculties granted to man in the absence of

supernatural grace: "with understanding and with art."
They are no mean endowment, and they have carried
Dante to the point of being able to trust in his own rightly
ordered faculties and to take his purified "pleasure" as his
safe guide. Adam, before he fell, dwelt naturally in the
Earthly Paradise. Dante, as a "figure" for humanity, has
made his return there, though—unlike Adam in his original condition—he remains mortal. The landscape of the
Earthly Paradise is before his eyes (27. 133–35): the sun,
the grass, the flowers and trees that spring, as they must
have done for Adam in his original paradisal state, spon-
taneously from the soil. Further than this Dante, by his
own unaided effort, cannot go. He must wait, in peace and
contentment, for "the fair eyes" (27. 136) that once, inter-
ceding for him, brought Virgil to his salvation and that will
now, in their own good time, reveal themselves to his ex-
pectant gaze in joy. Grace, though its arrival in response to
the purified will is assured, cannot suffer constraint. Pend-
ing its coming, he is free to take pleasure in the Garden
according to his will, dispensed of need for the guidance
that has so far sustained him:

> Non aspettar mio dir più né mio cenno;
> *libero, dritto e sano è tuo arbitrio,*
> e fallo fora non fare a suo senno.

("No longer expect word or sign from me. Free, upright, and whole is your will, and it would be wrong not
to act according to its bidding": 27. 139–41; italics
mine.)

Dante's will has been made free, upright, and whole: not
to act at this point in recognition of his freedom would be
in him a sin. In confirmation of this achieved state, the
spiritual and civic vocations, which are inseparable parts of
any full human life, have been finally joined in his person.
As his last act in the poem, Virgil crowns Dante—
Florentine poet, exile, and "figure" for mankind—
"bishop" and "king" over himself (27. 142), joining the

spiritual and temporal powers, harmonizing body and spirit in the attainment of his restored humanity.

NOTES

1. This is the sense of the Cacciaguida episode, significantly placed at the very center of the *Paradiso* (canto 17. 43–135).

2. Canto 21. See pp. 26–28 below.

3. Cantos 18 to 20.

4. The episode has been recalled by Farinata degli Uberti in *Inferno* 10. 91–93.

5. Canto 26. See pp. 33–38 below.

6. See *Purgatorio* 13. 136–38.

7. See ll. 98–99, quoted on p. 23 above.

8. *Inferno* 26. 116.

9. It is interesting that Dante at this point changes the emphasis of the story in a manner calculated to stress the danger to the hero rather than his capacity to withstand it. In Homer, Ulysses did *not* allow himself to be beguiled by the fascination of the Sirens' song.

10. *Eclogue* 4. 4–10.

11. *Paradiso* 19. 45.

12. *Purgatorio* 30–31.

13. *Purgatorio* 23. 49–51.

14. *Vita Nuova*, ch. 19.

15. Giacomo da Lentini, a poet of the Sicilian school that flourished at the court of Frederick II.

16. Guittone d'Arezzo (c. 1230–94) wrote in Florence and may have been known to Dante in his early years.

17. *Paradiso* 33. 145.

18. Mark Musa, in his interesting and often perceptive chapter on *The "Sweet New Style" That I Hear*, in *Advent at the Gates* (Bloomington: Indiana University Press, 1974), prefers to translate *le vostre penne* (generally rendered as "your pens") as "your wings" and to introduce the idea of "winged flight" under the guidance of Love, the "dittator"; but the balance of probability seems to me to fall more convincingly on the side of the traditional interpretation.

19. Compare similar warnings at the opening of the Ulysses canto (*Inferno* 26. 19–24; 43–45).

20. This preoccupation, and the attempt to relieve it, accounts for Dante's writing of his treatise on language, the *De Volgari Eloquentia*.

21. As Virgil explains to Dante, "Not every love is in itself a praiseworthy thing" (*Purgatorio* 18. 36).

22. "Libertà va cercando" (*Purgatorio* 1. 72).

23. Compare T. S. Eliot's repeated "Redeem the time" in *Ash Wednesday*.

2

Why is Ulysses in Hell?

NO reader of Dante's *Inferno* who comes for the first time to canto 26 and the story of Ulysses' last voyage can fail to respond to the splendor of the conception and the fascination of the narrative. Nor, indeed, is he likely to find himself refusing this sympathy after further readings. The imaginative range displayed in Ulysses' story, and the poetic power displayed in its telling, are such as to compel a true measure of identification. The identification, however, produces in turn a problem, which the reader must also feel. If the story of Ulysses' adventure induces, even forces, from us a powerful sense of admiration, how can it be explained, not only that he is eternally condemned but that Dante has chosen to place him at a point not far removed from the bottom of the infernal pit?

A possible answer to this question might begin by stressing the importance of not reading a medieval poem in the light of a modern experience. Such an answer would go on from this general proposition to argue that a reader of Dante's time would have found nothing to question in the treatment of a pagan hero who chose to defy the limitations that divine decree imposed upon mortal beings, and who suffered the consequences of his act of hubris. It might even be argued that the fact that we have found it natural to invoke this Greek word to describe Ulysses' "sin" suggests that his fate might not have seemed inappropriate to a reader in classical antiquity. Properly under-

stood, the notion has some merit for an understanding of
Dante's conception, and it would be wrong to dismiss it as
oppressively or insensitively moralizing. Dante certainly
wrote with a moral purpose in mind and adjusted the successive stages of his journey to it; but a reading that limits
itself to this truth does not account for the admiration that
we feel—and, more important, that Dante, through the
power of his poetry, seems to require us to feel—for the
spirit in which the great adventure is undertaken. We find
ourselves drawn to identify ourselves with the spirit of the
"brief oration" in which Ulysses incites his aging followers
to accompany him on his unprecedented voyage in pursuit
of "experience"; and it is impossible, surely, not to feel that
Dante could not have written as he did unless he shared
imaginatively in this identification.

It seems, then, that in the case of Ulysses we are being
asked both to admire a "sinner" and to acquiesce in the
justice of his condemnation. No solution of the "problem"
that fails to meet *both* these requirements can stand up to
what the poem actually and inescapably offers. It may be
helpful to begin by reflecting that this is not the first or the
only occasion in the poem—and more particularly in the
Inferno—that we are aware of a tension of this kind.
Francesca's story of her love for Paolo, as it is told in canto
5, evidently requires that we recognize a distinction between the justice of her condemnation and the pathos of
her history. In this case we are asked to distinguish between Dante the traveler, involved in his journey and
reacting emotionally to the successive situations he encounters, and Dante the poet who—having completed the
journey and understood its meaning—is "remembering"
the encounter and relating it to the totality of what he has
seen and understood. Dante the traveler weeps for
Francesca in her presence and loses consciousness at the
end of her story;[1] Dante the poet-creator recognizes the
"justice" of the condemnation that she has brought upon
herself in relation to the complete plan of his poem. We
might say, perhaps, that in the Francesca episode Dante

requires that we avoid the opposed excesses of the sentimentalist and the Puritan where the "sentimentalist" is defined as one who loves without judging and the "Puritan" as one who judges without loving. To "love" without judgment—Dante would seem to imply—is to live in the illusion that "desire" can be pursued for its own sake and as an exclusive end: that it is possible to desire only to desire. That illusion ends, for Dante, inevitably in "Hell": "Hell" not as a theological abstraction but rather as a realistic fact in human experience. To recognize this reality is not to ignore the opposite truth that to judge without loving is to bring into being a frigid monstrosity that ends equally in the death of the spirit. We are required, as a condition of living humanly, both to "love" and to exercise "judgment," and to exercise it not only with reference to others, which (as Dante surely knew from his own experience) is easy and apt to prove flattering to our self-esteem, but in relation to our own lives.

Something of the same kind can be said of other cantos of the *Inferno*, which tend—significantly—to be among the most memorable in one's reading. It is clear that Farinata degli Uberti, in canto 10, is appropriately punished for the ferocious and sterile pride that inspired, in the "sweet light"[2] of the world "above," his pursuit of the factional rivalries which, in Dante's view, undermined the possibility of a fruitful social order. The preoccupation with aristocratic lineage that leads him to bandy words with his fellow countryman—who is not above responding in kind[3]—is evidently perverse, even grotesque to the point of absurdity; but the absurdity is itself human, and there is dignity, a mixture of pathos and futility, in the bearing of one who rises from the tomb that is his eternal residence, "Com' avesse l'inferno a gran dispetto" ("as if he had great scorn of hell": *Inferno* 10. 36). Similarly, Brunetto Latini, whom Dante addresses so feelingly in canto 15, is evidently a sinner who has trespassed against his God-given "nature" and who now recognizes the secret squalor that has involved him in the fate of men whom he refers to as "tigna" ("scurf": *Inferno* 15. 111), and who were in every way his inferiors. Recognition of the sin and its consequences does not prevent Dante from expressing astonishment at finding his former teacher in so unexpected a situation[4] or from carrying on with him a conversation in the course of which he recognizes in feeling terms his debt to one who taught him "come l'uom s'etterna" ("how man makes himself eternal": *Inferno* 15. 87). Evidently Brunetto was unable to make himself in any positive sense "eternal." That is the pathos and the irony of his situation; but the contrast between the potentiality and the outcome, between what Brunetto might have made of himself (and actually achieved for his pupil) and what, through the corroding influence of a single secret flaw he became, dominates the entire episode.

The pattern of contrasts established in these memorable episodes runs through the *Inferno* consistently enough to be read as a central motive for this part of the poem. So much was implied from the outset, when Dante, standing with Virgil at the foot of the great "Roman" triumphal arch that rises so unexpectedly before them and seeking to decipher the lapidary inscription that crowns it, turns to his guide and says of the words he has just read: "Maestro, il senso lor m'è duro" ("Master, their meaning is hard for me": *Inferno* 3. 12). The difficulty evidently goes beyond the matter of mere deciphering. It concerns the incompatibility that, to a human understanding, separates the visible reality of Hell from the assertion that it reflects the *just* operations of a loving and all-powerful Creator:

> Giustizia mosse il mio alto fattore;
> Fecimi la divina podestate,
> La somma sapienza e 'l primo amore.

("Justice moved my high maker: the divine power made me, the supreme wisdom and the primal love": *Inferno* 3. 4–6.)

Hell, then, as the creation of the "divine love," is a reconciliation of opposites barely conceivable in terms of an ex-

perience necessarily limited to the human order. The tension established in this way at the very outset of Dante's
infernal journey makes itself felt at every stage in his progress. Even at the very bottom of the pit, where the isolating
ice prevails as a fitting environment for the ultimate negation, and where poetry seems to have died and the last
vestiges of human feeling (including the poet's own) have
been replaced by frozen insensitivity, we feel for the pain
inflicted by the traitor Ugolino upon the fellow in betrayal
to whom he is bound in an ultimate parody of relationship.[5] The episodes by which we remember the *Inferno*
begin and end with a pair of sinners eternally joined:
Francesca and Paolo, Ugolino and Ruggieri. In each case,
only one of the pair speaks while the other remains a silent
presence; dialogue tending to the affirmation of community is necessarily excluded from the reality of the sinners'
condition. The process that began with the "sweet" words
of "desire" beloved of the poets ends on the breakdown of
language itself, in inhuman cries of hatred and in the tears
of frustration that freeze to prevent the outward expression of suffering.[6] The process has a logic of its own that
reflects the death of feeling which accompanies the various
stages of the descent into Hell. The reiteration upon so
many levels of what is in effect a single theme should warn
us against the temptation to read into Dante's judgments,
as recorded in the poem, a simple moralizing intention.

Yet, when all this has been said, it is hard not to feel that
the case of Ulysses is in important ways different. In each
of the episodes we have considered we feel, no doubt, for
the sinners in their plight, but recognize the essential justice of a condemnation that, in each case, answers to their
natures and that they have brought upon themselves.
Ulysses, on the other hand, we have been led to admire
and, under the spell of his narration, we find it easy to
forget his condemnation. In spite of the classical tradition,
it is hard for us to think of him as a deceiver, a giver of
false counsel. Indeed, that Dante shared this difficulty is
suggested by the fact that he seems to have felt the need to

introduce in the following canto Guido da Montefeltro, who emerges as a self-confessed false counselor and a very convincing one at that. Guido's story is one of the most effective in the *Inferno,* and it would no doubt be more often recognized as such if it did not suffer from the proximity of Ulysses' great narrative. Given this situation, it seems necessary to turn to the canto in which Ulysses relives his adventure and to study it carefully for indications of what Dante may have intended in writing it. The *Inferno* as a whole evidently follows a plan in which each episode has a part to play and in which the various sins, presented through their "examples," follow one another in accordance with a strict and embracing logic. It is hard to believe that the Ulysses story constitutes an exception to the general rule or that it represents a fortunate surrender on the part of the poet to the leading of his imagination at the expense of the internal logic of the poem conceived as a reflection of human experience. Like all great writers, Dante no doubt places trust in the leading of his imagination, allowing it to take him where it will; but, more than most, he obtains some of his most powerful effects by setting this freedom within the context of a general plan that, in the very act of imposing its own constraint, intensifies the emotional power of his conception.

A close look at what is actually said in the course of the canto even before the entry of Ulysses offers certain clues concerning the poet's intention. The opening lines (26. 1–12), ironically addressed to Dante's own city, establish a connection (26. 4) with the episode immediately preceding, a fact that may have some significance for our purpose. Canto 25 was dedicated to the thieves and culminated in the elaborate description of the interchange of bodies between sinners and serpents, treated in a fashion of which Dante, as an artificer or craftsman in verse, is evidently proud.[7] The connection between the two cantos has some relevance to our problem inasmuch as the "false counselor" can be thought of as a special kind of thief. Whereas the sinners of canto 25 misappropriated material goods, Ulysses and those who are punished with him mis-used their exceptional gifts of intelligence and—above all—their eloquence to lead their fellow human beings on a false quest and in effect to "steal" from them their God-given ability to govern their lives by making reasonable acts of choice. In this sense, Ulysses can be seen as a par-ticularly subtle and insidious kind of serpent, using his intellectual and rhetorical gifts to insinuate himself into the hearts of men, taking possession of their very natures and substituting his own mind and will fraudulently and arrogantly for theirs. One of the results of this misuse of the gifts of reason is the civil strife that, in Florence, has so bitterly affected Dante's own life and to which he refers ironically in these opening lines of the new canto. We are being forewarned, in other words, that the sinner whose fate is now to be the concern of the poem is a particularly subtle kind of thief whose activities are the more grievous for being cloaked in a noble form and for being directed not merely to the appropriation of worldly goods but to manipulating and perverting the natural and distinctively human faculties of the mind.

After this introduction Dante and Virgil resume their journey, climbing up the steep wall of rock that affords access to the new "bolgia": here as on other occasions the pilgrim-poet needs the assistance of his guide (26. 15) in overcoming the difficulties that his mortal body presents to the ascent. At this point Dante chooses to emphasize a danger, not merely physical in kind, which the present stage in his poetic journey seems to foreshadow:

> Allor mi dolsi, e ora mi ridoglio
> > quando drizzo la mente a ciò ch'io vidi,
> > e più lo 'ngegno affreno ch'i'non soglio,
> perché non corra che virtù nol guidi;
> > sì che, se stella bona o miglior cosa
> > m'ha dato 'l ben, ch'io stessi nol m'invidi.

("I sorrowed then, and sorrow now again, when I turn my mind to what I saw; and I curb my genius more than

I am wont, lest it run where virtue does not guide it; so that, if a kindly star or something better has granted me the good, I may not grudge myself that gift": 26. 19–24.)

It seems clear that the passage is written with the following Ulysses episode in mind and that the poet is reflecting upon dangers of a personal nature involving his life and his creative endeavor that the experiences reflected in the story may have for him. He writes in the present, as the author looking back on his fictional experience in the act of re-creating it in his verse. He remembers that he "sorrowed" then (at the time of his journey) and the memory is such that it makes him "sorrow" again, at the present moment of writing and recalling.

The effect of remembering and of having at the time of the journey experienced the "sorrow" that the memory offers is to remind the poet of the need to "curb" his "genius," the "genius" of which he is so often conscious in the course of the poem and which is both the recognition in himself of a unique vocation and a possible source of pride. At this point it is the element of pride that prevails and leads to the warning Dante addresses to himself—as poet rather than as pilgrim—in the lines quoted. Not for the first or the last time, Dante shows himself acutely aware that his "genius" (the inspiration that allowed him to conceive his poem and the power of language that has enabled him to give it expression) could lead him, if allowed free expression, into places "where virtue does not guide it." The reference to Ulysses' coming story of his epic journey, which also includes an appeal to "virtue" (26. 120), is apparent. "Virtue" can easily be confused with self-approval and self-justification.[8] In a poem such as Dante's, the product in no small degree of a need to find compensation for apparent failure and the bitterness of exile,[9] the expressed intention of bringing a saving message to humanity—and the claim that this message is in some sense the result of a divine revelation granted to a mortal poet—can readily turn into a dangerous assertion of self. It is this

danger that is involved in the compelling imaginative quality that so splendidly imposes itself upon the reader in
Ulysses' telling of his story; and it is a danger to which the
gifts of the poet—his ability to transform the "real" in
pursuit of what could easily become self-absorbed and self-
justifying goals—make him peculiarly and dangerously
subject.

It should be noted, in relation to this same passage, that
there are other occasions in the poem where references to
the physical dangers of the journey are used by Dante to
underline the existence of perils of a moral kind, which
need to be met by watchfulness and by the exercise of a
strict control upon the free motions of the spirit. At the
end of the poets' ascent of the Mount of Purgatory (and,
curiously enough, in a canto that is also numbered 26)
Virgil has occasion to warn his protégé that he is approaching a moment of particular danger in his journey
and that it behooves him to take care. "Guarda: giovi ch'io
ti scaltro" ("Take heed: let my warning avail you": *Purg.*
26. 3). Nor does the admonition stand alone. Already, at
the end of the preceding canto, Virgil has expressed himself in terms that are notably close to the passage of the
Inferno that now concerns us:

> "Per questo loco
> si vuol tenere a li occhi stretti il freno,
> però ch'errar potrebbesi per poco."

("Along this place the rein must be kept tight on the
eyes, for one might easily take a false step": *Purg.* 25.
118–20.)

Given Dante's procedures throughout the course of his
poem, this coincidence can hardly be accidental. In both
passages we are touching upon themes that seem to convey
a strong sense of personal danger. In the *Purgatorio*, it is
the purification of lust and the conception of poetry as a
function of "love" that is in question. It is not an accident
that the souls encountered by Dante—the last whom he

meets before he passes through the purifying fire that stands between him and the entry into the Earthly Paradise—are those of two poets, Guido Guinizelli and Arnaut Daniel, whose work is held to stand in close relation to his own. In the *Inferno* a more fundamental danger—that of perverting the true sense of his work to accommodate his own consciousness of personal worth in an uncomprehending world—is the underlying theme of Virgil's warnings to the pilgrim-poet.

In both passages, then, Dante is warned by Virgil—in whom we are to see the higher operations of his own reason—that he stands in grave danger: the danger, in relation to Ulysses' story, of allowing his gifts of language and reasoning to make of him a false guide, a deceiver who has allowed his pleasure in his own powers to outrun "the curb of virtue," turning these gifts to uses that he would later have occasion to repent. The gifts have come to him both from his "kindly star," the confluence of favorable influences that accompanied his birth,[10] and from the higher source, the "something better" that is "grace"; but the awareness of carrying out his poetic task under such propitious auspices, both natural and supernatural, must not become for the poet an invitation to lose control of his gifts or to allow them to become false guides to lead astray those who are induced by them to follow him. It is significant that, a few lines further on, Dante remembers that he needed to grasp a rock in order to save himself from the real peril, caused by his own eagerness to see, of falling into the pit below:

> Io stava sovra 'l ponte a veder surto,
>   sí che s'io non avessi un ronchion preso,
>   caduto serei giù sanz' esser urto.

("I was standing on the bridge, having risen up to see, so that if I had not laid hold of a rock I should have fallen below without a push": 26. 43–45.)

A few further passages in these preparatory lines may

also stand in some relation to what follows. The bucolic evocation of the fireflies (26. 25–33) seen from the hillside by the peasant as he rests from his tasks may serve to remind us, in Hell, of the existence of a natural order of living that Ulysses has ignored; and the references to the Old Testament prophets Elijah and Elisha (26. 34–39)— prophets who were rejected by those to whom they brought their message but who received, in the event, supernatural confirmation for their efforts—recall the existence of true counselors whose warnings were set aside with disastrous consequences. The effect is to balance the intimacy of the previous description with a corresponding sense of distance, of great issues brought to a dramatic conclusion. This again leads to a return to the spectacle of the flames moving along the floor of the *bolgia* below and to an intimation of their still-hidden significance:

> tal si move ciascuna per la gola
>   del fosso, ché nessuna mostra'l furto,
>   e ogni fiamma un peccatore invola.

("so—like the flames of the prophet's chariot rising to heaven—each flame moves along the gullet of the ditch, for not one shows its theft, and each steals away a sinner": 26. 40–42.)

"Theft"; "steals away." Once more the idea of thieving is put forward in anticipation of the coming episode. It is put forward and involved in a deliberate mystery, a sense of things seen but not revealed beneath their appearance, which the studied complexity of the expression insinuates. The sinners are hidden, their identities concealed, within the tongues of flame that correspond to the organs of speech which they used in their mortal lives, to involve the sense of their words in enticements of deception. There is similarity of an almost syntactical kind between the conception of the sinners not "showing their theft" and yet involved in the flame that "steals them away" and the warning, secretly addressed by Dante to his own person, against "grudging himself his own gift" (26. 24).

At this point Virgil confirms to Dante the truth of what he has in fact been quick to understand: that the flames conceal spirits within them, and that "ciascun si fascia di quel ch'elli è inciso" ("each swathes himself with that which burns him": 26. 48). The revelation, typically, is of a concealment: just as the operations of the false counselors during their earthly lives involved them in the hiding of their true meanings, so they are now, in the afterlife, involved in the "tongues" of flame that have become their torment. Dante, in response, asks to know the identity of those who are concealed with a flame "so divided at its top that it seems to rise from the pyre where Eteocles was laid with his brother" (26. 52–55). The reference is to the sons of Oedipus who, having been compelled to abdicate, prayed that they should be eternally at war with one another. The refusal of Eteocles to respect the agreement between them and to allow his brother to reign alternately with him led to the war of the Seven against Thebes and to the death of both brothers. Dante's reference to the double flame is probably the result of his reading of Statius, who records that the flames which issued from the funeral pyre of the dead brothers divided as a sign of the hatred that separated them even in death.[11] The introduction of these elaborate classical references to strife and mutual hatred has the further effect of contributing to the epic quality of the following narrative.

From the opening part of the canto, then, we have learned a number of things that contribute to establishing the sense of what follows. It has been indicated that Ulysses' sin amounts to an aggravated form of theft and that its consequences for society are grievous. There has been a suggestion that Dante himself is personally involved in the story and its telling and that both represent a danger for himself. Moreover, there have been indications of the poet's desire to give a tragic dimension to Ulysses' narrative by distancing it from common speech and from the ordinary concerns of men. And, as a final step before the hero embarks upon his extended speech, we are reminded through Virgil of the multiple acts of "theft" and deception associated with his name. Ulysses was the instigator of the stratagem of the wooden horse that led to the downfall of Troy and of the Trojans who became, through Virgil's hero Aeneas, the ancestors of the Romans: a providential event in which Ulysses appears, in Virgil's poem, in an unfavorable light. He also persuaded Achilles to abandon Deidamia, the mother of his child, and to go to the seige of Troy, where—as the "gods" had foretold through a prophecy known to Ulysses but deliberately suppressed by him—he was fated to meet his death. Finally, together with Diomed, he entered the beleaguered city and stole the Palladium, the sacred image of Athena with which the safety of Troy was bound up and the loss of which foretold the fall of the city. Such, between them, are the traditional reasons that led Virgil, like other Latin authors, to present Ulysses and his activities in a hostile manner.

Dante, as a reader of Virgil, was of course aware of these aspects of the Ulysses story and ready to incorporate them into his poem where they suited his purpose. It is not, however, to thoughts of this kind that he is immediately moved by the presence of the Greek hero. As on other occasions, but to a degree scarcely paralleled in the poem, his imagination is stirred to life by the thought of a great character of classical antiquity, and he expresses himself with urgent anxiety in his desire to speak to the legendary figures hidden from his view in the concealing flame. His words to Virgil advancing his desire acquire a solemnity that reflects his involvement. Addressing Virgil as "maestro," "master," he pleads with him for help in attaining his desire:

> assai ten priego
> a ripriego, che'l priego vaglia mille,
> che non mi facci de l'attender niego.

("I earnestly pray you, and pray again, that my prayer

avail a thousand, that you deny me not to wait": 26. 65–
66.)

Then, as if this expression of concern were not sufficient,
he supports his plea with a further request to Virgil to take
note of the eagerness reflected in his attitude: "Vedi che
del disio ver' lei mi piego!" ("You see how with desire I
bend towards it": 26. 70). "With desire": the word invariably acquires in Dante's use a sense of urgent commitment,
and here it serves to underline the intensity of emotions
that are leading the pilgrim-poet to forget himself at the
prospect of being satisfied in his request.

Virgil, in replying, accepts the plea of his protégé and
fellow poet, finding it "worthy of much praise" (26. 71–
72); but he advises Dante to "restrain his tongue," leaving
it to him to address the heroes, who "since they were
Greeks would be disdainful of your words" (26. 74–75).
The reason for this reply, which has puzzled many com-
mentators, are no doubt various. Dante, as an Italian (a
"Latin"), is a descendant of those Trojans who were
enemies of the Greeks who destroyed their city. The
Greeks now in question, moreover, are the very ones
whose strateagems made that bitter outcome for Troy possible. Further, Virgil as a great poet of classical times and
as author of the *Aeneid* (which includes Aeneas's long account of the fall of Troy) was closer to the heroes than any
Italian poet could be. Whereas in the next canto it is Dante
who addresses his fellow Italian Guido da Montefeltro, it is
suitable that Virgil should address the heroes of classical
antiquity, whom he has already celebrated in his great
poem. Finally, the effect is once more to prepare for the
lofty tragic content of the story we are about to hear.

Virgil, indeed, having obtained Dante's silence, addresses the two heroes hidden within their single flame
with a proper degree of emphasis:

> "O voi che siete due dentro ad un foco,
> s'io meritai di voi mentre ch'io vissi,

s'io meritai di voi assai o poco
quandro nel mondo li alti versi scrissi,
   non vi movete; ma l'un di voi dica
   dove, per lui, perduto a morir gissi."
("O ye who are two within a fire, if I deserved of you
while I lived, if I deserved of you much or little when in
the world I wrote the lofty lines, move not; but let the
one of you tell me where he went, lost, to die": 26. 79–
84.)

The double appeal contained in the repeated phrase "if I
deserved" and the reference to Virgil's own "lofty lines"
serves the double end of stressing the desire (both of the
pilgrim-poets and, by extension, of the reader) to hear the
tale about to be told and of relating it by anticipation to
ends of high tragedy; and the indication that the two
heroes were "lost" refers both to the lack of certainty concerning their earthly ends and to what is now seen to be
their destiny among those eternally "lost." Literally, of
course, Ulysses was "lost" inasmuch as he did not return
from his last journey and no word of his fate transpired
for the enlightenment of future generations; and his story
of his end will be completed by the fact of his actual presence among the damned.

In response to Virgil's eloquent invocation, and while
Dante stands by in wondering silence, "the greater horn of
the ancient flame . . . flung forth a voice" (26. 85, 88) and
embarks upon its eloquent narration. This carries us with
it, as no doubt we are to understand that it carried those
who first heard it; but there are in it a number of indications that are germane for an understanding of Ulysses'
condemnation. In the first place, he chooses to begin his
story by referring, among all his adventures as narrated by
Homer, to the period of subjection to the sorceress Circe
who, he says, "detained me more than a year at Gaeta" (26.
91–92). One might see at this point an invitation on the
part of the poet to look forward to the reproaches that
Beatrice, at the end of the *Purgatorio*,[12] will address to him
for having deserted her memory in the pursuit of lesser

and baser satisfactions. Whether those are to be thought of as surrenders to actual "sins" of a sensual kind or whether they represent a recognition on the poet's part of having been led astray in his intellectual and poetic vocation can—perhaps must—remain an open question. What matters at this point is that Ulysses, like Dante, is aware of having been led astray, induced to forget—at least for a period of time—his true destination; and this forgetfulness, moreover, is conceived—as it is in Dante's own case at the end of the *Purgatorio*—in terms of a surrender to base and unworthy elements in his own experience.

More important, in the lines that follow, Ulysses, after overcoming the temptation represented by Circe and after bringing his journey to a proper conclusion by returning to Ithaca, undertook a new adventure that—as he now recognizes from the perspective acquired in Hell—involved the abandonment of all the natural ties and responsibilities that should have kept him at home after the completion of his first long voyage:

> né dolcezza di figlio, né la pieta
> del vecchio padre, né'l debito amore
> lo qual dovea Penelopè far lieta
> vincer potero dentro a me l'ardore
> ch'i' ebbi a divenir del mondo esperto
> e de li vizi umani e del valore.

("neither my fondness for my son, nor reverence for my aged father, nor the due love which would have made Penelope glad, could conquer in me the longing that I had to gain experience of the world, and of human vice and worth": 26. 94–99.)

It is essential to the state of the damned to recognize their error without being able or willing to correct it. Ulysses recognizes that commitment to his adventurous project led him to set aside the natural ties and obligations that should have detained him from further adventures in his old age. In this aspiration he was moved by a désire, a "longing," to gain "experience" of all human qualities, both those which lead to the enhancement of human life *(valore)* and those *(vizi)* which occasion its loss. In embarking upon his last journey in a spirit of adventure that contemplated an endless horizon, Ulysses both responded to a fundamental and innate human urge and refused to recognize the need for those "curbs" and "tight reins" of which Dante has already spoken in reference to his own case and which reflect a necessary sense of human limitation.

It is not hard to see in these words of Ulysses an application to the poet's own case. His poetic "journey" too is an adventurous voyage of the spirit: a voyage in search of "experience"—the word recurs frequently in the course of Dante's progress[13]—which has led him into dangerous places and involved him in the very real peril of losing his soul. Ulysses' burning desire for "experience," so eloquently conveyed in his own words, has led him to ignore the boundaries, moral and physical, that define and delimit human life in the process of making "vice" and "value," or "worth," equally objects of his craving. There is at least the suggestion here of a parallel between the great pagan adventurer and the Christian poet. Dante too has undertaken in his poem a "journey" that is taking him through Hell, the abode of "vice," and that is to bring him, with the help of Virgil and Beatrice, "reason" and "grace," to a right understanding of "value." Unlike Ulysses, however, Dante will not be undiscriminating in his pursuit of experience. The object of his journey is to arrive at a proper understanding of "vice" and "virtue," leading to the rejection of the one and to the right pursuit of the other. If Dante, in the course of his downward journey through Hell, experiences "vice," he does so in order to repudiate it and to build his life on foundations of humility and repentance that lie outside the pagan hero's perception. The difference between the two journeys does not, however, exclude in each case a real measure of emotional involvement in the fascination of the quest.

It seems, in other words, that Dante at once responds, as poet, to the imaginative venture represented by Ulysses' story and passes judgment upon him for the refusal to accept human limitations. Some critics have associated this passage, and the sense of the episode as a whole, with Dante's writing, presumably between the *Vita Nuova* and the *Commedia,* of his unfinished "philosophical" treatise, the *Convivio.* Dante, they say, conceived of this work in prose as an adventurous journey in the "open sea" of thought, a journey inspired by the desire to follow "philosophy" and "science" as self-sufficient means for the attainment of truth. The writing of the *Convivio,* as seen by Dante at a later stage in his life, would seem—according to this line of interpretation—to represent for him the turning away from a more "spiritual" conception of life, a turning away for which Beatrice, in the *Purgatorio,* seems to reproach him and which inspired the writing of the *Commedia.*

One need not, perhaps, press too far these possible "biographical" antecedents, which may or may not have relevance for what emerges in the poem as the statement of what Dante has come to understand as a reality of the human condition. We can hardly fail, in any case, to recognize in him a natural tendency to place confidence in the ability of reason (the exercise of which he associated with man's central obligation to make right use of his privilege of free will) to arrive at truth. This is plainly stated, in significant connection with the exercise of freedom of choice, by Dante in response to Beatrice in the fourth canto of the *Paradiso:*

> Io veggio ben che già mai non si sazia
> nostro intelletto, se'l ver non lo illustra
> di fuor dal qual nessun vero si spazia.
> Posasi in esso, come fera in lustra,
> tosto che giunto l'ha: e giunger puollo:
> se non, ciascun disio sarebbe frustra.

("Well do I see that never can our intellect be wholly satisfied unless that Truth shine on it, beyond which no truth can range. Therein it rests, as a wild beast in his lair, so soon as it has reached it; and reach it it can, else every desire would be in vain": *Paradiso* 4. 124–29.)

The discussion started with Dante's question, addressed to Beatrice, concerning the sanctity of vows. The nub of her argument is stated in the following canto, when she tells him that the importance of the vow consists in the fact that it represents a free decision, on the part of a human being, acting in full awareness, to return to God the highest gift— that of freedom of choice—that God conferred upon him.[14]

The reason given to men expresses itself, accordingly, above all in the making of right choices. Dante's faith in reason is such that he is willing, in the lines that immediately follow in the passage we are considering, to see the possibility of doubt as inseparable from its exercise:

> Nasce per quello, a guisa di rampollo,
>   a piè del vero il dubbio; ed è natura
>   ch'al sommo pinge noi di collo in collo.

("Because of this, doubt springs up like a shoot, at the foot of the truth; and this is nature which urges us to the summit, from height to height": *Paradiso* 4. 130–32.)

To be human, as Dante understands it, is to be capable of "doubt," to raise "questions" that present themselves in succession and that, when answered by the exercise of reason, lead step by step, in an ascent towards the "summit," to a truth that, in its final completeness, must always lie beyond our attainment in time, in the "infinite excess"[15] that of necessity separates a timeless creator from his temporal creation.

Reason, then, at once confirms man in the exercise of his choices and makes it clear to him that these choices cannot, in time, be final or self-sufficient. The paradox that, for Dante, lies at the heart of the human situation is summed up by Marco Lombardo in the course of the discussion on the relation of "free will" to "love" that is placed at the center of the *Purgatorio* and indeed of the whole poem. Speaking of man, Marco says:

> A maggior forza e a miglior natura
>   liberi soggiacete; a quella cria
>   la mente in voi, che'l ciel non ha in sua cura.
> ("You lie subject, in your freedom, to a greater power and to a better nature, and that creates the mind in you which the heavens have not in their charge:" *Purgatorio* 16. 79–81.)

The God-given faculty of reason, which expresses itself in the definition of free choices, proceeds from the "mind," which in the exercise of its freedom is not subject to the determining influence of the stars. To choose freely and rationally, in accordance with a true understanding of one's nature, is the distinguishing mark of a human being; but in its exercise he will be led, by this same reason, to recognize the necessity of his subjection to the "greater power" and the "better nature" that conferred upon him the privilege of choice. It is this recognition that Ulysses failed to make and for which he is finally condemned; and the condemnation, far from being the expression of an obscurantist hostility to reason and adventurous speculation, is central to his creator's understanding of the paradox involved in being human.

In the light of these considerations we begin, perhaps, to understand the sense of the Ulysses episode and to grasp its place in the conception that governs Dante's poem. In creating the figure of Ulysses, Dante is balancing his faith in human reason—a faith that borders at times on the arrogant[16]—with a recognition that "reason" has its limits, that "truth" is revealed by God as well as approached by "reasonable" philosophic and scientific speculations. With or without the example of the *Convivio* Dante is both expressing and judging an unprecedented journey on the "open sea" of thought: living an adventure to which his imagination responded, and still responds, powerfully, but

which seems to him, as he looks back upon it in the light of
his own more recently acquired understanding, to have
led him to the intimate danger of shipwreck.

Nothing in this argument means that we should deny to
Ulysses' story a full measure of imaginative identification.
Indeed, to fail in this would be to subvert the entire sense
of the episode. From the moment in which the hero recalls
himself as "putting forth" on "l'alto mare aperto" ("the
deep open sea": 26. 100), with "one vessel only" and a crew
composed of that "small company which had not deserted
me" (26. 102), we sense his thrilling (and that of the poet
with him) to the prospect of an unprecedented adventure.
Beyond the powerful emotional identification, however,
there are questions to be asked. We are told that Ulysses'
companions were "old and slow" (26. 106) when they set
out on their voyage; we also learn that most of his original
followers had "deserted" him. In other words, what he
required of his followers amounts to an act of faith in the
compelling validity of his vision. The responsibility for the
voyage rested upon him alone and, as we respond to his
retelling of it, we are led not only to grant him in proper
measure our admiration and wonder but to ask ourselves:
Where is he leading them? and was he not, in one sense at
least, using the fascination of his imagination and his
oratorical gifts to impose upon them what turned out to be
a deception? These are questions that we can readily take
beyond the Greek hero's situation to involve the use by the
poet of his mastery of language and power of imaginative
transformation in his creation of what he repeatedly calls
his unprecedented poet effort.[17]

These balanced contraries of danger and adventure are
more urgently felt as Ulysses and his companions approach "that narrow outlet where Hercules set up his
markers, that men should not go beyond" (26. 107–9).
These are, of course, the Pillars of Hercules, the limit for
human endeavor set up by the pagan gods. It is, however,
the specific human vocation to "go beyond," in pursuit of
that "truth" that men are impelled by their natures to seek

and that presents itself to them, of necessity, as always incomplete. This seeking of what is "beyond" is at once an invitation to adventure, which corresponds to man's sense of his highest capacities, and a possible cause of hubris. Both are present when Ulysses, responding to the challenge facing him, inspires his men with splendid eloquence, addressing them as "brothers" in the endeavor he urges upon them:

> "O frati," dissi, "che per cento milia
>   perigli siete giunti a l'occidente,
>   a questa tanto picciola vigilia
> d'i nostri sensi ch'e del rimanente
>   non vogliate negar l'esperïenza,
>   di retro al sol, del mondo sanza gente.
> Considerate la vostra semenza:
>   fatti non foste a viver come bruti,
>   ma per seguir virtute e conoscenza."

("'O brothers!,' I said, 'who through a hundred thousand dangers have reached the west, to this so brief vigil of our sense that remains to us, choose not to deny experience, following the sun, of the world that has no people. Consider your origin: you were not made to live like brutes, but to pursue virtue and knowledge'": 26. 112–20.)

Here we have what is in effect the heart of the episode: and our response to Ulysses' eloquence should not lead us to ignore the underlying sense of a double significance. That the eloquence *is* splendid and that we are required to respond to it is not in question. Ulysses is giving expression to what he sees, and sees truly, as that innate thirst for "experience" that drives man always beyond and that constitutes the highest affirmation of human potentiality. This, for Ulysses as for Dante, is man's nature, and in his pursuit of it he can conceive no limit to what he (and his creator with him) are disposed to see as the specific human vocation. The sense of human experience as incomplete, as necessarily pointing beyond itself, is indeed the foundation of any "religious" reading of life.

For Dante, however, by the time he came to write the *Commedia*—whatever he may have felt in his earlier years—this affirmation cannot answer to the complete truth. Having journeyed through Hell and having experienced the infernal reality in his own flesh Dante requires us to balance our real admiration for Ulysses with a recognition of limits, an acceptance of the fact that there are frontiers, imposed on men by the reality of their temporal situation, beyond which they cannot go. To the extent that this is so Ulysses' magnificent project is doomed by its very nature to failure. In addressing his followers as "brothers," he was in effect deceiving them, asking them to sacrifice the reality of their human lives in pursuit of a noble and grandiose fiction that reflects his own special form of pride. In the last analysis, Ulysses proposed to refuse to live humanly, to reject the human measure that his nature, when rightly understood, imposed upon him.

Genuinely moved (and deceived) by this eloquence, Ulysses' companions are induced to share his enthusiasm for the journey before them: his words have made them so "keen" ("aguti": 26. 121) that he "could hardly have kept them back" (26. 123). Thus inspired, and—significantly—turning their backs upon the source of light ("turning our stern to the morning": 26. 124), they enter upon their "mad flight" (26. 125). Now, from the perspective of Hell, Ulysses knows his adventure to be that: but his imagination, fixed in his ultimate sense of his own nature, still thrills to the memory of the conception that moved, and still moves, his eloquence. The stages of the journey are related (26. 127–29) to the motion of the unfamiliar stars of the Southern hemisphere: stars that are absent from Hell, but here—uniquely, to this degree—present in the memory of a sinner. Dante's own journey through Purgatory and Paradise, which is at once parallel to and contrasted with that of the Greek hero, will be related at each stage to the motions of the firmament: but that journey, of course, will have an end of life, whereas the "mad flight" can lead only to death, for Ulysses and those whom he has induced to follow him.

At the end of the adventure the seafarers are offered the distant view of a destination that is not to be theirs: a mountain

> bruna
> per la distanza, e parvemi alta tanto
> quanto veduta non avëa alcuna.

("dark in the distance, and to me it seemed the highest I had ever seen". 26. 133–35.)

Like Dante on his journey, Ulysses is offered the prospect of a mountain, and there is a clear parallel between what he sees and the Mount of Purgatory. The end of the two journeys is, however, different. The pilgrim Dante, when at the beginning of the poem he came out of the "dark wood" in which he was lost,[18] stood at the foot of a hill illuminated by the light of the sun: a hill that he desired to climb but that he was prevented from approaching directly by the action of the leopard, the lion, and the wolf.[19] Only after a journey that took him, under the guidance of "reason" set in motion by "grace," through the entire depth of Hell; only after he has emerged from these mortal perils to stand in the renewed light of the morning sun at the foot of the Mount of Purgatory; and only after he has wept for his sins and been girded with the rush that represents humility,[20] is he in a proper state to embark upon the ascent. Unlike Dante the pilgrim, Ulysses failed to approach the mountain in a proper spirit, recognizing his own sins and his share of the limitation that his mortality implies: and so the "joy" with which he and his followers greeted the sight of the distant height (26. 136) becomes an act of presumption and turns to tears as their vessel, struck by a rejecting blast that reflects the will of

"Another" (26. 141), founders within sight of its unattainable objective.

Our reading of the episode has made it clear that its sense is not to be understood in terms of any one reading but depends rather upon a fruitful tension of the kind that marks so many of the most memorable episodes of the *Inferno*. For a full answer to the question we posed at the outset, concerning the reason for Ulysses' condemnation, it may be helpful to move beyond the story itself and to consider certain connections that seem to bind it to the larger themes of the poem. We may perhaps best begin by considering that certain images connected with the story recur in the course of the work, with an imaginative reverberation that seems to answer to its deepest sources of inspiration. Among these there figures prominently the image of seafaring, of a voyage of discovery in unknown and dangerous waters: an image applied to life, and more particularly to the "adventure" recorded in, and synonymous with, Dante's poem. Dante too thinks of his work as a journey of discovery in uncharted waters. At the very beginning of the poem, he compares his delivery from the "dark wood" to the situation of a swimmer who

> con lena affannata,
> uscito fuor del pelago a la riva,
> si volge a l'acqua perigliosa e guata.

("who with laboring breath has escaped from the deep to the shore (and) turns back to look upon the dangerous waters": *Inferno* 1. 22–24.)

It should be noted that Dante describes himself as coming out of the "dangerous waters" to stand at the foot of a hill that—like Ulysses, and as I have already indicated—he is unable to climb by direct effort.

The line of imagery initiated in this way has various ramifications in the course of the poem. At the beginning of the *Purgatorio* Dante speaks of "la navicella del mio in-

gegno" ("the little bark of my genius": *Purgatorio* 1. 2), and
says that he is about to "course over better waters" (1. 1);
while at the end of this opening canto he refers to himself
and Virgil in these terms:

> Venimmo poi in sul lito diserto,
>   che mai non vide navicar sue acque
>   omo, che di tornar sia poscia esperto.

("Then we came to the desert shore, that never saw any
man navigate its waters who afterwards had experience
of return": 1. 130–32.)

The parallel with Ulysses' unprecedented voyage seems
clear: that a connection exists is confirmed by Dante's use
of the word *esperto,* paralleled in *Inferno* 26. 98, as well as
by the echo, in the next line, of the phrase "com' altrui
piacque" ("as pleased another": *Purgatorio* 1. 133; *Inferno*
26. 141). The effect of the echo is not annulled by the fact
that Ulysses is referring to the God who has rejected him
and Dante to Virgil in his guiding action. Both Dante and
Ulysses stand in significant relation to a mountain that
they aspire to climb. Unlike the Greek hero, the Christian
poet has learned to approach it in a proper spirit and this
will make it possible for him to make the ascent from
which Ulysses was barred.

In the *Paradiso,* the references to seafaring become
more insistent as Dante's sense of the difficulties that face
him in that last stage of his poetic undertaking grows.
There are abundant signs that he is aware both of the
immense literary challenge represented by an attempt to
find language to convey the paradisal experience and of
the possible presumption involved in the assertion on the
part of a mortal being that he has been given the grace, on
this side of death, to see the state of the blessed and to
enjoy, however fleetingly, the Vision of God. In *Paradiso*-1,
Dante speaks of the entire creation as moving in accordance with the divine design over "the great sea of being"
(1. 113). At the opening of canto 2 he develops to unusual

length the comparison of his poetic undertaking to a journey over uncharted waters (2. 1–18), and addresses those
who are disposed to follow him—his readers—as voyagers
in their "little bark" whom he advises of the peril involved
in following "dietro al mio legno che cantando varca" ("following behind my boat that singing makes her way": 2. 3).
Ulysses' boat, we remember, was also twice described as a
"legno" (a wooden vessel: *Inferno* 26. 101, 138) to indicate
both its fragility and the daring of the human being who
entrusted his safety to it.

The comparison, indeed, goes further than this. In the
passage from the *Paradiso,* those who may aspire to follow
the poet in his voyage are urged to return to the safety of
the shore and not to commit themselves to the perils of the
"pelago," "the open sea" (2. 5). In other words, where
Ulysses persuaded his followers to ignore the dangers of
the journey, with the effect of deceiving them, Dante issues a warning to those who may be persuaded to follow
him in his project without a true understanding of what it
entails. The lines that at once follow combine the poet's
sense of pride in his venture with a stressing of the dangers involved in its persecution. Once again, the terms in
which he describes his projected adventure remind us of
those already used by Ulysses: "L'acqua ch'io prendo già
mai non si corse" ("The water that I take was never
coursed before": 2. 7). Unlike Ulysses, however, Dante
does not rely exclusively upon his own resources but takes
confidence from his sense of divine guidance. Minerva,
the goddess of wisdom, "breathes," and Apollo, the god of
poetry, "guides" him, and "nine Muses point out to me the
Bears" (2. 8–9). The Bears make up the constellation that
guides mariners on the open waters safely to their destination.

Dante's poetic journey, then, like Ulysses' adventure, is a
perilous undertaking in which the Christian poet, unlike
the pagan adventurer, is aware of the need for divine
guidance, and in relation to which he is conscious of the
responsibility involved in offering to induce others—his

readers—to follow him. He has warned incautious travelers of the danger of following in his steps; but, having
done this, he also recognizes that there are among them
those who will approach the adventure in a proper spirit
and who can make the journey. These are those who, following a Eucharistic line of imagery that is variously present in the poem,[21] "have lifted up their necks betimes for
the bread of angels, on which we here subsist but never
become sated of it" (2. 10–12). The "bread of angels" is
Wisdom, which constitutes the object of the human quest.
Ulysses sought to acquire "conoscenza," knowledge of "human vices and value"; but the use at this point of imagery
with Eucharistic associations serves to remind us that
Dante's undertaking, unlike that of Ulysses, is supported
by true supernatural resources that come to him from his
access to Christian belief. Those who share this source of
strength may follow him on his journey. They, and they
alone, may "commit their vessel to the deep brine" ("l'alto
sale": 2. 13) and trust to Dante's poem as a true guide:

> servando mio solco
> dinanzi a l'acqua che ritorna equale.
> ("holding to my furrow ahead of the water that turns
> smoothe again": 2. 14–15)

The extended comparison comprises an introduction as
long and elaborate as any in the poem. It is brought to an
end (2. 16–18) by a reference to the Ulysses-like figure of
Jason, the first human being who adventured into unknown seas in the quest for the Golden Fleece and whose
companions were amazed by what they saw, or experienced, on the way. It is significant that at the very end of
the *Paradiso,* when the pilgrim attains the final end of his
journey and is granted for a moment the vision in which
all reality is gathered,[22] the thought of Jason as a traveler
breaking into unknown waters and inducing wonder in
the god of the sea, Neptune, as he sees for the first time
the shadow of a man-made keel breaking into his do-

main,[23] recommends itself as an image for the unprecedented and perilous nature of his undertaking.

Side by side with these references are others, scattered through the poem, that refer more explicitly to Ulysses and his adventure. At *Purgatorio* 19. 19–24, there is a direct reference to the song of the Sirens that tempted the wanderer on his path:

> "Io son," cantava, "io son dolce serena,
>   che' marinari in mezzo mar dismago;
>   tanto son di piacere a sentir piena!
> Io volsi Ulisse del suo cammin vago
>   al canto mio; a qual meco s'ausa,
>   rado sen parte; sì tutto l'appago!"

("'I am,' she sang, 'I am the sweet Siren who leads mariners astray in mid-sea, so full am I of pleasantness to hear! Ulysses, eager to journey on, I turned aside to my song: and whoever abides with me rarely departs, so wholly do I satisfy him!'": 19. 19–24.)

Ulysses, we remember, began his narrative by referring to Circe, who detained him from his journey for a year. Here it is interesting to note that the Siren is said to have turned him aside from his purpose in spite of his eagerness to continue the homeward voyage. This is a departure from the Homeric story, which presents a hero who successfully resisted these advances by having himself tied to the mast of his ship.[24] Dante seems to be comparing himself to Ulysses and referring to circumstances in his own career that represented a temporary deviation from the goal he had set himself.

At a later stage in the *Paradiso,* Dante, as he approaches the end of his journey, describes himself as standing at the upper limits of the created universe and is urged by Beatrice to look back from his point of vantage in the Primum Mobile in order to consider from this new perspective the insignificance of what he has left behind:

> io vedea di là da Gade il varco
> folle d'Ulisse.
>
> ("I saw, beyond Cadiz, the mad track of Ulysses": *Paradiso* 27. 83–84.)

What lies beyond Cadiz, beyond the limits imposed by the gods and ignored by Ulysses, is the endless open sea of his adventure. Dante has reached a point from which this can seem to be insignificant in relation to the greater, true journey that is now approaching its goal. He speaks of the "mad track" of Ulysses, echoing the hero's own description of his adventure as "il folle volo," "the mad flight."[25] Taken together, the phrases point to a similarity (and a difference) between Ulysses' adventure on the sea and that of Dante over the uncharted waters of "experience" that is the subject of his unprecedented poem. In each case, though to different ends, the effect is to balance the joy of adventure into the unknown, conceived as an essential affirmation to man's true nature, with the perils represented by self-deception and eventual shipwreck. Ulysses' first voyage, at least, was a positive adventure, and the fact that—in Dante, if not in Homer—the Siren was able to entice him from pursuing it, points to the essential ambivalence with which the poet approached the whole question of intellectual and spiritual voyaging. It is an ambivalence that permeates the *Commedia* and constitutes a presence sufficiently powerful to provide a ground-theme for the entire work.

The story told by Ulysses, then, conveys a fascination and—with it, inseparable from it—a sense of danger. Both have to do with the thirst for "experience" (26. 116) that moved him to exploration and that emerges both as the response to an innate human need and as bearing within itself the potentiality for mortal peril when it is pursued without a recognition of the limits imposed upon man by his time-conditioned nature, by the fact of his mortality, and by the inescapable realities of his human life. Ulysses, in other words, used his remarkable powers of imagination and his mastery of the resources of language to lead those less gifted than himself away from their homes and families to death in the infinite emptiness of the sea. In developing this conception of Ulysses' voyage, Dante was no doubt influenced by the existence of a classical tradition that saw in the Greek hero and in his adventures a "symbol" for the "philosopher" in his pursuit of wisdom. The following passage from Cicero, with its explicit reference to the temptation of Ulysses by the Sirens, is relevant:

> Homer was aware that his story would not sound plausible if the magic that held his hero inmeshed was merely an idle song! It is knowledge that the Sirens offer, and it was no marvel if a lover of wisdom held this dearer than his home. A passion for miscellaneous omniscience no doubt tempts a man as a mere dilettante; but it must be deemed the mark of a superior mind to be led on by the contemplation of high matters to a passionate love of knowledge.[26]

In these terms, Dante could clearly identify himself with Ulysses in his "passionate love of knowledge" and in feeling himself driven by a "passion" that is more than the desire for "miscellaneous omniscience."

The following passage from Horace, writing of Homer in the *Epistles,* points in the same direction:

> Again of the power of worth and wisdom he (Homer) has set before us an instructive pattern in Ulysses, that tamer of Troy, who looked with discerning eyes upon the cities and manners of many men; and while for self and comrades he strove for a return across the broad seas, many hardships he endured, but could never be overwhelmed in the waves of adversity.[27]

Once again, and though it is not necessary to suppose that Dante had this or similar passages in mind, the relevance to the poet's own case is evident. That Dante thought of his vicissitudes in exile in terms of a sea voyage is evident from a passage in the *Convivio* in which he says of himself: "I have been a ship without sail or steering wheel, carried to different ports, estuaries, and shores, by the dry wind of dolorous poverty."[28] Like Dante in exile, Ulysses was a wanderer cast adrift from his natural moorings: a wanderer who sought to impose upon his journey the sense of a goal, an end, always sought and never, in time, to be finally attained. That Ulysses had already acquired in classical times a moral significance is evident from passages like the following from Seneca's *Letters:*

> Do you raise the question, "Through what regions did Ulysses stray?," instead of trying to prevent ourselves from going astray at all times? We have no desire to hear lectures on the question whether he was sea-lost between Italy and Cadiz, or outside our known world (indeed, so long a wandering could not possibly have taken place within its narrow bounds); we ourselves encounter storms of the spirit, which toss us daily and our depravity drives us into all the ills which troubled Ulysses.[29]

Here the tendency to interpret Ulysses' voyage in a moral sense is apparent. A discrepancy is recognized between the time employed in the journey and the narrowness of the geographical setting: "depravity" and "ills" are associated with the venture and its relevance for the situation of all men is plainly stated.

As far as Dante's work is concerned, it seems useful to connect the Ulysses' story with the circumstances of the confrontation with Beatrice that constitutes the goal of his journey in the *Purgatorio*. Directing her indictment to the assembled "court" of angels that is witness to the encounter, she stresses the gifts—both of "nature" and of "grace"—that she accuses him bitterly of having turned to perverse use:

> Non pur per ovra de le rote magne,
>   che drizzan ciascun seme ad alcun fine
>   secondo che le stelle son compagne,

> ma per larghezza di grazie divine,
>> che sì alti vapori hanno a lor piova,
>> che nostre viste là non van vicine,
> questi fu tal ne la sua vita nova
>> virtualmente, ch'ogni abito destro
>> fatto averebbe in lui mirabil prova.

("Not only through the working of the great wheels, which direct every seed to some end according as the stars are its companions, but through largess of divine graces that have for their rain vapors so lofty that our sight goes not near thereto, this man was such in his new life, virtually, that every right disposition would have made a marvelous proof in him": *Purgatorio* 30. 109–17.)

The emphasis lies on the exceptional gifts conferred upon the poet and upon the responsibility placed on him for turning to good use what was granted to him "virtualmente," "in potentiality." As a result of the process recorded in the *Vita Nuova*, Beatrice says, Dante was given an understanding of the true nature of love that would have enabled his gifts, both of the natural and supernatural order, to come to "marvelous proof": to bear fruit, in other words, in a great work that would reflect upon the common good. For a time, she says, it seemed that the promise would come to fruition, inasmuch as she "sustained" him with her presence and "led him with me turned towards the right goal" (30. 121–23). After her death, however, which is the point at which the experience recorded in the *Vita Nuova* ends, Dante—she says—allowed himself to be led into paths of error," following false images of good, which pay no promise in full" (30. 131–32). Indeed, his situation became one of moral danger:

> Tanto giù cadde, che tutti argomenti
>> a la salute sua eran già corti,
>> fuor che mostrarli le perdute genti.

("He fell so low that all means for his salvation were now short, save to show him the lost people": 30. 136–38.)

The relation of this to Ulysses and his story is not difficult to establish. Like Ulysses, Dante was the possessor of faculties that offered great potentiality for good and that should have been displayed in a project which benefited those who relied upon him for guidance. This potentiality, however, ran for a time the grave risk of being directed into deceptive ends. Like Ulysses, Dante allowed his possession of these gifts to seduce him into false paths in the process, as Beatrice says, of "taking himself from me and giving himself to others" (30. 126).

From this mortal danger, the result of undue confidence in his own attainments, Dante has been saved by Beatrice's intervention. The rescue, however, has entailed a cost. It has been necessary that, like Ulysses, he should make the descent into the infernal regions, with all that this implies in terms of pain and self-alienation. He too has had "experience" of Hell; but his sufferings, unlike those of the Greek hero, who remains unrepentantly fixed in his predicament, have proceeded from a recognition of error that Ulysses was unwilling or unable to make, and they have opened for him the possibility of salvation. Since he has approached the Mount in a proper spirit of humility and has shown recognition of his human error, he is permitted to make the ascent and to reach the summit; whereas Ulysses, who may be said to represent what Dante, or any man, might easily have become, founders at a distance from the goal.

The following canto (31) of the *Purgatorio*, which continues the repentant poet's meeting with Beatrice, may also be relevant to our purpose. There Dante is accused of having been unfaithful to the memory of his love with a "pargoletta" ("a young girl": *Purgatorio* 31. 60) who may have some connection with the "window lady" of the *Vita Nuova*,[30] and eventually with the "Lady Philosophy," who seems to have replaced Beatrice in the *Convivio*.[31] The change is due no doubt to the shift in emphasis that can be perceived in comparing the two works. The *Vita Nuova* is an exploration of love, its alternate joys and disappointments, and an indication of the way in which this subjection to the vicissitudes of desire can be overcome. The *Convivio,* which Dante seems to have left unfinished when he embarked on the *Commedia,* is written in what emerges as a spirit of confidence in human reason and in its ability to achieve "truth." That confidence is, indeed, a constant feature of Dante's genius. It is maintained in the *Commedia* where—as we have seen—he reaffirms to Beatrice his belief that reason can arrive at truth:

> e giugner puollo:
> se non, ciascun disio sarebbe *frustra.*[32]

The affirmation is made, however, in a new context, which establishes an important difference between the prose treatise and the poem. The difference is indicated, interestingly enough, in a passage in the *Paradiso* where Dante, to convey his new understanding, returns once more to his favorite image of the open sea. In canto 19 the eagle of Divine Justice addresses the pilgrim-poet in response to his question concerning the fate of the "virtuous heathen" in relation to the divine plan for salvation. The eagle stresses that the purposes of the Creator are of necessity beyond the grasp of unaided human reason:

> Però ne la giustizia sempiterna
>   la vista che riceve il vostro mondo,
>   com' occhio per lo mare, entro s'interna;
> che, ben che da la proda veggia il fondo,
>   in pelago nol vede; e nondimeno
>   èli, ma cela lui l'esser profondo.

("Therefore the sight that is granted to your world penetrates within the Eternal Justice as the eye into the sea; which, though from the shore it can see the bottom, in the open sea it sees it not, and none the less it is there, but the depth conceals it": *Paradiso* 19. 58–63.)

Man in the exercise of his gift of reason stands in relation to the order of the eternal in the situation of a seafarer proposing to voyage on the deep. Standing on the shore before embarking he is able to perceive the shallow bottom; but once he has entered upon the "open sea," he necessarily loses the ability to see what his reason can tell him is still there. Moved by a faith to which his reason directs him but which it cannot of itself exhaust, the seafarer is able to proceed with confidence on his path; lacking that faith the very possibility of the journey becomes problematic and its end uncertain.

The relation to our problem is clear enough. By the time he came to write the *Commedia* it seems that Dante, while still ready to stand by his affirmation of the validity of human reason, had come through reflections on the circumstances of his own life to believe that "reason" unaided could not provide the answers he needed to the questions raised by his own situation and by its reflection in the world around him. As always, we have to remember in this connection that the pilgrim of the poem is not only the Florentine poet Dante Alighieri, but—through and beyond that intensely personal identity—a "figure" for man in his journey from time to eternity. One might say, perhaps, that he had come in the light of his own experience to reflect more fully upon the necessary disproportion between the temporal and what I choose, for want of a better word, to call the "eternal": the gap that must logically separate time-conditioned human experience from the perception of a reality that is by definition timeless and incommensurate with that experience. Reason, indeed, can convince us of the necessity of this gap. The "bottom" of the sea is there, though the human voyager embarked upon it can no longer perceive it; but the gap that renders direct vision of it impossible can only be bridged by an act or "leap" of faith. Once the necessity for that act has been accepted, Dante would no doubt say that "reason" can build fruitfully upon the acceptance: what it cannot do, as "reason" itself can show, is dispense with the initial "leap" that the circumstances of the case require. Dante—to put the matter in another way—may have come to feel that something, which we might call "grace," had been left out of the earlier picture, and that without it man can neither understand his nature nor satisfy his deepest aspirations. This would suggest that in creating the Ulysses episode, Dante is looking back on what he has come to see as a decisive crisis in his earlier life, the result of an adventure in the realm of "experience" that seemed to offer promise but that—when embarked upon—led finally to personal failure and moral "shipwreck."

The point, of course, is one that does not only concern Dante's hypothetical reading of his own experience. The tensions reflected in the Ulysses story have to do with what the poet saw as inescapable realities built into the human situation: realities that the bitter experience of exile, accompanied by exposure to the vicissitudes of a chaotic world, brought home to him with devastating force. One might say that, finally, Ulysses is condemned in spite of the real fascination that his story holds, because he followed, and induced others less gifted and imaginative than himself to follow, an attempt to satisfy in time a "thirst" that men and women, by the very facts of their human nature, are unable to fulfill within the limits imposed by their temporal situation. To use one of Dante's favorite biblical parallels, the water offered to Christ from her well by the woman of Samaria in Saint John's gospel[33] is insufficient to quench the ultimate human "thirst," which can only be satisfied by "the living water" that he offered in return. It is the recognition of *this* thirst, as he repeatedly states, that Dante aims to promote in his poem;[34] and once it has been satisfied—but only then—all lesser "thirsts" fall naturally into place. On this side of "eternity" there can be, for Dante, no finality in human life, no valid end to the journey; and to seek finality where it is not to be found is to invite disappointment and failure. The satisfaction of the true "thirst" lies in "eternity," even though it is true that the word can only be defined, in terms of reason, through negation. The "eternal" is what man, in time, is *not;* more than that reason cannot tell us. The rest belongs, for

Dante, to an order of the real in which "grace," the free gift of God's love, prevails. The road to the true satisfaction of this innate "thirst" passes, like that of the poet's own journey, through the Mount of Purgatory: it lies in the recognition, which Ulysses failed or was unable to make, of "sin," or, more simply, the insufficiency, the incompleteness, of all that is merely human. Man, it seems, is the creature who, involved in time, and conditioned by the limits of his temporal nature, seeks or aspires through his experience to a timeless fulfillment. Ulysses' error was to have sought this necessary consummation, which the fact of his humanity imposed upon him, in an unending extension of human consciousness in time: in other words, in an unreal, or at least an incomplete understanding of what "experience," properly understood, must imply. To think of the "eternal" as an endless extension of the temporal is to invite a contradiction: for the "eternal" does not "become" or "cease to be," but simply and simultaneously *is*.

The point made in this way is, if we will, a moral one, and a moral judgment is passed on Ulysses that stands firm, in spite of the fascination of his endeavor; but, when the necessity of the condemnation has been granted, as the logic of the poem requires, we must further recognize that there is in this case, as there is so often in the *Commedia,* an element of real tension between "doctrine" and "experience." Man, it would seem, begins to understand himself when he is conscious of living between "time" and "eternity." It is the recognition of a necessary tension between these two poles that makes Dante's poem something more than a moralizing blueprint for the conduct of human life; and the tension, once accepted, requires from us a full measure of respect for *both* terms in the equation. Once more, the poem asks us to avoid a one-sided or "romantic" reading that identifies with a sinner in his "lost" situation. We need to respond to the fascination of Ulysses' adventure but at the same time to refuse simple identification with a hero rhetoricizing his predicament and demanding our pity: or, better, demanding it beyond the measure of what can, reasonably and humanly, be given.

NOTES

1. *Inferno* 5. 142.

2. *Inferno* 10. 69.

3. *Inferno* 10. 49–51.

4. *Inferno* 15. 30.

5. *Inferno* 33. 4–9.

6. *Inferno* 33. 94–99.

7. *Inferno* 25. 94–99.

8. It is interesting to compare Dante's use of the word with that of Machiavelli in *The Prince* and elsewhere. Machiavelli tends to separate the word from its usual moral connotations and to use it to describe the self-reliance, the ability to conceive a political purpose clearly and to will its execution firmly and decisively, which he associates with successful public affirmation.

9. The long Cacciaguida episode (*Paradiso* 15–17) represents Dante's final effort to come to terms with and to justify the seeming failure of his life.

10. In *Paradiso* 22. 110–20, Dante mentions that he was born under the constellation of Gemini and recognizes that "influence" as formative of his "genius, whatever it be."

11. Statius, *Thebaid* 12. 429–32, quoted by C. S. Singleton in his edition of the *Inferno* (Princeton N.J.: Princeton University Press, 1970).

12. *Purgatorio* 30 and 31. See pp. 78–80 below.

13. Compare, for example, *Purgatorio* 26. 73–75, where the shade of the poet Guido Guinizelli addresses Dante in the following terms:

> Beato te, che de le nostre marche . . .
> per morir meglio, esperienza imbarche!

("Blessed are you . . . who in order to die better do ship experience of our regions.")

14. *Paradiso* 5. 19–33.

15. *Paradiso* 19. 45.

16. In *Purgatorio* 13. 136–38, Dante expresses vividly his fear that he will have to return after his death to undergo purgation for what he recognizes to be his sin of pride.

17. *Paradiso* 2. 7.

18. *Inferno* 1. 1–3.

19. *Inferno* 1. 31, 45, 49.

20. *Purgatorio* 1. 133–35.

21. The sequence for the feast of Corpus Christi, written by Thomas Aquinas, contains the phrase "Ecce panis angelorum" ("Behold, the bread of angels").

22. *Paradiso* 33. 79–93.

23. *Paradiso* 33. 94–96.

24. *Odyssey* 12. 39–54.

25. *Inferno* 26. 125.

26. Cicero, *De Finibus* 48–49, quoted by C. S. Singleton in the notes to his edition of the *Inferno*.

27. Horace, *Epistles* 1. 2. 17–26. Quoted by Singleton in his edition of the *Inferno*.

28. *Convivio*. 1. 3. 5.

29. Seneca, *Epistolae morales*, quoted by Singleton, ed., *Inferno*.

30. *Vita Nuova* 35–39.

31. "I say that this lady is that lady of the intellect who is called Philosophy" (*Convivio* 3. 11. 1).

32. *Paradiso* 4. 128–29.

33. *John* 4:5–14.

34. *Inferno* 21. 1–4.

[3]

The Franklin's Tale

THE Franklin's Tale is commonly thought of as providing a kind of resolution to round off a series of tales in which Chaucer is said to be engaged in developing a varied and subtle exploration of the realities of marriage as a central and dominating reality of human life.[1] The idea is not without its merits but needs to be approached with caution, for reasons that have to do with the very nature of Chaucer's art: an art that tends to be distrustful of final "solutions," and that shows itself increasingly conscious of the inadequacy of "tale-telling" in relation to whatever "truth" may be presumed to exist beyond the varied and intractable waywardness that constitutes the reality of human life in time. In any consideration of the so-called marriage theme, it is necessary to stress two points: in the first place, the theme, inasmuch as it can be said to exist, is conceived as part of a larger design in which "patience" and "grace" are the ultimate realities; and, secondly, that any conceivable resolution of the issues raised in the course of its development must lie, not primarily in the "dramatic" development of their relation to one another, but rather in the referring of them all to the ultimate end, essentially outside and beyond the pilgrimage, which may be presumed to govern their existence. Any skepticism that we may think we detect in the poet's attitude to that "end" concerns, not so much his readiness to believe in its

87

reality as his sense of the necessary inadequacy of all human speculation to give it definition.

After the powerful exercise in disillusioned realism provided by *The Merchant's Tale*, Chaucer returns to the marriage theme in *The Franklin's Tale*. This is connected with
the intervening story by the Squire, a tale of "romantic"
marvels, appropriate to the youth and inexperience of the
teller, and as such incapable of being meaningfully con-
cluded. The Franklin admires the Squire for his "gentility," which reflects his social standing as the son of the
Knight, though the older man's conception of the chival-
rous life, as suggested in the General Prologue[2] and developed at length in his tale, rests on deeper, less "decora-
tive" foundations than that of his son. He draws an
unfavorable comparison with the conduct of his own offspring, whom he has, he says, reproved—"snybbed"—for
his lack of concern for the social graces and the virtues that
they represent. "Fy on possessioun," he says, "But if a man
be vertuous withal" (V. 686–87). The portrait in the General Prologue,[3] however, was less suggestive of a man who
was careless of possessions than of one who had enough of
them to support a show, not necessarily insincere, of indifference in their regard. We may see here, if we will, a
mixture of social ambition and cultured aspiration that
provides a relevant and in some measure a limiting comment on the tale he is about to tell. It is noteworthy that
part at least of the Franklin's disappointment concerns his
son's thriftlessness. His lack of care for "virtue" is associated, in his mind, with his inclination to "pleye at dees"
and

> to despende
> And lese al that he hath,
>
> (V. 690–91)

as well as to waste his conversation on a "page" rather than
to commune with any "gentil wight," by which we may
understand a person of suitably "aristocratic" status and
refinement.

Not all the pilgrims are ready to accept these expressions of pardonable snobbery. The Host declares his impatience when he breaks into the Franklin's words with his habitual bluntness—"Straw for youre gentillesse!"—and roughly commands him to proceed with his story. To say this is not necessarily to identify with the Host's reaction. The Franklin's attitude toward the Squire, and toward his own son, no doubt reflects a disappointment that derives ultimately from the failure to see his own ambition suitably sustained by his offspring; but the phrase about "possession" and its relation to "virtue" surely rings true, and there is no reason we should think that the Host's impatience reflects in any really adverse way upon it. It may be that "gentillesse" is a remote, even in some respects an unreal conception. As much, indeed, has been suggested in the Squire's own tale; but it contains, even beneath the limiting forms of artifice, elements of sweetness and tolerance without which love is inconceivable and human life the poorer. As so often in the course of these tales, we see Chaucer engaged in a characteristic balancing of attitudes and to seek to impose any one-sided "solution" upon what he deliberately leaves open and unresolved is to be untrue to the thrust of his conception.

This, perhaps, is as good a place as any to stress the subtle balance involved in Chaucer's attitude to the courtly tradition and the "gentillesse" that is repeatedly asserted as its distinctive value. No one who has read his treatment of the hero in *Troilus and Criseyde* can doubt that he was aware of the elements of absurdity and presumption in that tradition and that he made it one of his purposes to deal faithfully with its aberrations. In this respect we might say that he was true to the elements of naturalism and bourgeois realism that were an important part of his inheritance from his age. But there are also passages in the *Troilus* that show him responsive to the elements of genuine idealism in the tradition, which suggest that he recognized that, while men cannot hope to live by an "idealism" divorced from reality without some kind of "idealism," some exercise of the creative imagination, their lives cease to be, in any real human sense, meaningful at all. To be "gentil" is, in Chaucer's terms and whether the Franklin so understood it or not, something more than to adopt a distinctive and limited set of social prejudices. It is to be aware of beauty, of the importance of sentiment in life, and so to make tolerable the otherwise brutish and mean concerns of what passes for unrelieved "common sense." "Gentility," the idealism of the world, is indeed a beautiful but vulnerable thing, and the "realism" that is so often set in opposition to it at once necessary and incomplete. If courtly "idealism" is fragile and unreal when carried beyond a certain point, practical "realism" is finally, in the absence of that idealism, rendered pointless and demeaning. Beyond both, reconciling and balancing these contraries, there has to be a reality that includes both in the process of looking beyond them; and to obtain a glimpse of this reality as reflected in the behavior of fallible and inconsistent human beings is a principal objective of the human "pilgrimage."

In any event, since the theme of true "gentillesse," its nature and limitation, is to feature largely in his tale it is reasonable to see in the exchange between the Franklin and the Host a comment, typically Chaucerian in its indirectness, on what we are about to hear. This is to be a story of romance, set in "Armoryk, that called is Britayne," essentially a country of the imagination. The fact is relevant when we are asked to think of the Franklin's story as some kind of "answer" to the challenge laid down by the Wife of Bath. It is as if Chaucer were from the very outset limiting the scope of this "answer," indicating that, related as it is to the problem of "maistrie" as experienced in the relationship of flesh-and-blood men and women, it is offered on a more remote, a less "real" level. The "answer," if it exists, is presented on the level of the imagination, provides something to which a man of genuine, if slightly "literary" sensibility might aspire, rather than a practical comment on the conduct of daily life. In this realm of "romance" a certain knight is said to have offered "service," in the terms of aristocratic and poetic convention, to the "lady" of his devotion. The relationship is of the kind sanctioned by the conventions of courtly poetry, which contain elements that any "realistic" view of marriage will do well to take into account but which can hardly be thought of as containing much that is of direct application to Dame Alice's more solid and tangible world. The lady is of "so heigh kynrede" that the knight is scarcely able, "for drede," to offer her the "service" by which he hopes to prove himself worthy of her. Accordingly, he has lived for a long period in the state of "peyne" and "distresse" associated, according to the poets, with those who pass their lives in subjection to the God of Love.

In this case, however, the lady has been persuaded to accept the knight's offer of dedication. On account of his "worthynesse" and, above all, of the "obeysaunce" that is the sign of his true devotion, she has been moved to show "pity" for his "penaunce," with the result that

> pryvely she fil of his accord
> To take hym for hir housbonde and hir lord,
> Of swich lordshipe as men han over hir wyves.
> (V. 741–43)

The marriage, in reference to the issues raised by the Wife of Bath, is to be one in which the knight agrees to assert no "maistrie" over his wife, but rather to "hire obeye, and folwe hir wyl in al" (V. 749); for this, we are told, is what is to be expected in terms of the view of love on which the tale is based: "As any lovere to his lady shal" (V. 750).[4]

There is, however, to be one curious exception to this arrangement. Arveragus, while renouncing the claim to exercise real "authority" in his marriage, will continue to claim its appearance in the eyes of the world:

> Save that the name of soveraynetee,
> That wolde he have for shame of his degree.
> (V. 751–52)

The whole meaning of the tale turns, in an important sense, upon the difference between the "name" of things, their nature as men conceive and will them to be, and their ineludible reality. It is necessary to give this situation its intended weight; for the effect is to place any simple reading of the story as a direct answer to the claims of domination advanced by the Wife of Bath largely out of court. We are being warned, in effect, that the tale to follow is based upon what, to a medieval mind, and indeed in most thinking upon this subject at times much later than that of Chaucer, is likely to have seemed an impossible contradiction. The knight proposes to enter upon the state of marriage while neglecting what such thought considers to be true and necessary to its nature. His proposal amounts to a wish to maintain in the eyes of the world the external forms of natural "soveraynetee" that rest traditionally, and, as Chaucer and his time would have assumed, naturally with the husband, while renouncing—beyond its abuse in the form of undue domination—the responsibility that circumstances, the daily realities of living, impose upon him. A real marriage, as distinct from one based on literary fantasy, implies the taking of real and often hard decisions, many of which had to be taken, in any world that either Chaucer or his age could conceive, by the male party to the relationship. To set out by evading this responsibility, the existence—to anticipate the central symbol of the tale—of real and solid "rocks" in any relationship worthy of the name, is to propose literature as a substitute for life and to try to live, comfortably but impossibly, in the shelter of the illusion that gave rise to the attempt.

The story, then, is set in motion under the sign of a typically Chaucerian ambiguity, and we are being warned—if we are ready to read it with the care, the capacity for maintaining necessary distinctions, which is part of the author's continuing requirement of us—against any one-sided or sentimental reaction. The aristocratic "service" of courtly love, which so engages the Franklin's essentially bourgeois aspirations, is at once attractive and insufficient. It is compatible with, indeed serves to advance, human and civilizing virtues that belong to any tolerable conception of life, and to these the tale is ready to give full value as providing part of the answer to the problem that the assertion of "maistrie" by the Wife of Bath has raised and which in effect her story of her marriages and the following tale largely, if unconsciously, underlined. It is true, and in a very real sense necessary, that personal relationships need to rest on a foundation of mutual respect, on the indispensable exercise of "trust." To the extent that it advocates this position, the tale affirms the true nature of the "gentillesse" that the Wife of Bath considered in her tale,[5] but which her "philosophy" of domination prevented her from displaying in her own life.

This, however, is not the whole story, and the tenor of *The Franklin's Tale* is to involve its hero and heroine in contradictions that cannot be resolved simply by affirming values that the Franklin, as teller, assumes to be true but which are misleading as sufficient guides for dealing with the problems of *real,* as distinct from literary or "romantic," living. The knight of the story is to be both commended and reproved: commended for his "gentle," courteous attitude and for the exercise of trust in his relationship with his wife, and reproved for his too-easy assumption that he can simply set aside the realities implied in a state that has its social context beyond that of the immediate bond between the man and woman directly affected. In that context the husband has obligations that call for recognition—the acceptance of a real, a natural situation—from all concerned if the marriage is to stand as a valid relationship.

This element of ambiguity emerges even more clearly in relation to the attitude of the wife. In return for her "servaunt" lover's renunciation of authority she agrees to be "youre humble trewe wyf," and expressly states that this is the natural and appropriate response to his gesture of "gentillesse." To his offer of "so large a reyne" of "liberty," she replies with an assertion of the normative virtue of trust upon which any valid relationship must rest:

> Have heer my trouthe, til that myn herte breste.
> (V. 759)

for on this mutual recognition they may reasonably aspire to live their lives "in quiete and in reste."[6] It should be noted, as once more central to the sense of the tale, that the Franklin in his comment makes this position rest on his understanding of the very nature of "friendship," the larger reality of which "love," considered as a relationship between persons of different sex, is only a single if a particularly valuable aspect:[7]

> For o thyng, sires, saufly dar I seye,
> That freendes everych oother moot obeye,
> If they wol longe holden compaignye.
> (V. 761–63)

The relationship so presented is commended insofar at least as "love" and "maistrie" are seen to be mutually exclusive of one another. "Love," comments the Franklin,

> wol nat been constreyned by maistrye.
> Whan maistrie comth, the God of Love anon
> Beteth his wynges, and farewel, he is gon!
> (V. 764–66)

It is significant, however, that the argument, which has already been introduced in terms of "gentillesse," or courtesy, has application to the activities of the God of Love. It is this god who will not suffer constraint, the operation of "maistrie": and it is this god whose values are stated to be incompatible with the attitudes so powerfully advanced by the Wife of Bath. Once more it will be prudent to reflect that these are not the poet's words but those of the character he has created for the purpose of telling the tale: a character who is contributing, in the light of his own understanding, to the greater picture of which his efforts form a part but who cannot safely be assumed to possess superior insight or to transcend the limitations of his own position among his fellow pilgrims.

By allowing his narrator to set the values he is advancing under the auspices of the God of Love, Chaucer is able to stress the element of real value in them while maintaining a tacit reservation; the position is familiar to anyone who has followed the device by which the narrator—"I, that God of Loves servantz serve"[8]—was allowed to advance, up to the point at which they finally fail his protagonists, the values of the god he professes to serve through the course of his story in *Troilus and Criseyde*. The kind of love tht Arveragus and Dorigen are pursuing demands "liberty" as a condition of its being—"Love is a thyng as any spirit free" (V. 767)—where "free" carries the common medieval sense of "generosity," but where also that central human virtue depends for its exercise on a proper recognition of freedom from the constraints that would make such "giving" impossible.[9] It is to be noted that the Franklin follows up his observation with an indirect comment on the extreme and one-sided subjection that was put forward as an ideal by the Clerk in his tale of the patient Griselda:

> Women, of kynde, desiren libertee,
> And nat to been constreyned as a thral.
>
> (V. 768–69)

The emphasis is on "kynde," on what is natural, normal in woman as a sex, and it leads to what can be read as a quiet but effective recall to reality of the Wife of Bath herself: "And so doon men, if I sooth seyen shal" (V. 770). Both men and women naturally desire what they call "liberty," and the key to a successful relationship in marriage lies in tolerance, the exercise of the indispensable virtue of "patience," by which things may be "vanquisshed"— achieved—"that rigour sholde nevere atteyne" (V. 775).

The point is gently, even sympathetically made, and we are intended to react to it with a proper measure of assent; but, when this has been done, the problem of adapting it to the real and sometimes intractable circumstances of mutual living remains to be posed and resolved.

The expression of the argument at this point is worthy of attention. What the Franklin says is this:

> Pacience is an heigh vertu, certeyn,
> For it venquysseth, as thise clerkes seyn,
> Thynges that rigour sholde nevere atteyne.
> For every word men may nat chide or pleyne.
> Lerneth to suffre, or elles, so moot I goon,
> Ye shul it lerne, wher so ye wole or noon;
> For in this world, certein, ther no wight is
> That he ne dooth or seith somtyme amys.
> Ire, siknesse, or constellacioun,
> Wyn, wo, or chaungynge of complexioun
> Causeth ful ofte to doon amys or speken.
> On every wrong a man may nat be wreken,
> After the tyme moste be temperaunce
> To every wight that kan on governaunce.
> And therfore hath this wise, worthy knyght,
> To lyve in suffraunce hire bihight,
> And she to hym ful wisly gan to swere
> That nevere sholde ther be defaute in here.
>
> (V. 773–90)

The whole passage is an admirable example of the care, the ability to maintain necessary distinctions, which Chaucer at his best demands of us. "Pacience" is, indeed, the "heigh vertu" that so many of the tales have assumed it to be. It is an essential aspect of that "governaunce," or self-control, which—as the Knight has already shown in his tale of Theseus—is supremely required of a man in responsible authority, but which every man is called upon to exercise in regard to his fellow men. Patience, in this sense of the word, is a central concept for understanding the whole pattern of the human "pilgrimage" in time. Finally, it amounts to a recognition of the real nature of things, to ignore or reject which in the pursuit of an illusory self-affirmation can only lead to unhappiness and frustration.

This "realism" tells us that "rigour," the pressing of selfish desires beyond reasonable limits, can only lead to the collapse of any valid understanding between human beings, whether in the married state or in any other relationship. A man may not "chide or pleyne" for "every word" that has been hastily spoken, and if he insists on doing this he will wreck any prospect of a fulfilled or reasonable life for himself and, in the state of marriage, for his partner. The entire life history of the Wife of Bath can be seen as an example of the consequences of ignoring patience, understood as the exercise of a realism indispensable to the reasonable and positive understanding of life in its human form. All men, too, are subject to alterations of circumstance beyond their control—"Ire, siknesse, or constellacioun" and the rest—both as a result of their own weakness and of their inescapable situation as mortal beings; and this reality they will do well to take into account. To recognize these things "patiently" is to bring into play the human virtue that follows from such recognition: the virtue of "temperance," without which no man can aspire to assert the measure of control—"governaunce"—which is required of him as a moral and responsible creature.

This is the positive side of the "doctrine" that is being put forward in the form of a "romantic" and deliberately remote tale, and we shall not underestimate its validity or deny its relevance to some of the main themes of the pilgrimage. *The Tale of Melibeus* will in due course give it added force, at considerable—even, it may be thought, excessive—length.[10] Neither, however, shall we take the Franklin's statement of it entirely at face value. The fact that we are told expressly that these are academic thoughts—"as thise clerkes seyn"—is indicative; we shall do well to recognize in Chaucer's frequent recourse to this or similar phrases a reminder of the claims of real life as opposed to even the most respectable theorizings about it. It is interesting too that we should be told that "this wise, worthy knyght"—and the adjective expresses the Franklin's admiration, which need not be quite the same as Chaucer's own—favored those attitudes of "sufferaunce" because he desired "to lyve in ese"; something, no doubt, that all men naturally and properly desire to do but that is not to be achieved through a simple assertion of what ought to be. The respective and mutually supporting attitudes of this "gentle" pair have their own attraction, which is not to be underestimated, especially inasmuch as they contain an implicit and humane reply to the positions advanced by the Wife of Bath. Theirs was truly, *as far as it went*, "an humble, wys accord," and humility and wisdom are central human virtues that the proper conduct of life requires.

The marriage that resulted from it, and which is briefly characterized in the lines that at once follow—

> Thus hath she take hir servaunt and hir lord,
> Servant in love, and lord in marriage—
>
> (V. 792–93)

is such, on the other hand, as to raise real questions that the undoubted fact of its attractiveness does not necessarily dispose of. The problem that the tale ultimately poses is whether a "solution" of this kind, feasible in terms of the tale, is valid in real life, or whether it does not, on deeper consideration, tend to cover the real problems of mutual relationship under the expression of something not very different from verbal casuistry. Perhaps the aspiration to "maistrie," perversely affirmed by the Wife of Bath, is also the reflection of a human reality; and perhaps some measure of recognition of this and some realistic resolution of the issue of responsibility in the real world, as distinct from that of "gentle" aspiration or clerkly theory, is central to the nature of marriage as a social relationship and so to the conduct of life itself. "Governaunce," it may be, is one of

the responsibilities that men and women are called upon
to exercise, both in respect of themselves and in their
mutual relationships; and upon their way of fulfilling this
obligation, upon the manner in which they decide to di-
vide up their several duties in a spirit that combines
mutual respect with an understanding of their real situation, the success of marriage—and with it, perhaps, the
stability of society—will finally depend.

Initially, at all events, Arveragus and Dorigen enjoy true
happiness in their married state. They lead their lives "in
blisse and in solas"; for who, as the narrator pertinently if
rhetorically asks,

> koude telle, but he hadde wedded be,
> The joye, the ese, and the prosperitee
> That is bitwixe an housbonde and his wyf?
>
> (V. 803–5)

The picture so presented of the marriage—the fruit, we
remember,[11] of an "accord" at once "humble" and
"wise"—is certainly positive, and we shall not be led to
undervalue it, as some have tried to do, in the light of the
Franklin's supposed "Epicureanism."[12] "Joy," "ease," and
"prosperity" are none the worse for being human aspirations capable of natural fulfillment. Marriage is a human
contract as well as a sacrament based on the law of love,[13]
and it is the human reality that is being recognized and
valued in no uncertain terms. We may also, however,
reflect on the contrast between it and what we have already
learned of the Wife of Bath's history and, even more, on
the very different effect of much of the same language
recently used in respect of marriage by the embittered
Merchant in his tale.[14] The earlier words and the bleak
reality that underlies them echo persistently and with a
disturbing effect upon those which come later. Apart from
this coincidence, the state of bliss that unites the pair is,
like all human relationships and aspirations, subject to
change. We are told that "a yeer and moore lasted this

blisful lyf" (V. 806), and we remember that the narrator
has himself recently spoken of the effects of "constellacioun," of "chaungynge of complexioun," upon *all* human affairs.[15] These, too, are realities with which men and
women are required to come to terms. At the end of the
period indicated the state of happiness between man and
wife is interrupted by the intervention of other, equally
human obligations. Arveragus is called, in the process of
seeking "in armes worshipe and honour" (values that belong, in the spirit of the tale, to his knightly status and so to
his nature as a man), to travel across the sea to England.
Dorigen is left behind in solitude and sadness to bewail her
husband's absence, "As doon thise noble wyves whan hem
liketh" (V. 818).

The suggestion, at least, is that hers is an excessive and
one-sided reaction to natural and inevitable realities.
Those who serve the God of Love are subject, as all men
are, to the natural vicissitudes of their temporal condition;
but their "service," of its very nature, offers them no stable
foundation upon which to build a reasonable acceptance
of this reality. Dorigen loves her husband "as hire hertes
lyf," and this no doubt is a virtue in her and an indication
of the essential truth of the marriage; but she is also "des-
treyned" by "desir of his presence" to such a degree that
"al this wyde world she sette at noght" (V. 821), and this is
contrary to a "patient" reaction to the reality that loss and
separation are built into the very fabric of human experience. "Desire" is a word that, in Chaucer as in other
medieval writers,[16] carries a sense of excess, of a failure in
necessary control. To desire is to follow an impulse of life,
but also to expose oneself to the risk of being overmas-
tered by it, carried to ends unforeseen and finally destructive of all reasonable determination. So is it at this point
with Dorigen. Her friends seek to bring her comfort, tell
her that "causelees she sleeth hirself, allas!" (V. 825). They
"preach," they tell her "night and day" what she should
feel and do, and no doubt their well-meant considerations
strike her as remote from the real sorrow of her situa-

tion;[17] but, equally, there is an important measure of truth
in their contention that so much dedication to grief is excessive, unreasonable, and finally impossible. Time, up to
a point, confirms their advice; for, as we are told, Dorigen
"may nat alway duren in swich rage" (V. 836), and she
finally agrees to drive away her "derke fantasye" (the word
is normally associated in Chaucer's use[18] with the loss of a
sense of reality) by accepting her natural instinct "to come
and romen hire in compaignye" (V. 843). Men and women
are, after all, sociable creatures. They fulfil themselves in
relationship to their fellows, and true marriage, far from
resting on an impossibly one-sided or exclusive devotion,
requires this recognition of the larger human reality of
which it forms a part.

Dorigen's grief, however, is not assuaged by this recognition. In her "fantasies" of foreboding solitude, she looks
out to sea in the hope of discerning the ship that will bring
Arveragus back to her:

> "Allas!" seith she,
> "Is ther no ship, of so manye as I se,
> Wol bryngen hom my lord? Thanne were myn herte
> Al warisshed of his bittre peynes smerte."
>
> (V. 853–56)

Even in the company of her friends these thoughts intrude
and leave her in an essential loneliness. Under their pressure, she begins to elaborate what we should call, in modern terms, "subconscious" images of fear and desolation,
in the course of which she projects her unhappy condition
upon the nature around her, fearing that her husband on
his return will be shipwrecked on the "grisly feendly
rokkes blake" (V. 868) that she sees below her during her
long and solitary walks along the cliffs of Brittany.

As a result, and by a notable extension of the implications of the story, she finds herself driven in the course of
these dark imaginings to question—in Boethian terms—
the workings of the divine "purveiaunce," the justice of a

God said to be "parfit," "wys," and "stable" (the terms echo those used by Theseus in *The Knight's Tale*[19]) and who seems to have been moved so incomprehensibly to create what presents itself to her anxious thoughts as "a foul confusion," "this werk unresonable" (V. 872). The vision corresponds to her unnaturally tense, "neurotic" condition:

> An hundred thousand bodyes of mankynde
> Han rokkes slayn, al be they nat in mynde,
> Which mankynde is so fair part of thy werk
> That thou it madest lyk to thyn owene merk.
> Thanne semed it ye hadde a great chiertee
> Toward mankynde; but how thanne may it bee
> That ye swich meenes make it to destroyen.
>
> (V. 877–83)

The question raised is evidently a large one, and the "romance" setting, while it acts as a warning to us against overstressing it, should not lead us to give it less than its proper weight. The fortunes of this pair in marriage are seen against the background of an ordered, end-directed universe that Dorigen is led by her unhappy inner state to question: in one order of things as in the other, the reestablishment of harmony depends upon a proper and therefore "patient" understanding of what the tale assumes to be the real order of things.

Dorigen's friends, seeing her weighed down by fears which they cannot share, do what they can to restore her to a normal, natural state. Seeing unsociability as the cause and sign of her unhappiness, they try to distract her from these dark thoughts by introducing her to "other places delitables"; for they consider that it is "no disport" for her

> To romen by the see, but disconfort
>
> (V. 896)

Accordingly, they "shopen for to pleyen somewhere elles," leading her to "daunce," to "pleyen at ches and tables," to

indulge in the social pastimes of sophisticated society.[20]
Finally, as the natural conclusion of their efforts, they
bring her—in Chaucer's favorite month of May—to a garden that—like many other gardens in the *Tales*—carries
persistent echoes of the traditional Garden of Love and
shows, beyond this, at least some of the features of Eden,
the lost paradise:

> And this was on the sixte morwe of May,
> Which May hadde peynted with his softe shoures
> This gardyn ful of leves and of floures;
> And craft of mannes hand so curiously
> Arrayed hadde this gardyn, trewely,
> That nevere was ther gardyn of swich prys,
> But if it were the verray paradys.
> The odour of floures and the fresshe sight
> Wolde han maked any herte light
> That evere was born, but if to greet siknesse,
> Or to greet sorwe, helde it in distresse.
>
> (V. 906–16)

Such indeed was Dorigen's "unnatural" condition, and in
the light of it the garden emerges as a fleeting aspiration
for something that in the real world—which includes the
possibility of "siknesse" and "distresse"—is no longer (if it
ever was) lastingly available to man. The theme is one that
Chaucer found suggestive, and to it he returns at moments
of central significance in his plan. The garden in which
Emelye walked in *The Knight's Tale*[21] seemed a remote and
inaccessible aspiration to Palamon and Arcite in prison.
The one created by Januarius in *The Merchant's Tale*
reflected the unnatural, senile possessiveness of its owner
and bore the fruit of corruption on the tree at its center.[22]
It also provided the setting for the activities, in the person
of Damian, of yet another intruding "squire." Dorigen's
real and natural sorrow prevents her from sharing in the
pleasure offered by a sight that has been "curiously"—
artificially—contrived by the "craft" of human hands and
that represents both the attraction and the limitation of

man-made or even "natural" achievement. She is unable to take part in the dancing in which the state of paradisal spring naturally expresses itself. The fact at once underlines the reality of her human grief and indicates the unsociable, unnatural depth of her isolated, life-rejecting reaction to the position in which she finds herself. The fulfillment that the garden offers and which seems to reflect a natural human aspiration in the eyes of those who have led her to it is not available to her in her distraught and insecure condition.

All this is the background to a new situation in the tale. In the garden Dorigen sees before her eyes a "squyer" (and we remember that the tale has been in part prompted by a story told by another squire, whom the Franklin has favorably and even enviously compared to his own son,)[23] engaged in the springtime occupation of the dance: a squire, we are told,

> That fressher was and jolyer of array,
> As to my doom, than is the month of May.
>
> (V. 927–28)

The young man's name is Aurelius, and we are told that he is a "lusty squier," servant to Venus," and a lover—albeit unknown to her—of Dorigen herself. We may remark that he also reminds us, perhaps not accidentally, of the very similar squire who wooed the "fresshe" May, though certainly not to the same end, in *The Merchant's Tale*.[24] Aurelius's love is throughout consistent with the requirements of courtly decorum, being at once worshipful, compounded of grief and reticence in extremity—we are told that he "langwissheth as a furye dooth in helle" (V. 950)—and incapable of expression:

> Ne dorste he nat to hire his wo biwreye,
> Save that, paraventure, somtyme at daunces,
> Ther yonge folk kepen hir observaunces,
> It may wel be he looked on hir face

In swich a wise as man that asketh grace;
But nothyng wiste she of his entente.

(V. 954–59)

Still following the convention, Aurelius is finally driven by
the compulsive "desire" he bears so uncomfortably within
himself to declare this concealed passion, for which he
affirms that he is ready, if need be, to die. Dorigen replies
as befits the devoted wife she is. She declares in the most
solemn and unequivocal terms the love that unites her to
her absent husband:

By thilke God that yaf me soule and lyf,
Ne shal I nevere been untrewe wyf
In word ne werk, as fer as I have wit;
I wol been his to whom that I am knyt

(V. 983–86)

But though this is given in all sincerity and is intended to
be her "fynal answere," the grief of separation and the
sinister thought of the black "rocks" still weigh heavily
upon her mind and she is incautious enough to tempt her
fate by adding, "in pleye," that she will be ready to grant
him her love if he can bring about the removal of the
dangers that, in her obsessed imagination, threaten her
husband's safe return.

In the state of despair that this rejection induces in him,
Aurelius does his best to achieve what he recognizes to be,
in sober reason, "impossible." His first efforts end in failure. He prays Apollo to cause Lucina, the moon goddess,
to raise a flood to submerge the offending rocks; but,
naturally enough, nothing changes, and Arveragus in due
course returns to restore his wife, for a certain period, to
the complete happiness of their married state. At this
point, however, Aurelius's brother recalls having read a
book of magic and takes him to a magician of "Orleans in
Fraunce," whom he persuades to use his power to cause
the rocks to become for a time invisible. The fantasy that
prevails in this part of the tale can be seen as a comment on

the element of unreality in the Squire's preceding tale of naively expressed wonders and magical appearances. The tale, incidentally, expresses a firm conviction that what the magician offers *is* an illusion and no more. Of his book we are told, "As in oure dayes is nat worth a flye" (V. 1132), although in the past, and in the romantic climate of the story, it may well have been otherwise. The pair return to Brittany in the company of the magician, who sets to work to achieve what the tale calls his "illusioun," until Aurelius is able to tell Dorigen that "the rokkes been aweye" (V. 1338) and to claim the fulfillment of her rash promise.

It is stressed that all this takes place in the world of "appearances," is the product of what Chaucer habitually calls "fantasy," the art of making things seem what they are not in order to satisfy the irrational cravings of men and to "change" the reality that they would do better to accept. As Aurelius's brother puts it:

> I am siker that ther be sciences
> By whiche men make diverse apparences,
> Swiche as thise subtile tregetoures pleye.
> For ofte at feestes have I wel herd seye
> That tregetours, withinne an halle large,
> Have maad come in a water and a barge,
> And in the halle rowen up and doun.
> Somtyme hath semed come a grym leoun;
> And somtyme floures sprynge as in a mede;
> Somtyme a vyne, and grapes white and rede;
> Somtyme a castel, al of lym and stoon;
> And whan hem lyked, voyded it anon,
> Thus semed it to every mannes sighte.
>
> (V. 1139–51)

The "tregetours" are jugglers, who appear to have the faculty of altering the nature of reality: a faculty that responds to the inveterate desire of men to see things as other than they are and to build the conduct of their lives not on a realistic recognition of incontrovertible fact but on the comfortable "illusion" that the "real" can, if necessary, be remolded to answer more closely to their desires. The human attraction for "illusion" and the dilemmas to which men and women are led by their desire to evade or change the "real" is a theme that is variously present in the pilgrimage and illustrated by the chief actors in this tale. It is also a theme that bears a relationship to Chaucer's persisting concern with the problem of "tale-telling" in its relation to "truth." The artist too is a kind of "magician," a creator of "illusions," who needs to believe that the illusions that he brings into being are in some important sense "true." What kind of truth is attained by his efforts and what may be its problematic relationship to whatever truth may finally be presumed to exist is a question recurrently posed in the course of the pilgrimage.

All the actors in this story, indeed, are in some measure shortsighted or deluded in relation to their declared motives for acting as they do. Arveragus was deceived, or deceived himself, in his belief that he could carry his renunciation of "sovereignty" to the length of neglecting the responsibilities proper to a husband and of covering the failure by a verbal subterfuge. Dorigen was ready to comtemplate the "removal" of the "rocks" that seemed to threaten her husband's safe return but that were in fact a part of the real order of things and, as such, were to be accepted. Aurelius, finally, was ready—because it suited his immediate infatuation—to believe that the permanent reality—the "rock," as it presented itself to him—of a marriage could be spirited away in order to gratify his love-fantasy. Each wished to rest the conduct of life upon "illusion," upon a particularly subtle, because natural, form of selfishness, and each was brought by events to a realization that nothing lasting or valid can be built upon these foundations.

It is interesting to note, in this connection, how the visit of the pair to the magician is conducted in an atmosphere of "romance" that is set in deliberate contrast to everyday reality. As they reach Orleans they meet a "yong clerk" who is said to be "romynge by hymself," and who declares that he is already aware of the nature of their mission. They are brought to the magician's house where an elaborate "illusion" of hospitality is set up for their benefit: visions of hunting and falconry, of knights jousting in a plain, and of Aurelius's own lady

> on a daunce,
> On which hymself he daunced, as hym thoughte;
>
> (V. 1200–1201)

but, immediately after the "maister" had worked this magic,

> he clapte his handes two,
> And farewel! al oure revel was ago.
>
> (V. 1203–4)

It should be noted that, for all his works of "illusion," the magician has a firm grasp of reality. "Lesse than a thousand pound he wolde nat have" (V. 1224) to perform the service required of him; and it is, significantly, Aurelius who is ready, in the "blisful" state that these fictions open up to him, to declare his readiness to give up the wide world itself in order to obtain the object of his desire:

> Fy on a thousand pound!
> This wyde world, which that men seye is round,
> I wolde it yeve, if I were lord of it.
>
> (V. 1227–29)

The point is, of course, that neither Aurelius nor any other mortal being has reason to think of himself as "lord of the world" or to indulge his imagination with the thought of disposing of it at will.

In the light of the bargain so disconcertingly driven, Aurelius goes to rest in the hope—or the illusion—that his "woful herte" has been relieved of the "penaunce" that has exercised it since he first saw Dorigen. All three—Aurelius, the magician, and his brother—return to Brit-

tany in what is expressly described as "the colde, frosty
seson of Decembre" (V. 1244). Their journey is made the
occasion for a passage compounded of elements of folk-
lore that make their own contribution to the mood of the
tale:

> The bittre frostes, with the sleet and reyn,
> Destroyed hath the grene in every yerd.
> Janus sit by the fyr, with double berd,
> And drynketh of his bugle horn the wyn;
> Biforn hym stant brawen of the tusked swyn,
> And "Nowel" crieth every lusty man.
>
> (V. 1250–55)

The combination of classical and pagan memories with the
Christian content, the sense of life withdrawn to the
hearth and affirming itself in the presence of winter: all
this runs in contrast to the Maytime associations of love
and life reborn that are so powerful throughout the *Tales*
to lend this story a fantastic, poetical quality of its own.

Against this subtly drawn background the magician
works the "illusion" proper to his "art." "Illusion," indeed,
is the essence of his contriving, and it is clear that what he
achieves is not any "real" removal of the rocks, which
would be beyond the power of all magic, but a conviction
on the part of those concerned

> That she and every wight sholde wene and seye
> That of Britaigne the rokkes were aweye.
>
> (V. 1267–68)

The illusion the magician produces with the help of these
devices is based finally on trickery and the exploitation of
man's instinct for the "mysterious," in the portrayal of
which Chaucer is, here and elsewhere, a master. This
worker of "wonders," manipulating his "japes" and
"wrecchednesse" with what is described as a "supersticious
cursednesse" (V. 1272), could be considered a fitting companion of the alchemist who will be presented in *The Ca-*

non's Yeoman's Tale.[25] The inveterate and finally self-deceiving tendency of men to seek to manipulate reality for their convenience is—together with their inability to achieve any lasting success in this impossible aspiration—one of the main themes of *The Canterbury Tales.*

For the moment, however, the magician seems to gain his ends. For a time—and *only* for a time—his "illusion" imposes itself:

> for a wyke or tweye
> It semed that alle the rokkes were aweye.
> (V. 1295–96)

Men can succeed, for a brief period, in imposing their desires upon the "real" so as to make it seem other than what it is. They can even do this to produce results in the "real" world that are disquieting and destructive of true human needs. What they cannot do is to make the "illusion" last or prevent the return of the obstinately real. The "miracle" is strictly temporary, and we know that in due course reality will reassert itself; but meanwhile Aurelius is able to go to Dorigen and ask her, in the name of the sacred quality of "trouthe," or trust, for the fulfillment of her promise. The irony of his appeal rests, of course, on the fact that his recourse to "truth" is not only founded on the apparent success of his manipulation of it by recourse to its opposite, "illusion," but is advanced in the interests of betrayal, of the denial of "trouthe" itself.

Aurelius's approach to his demand is very characteristically ambivalent. It is expressed in all the familiar terms of aristocratic "love," which require the lover to stress his misery—"Ye sle me giltelees for verray peyne" (V. 1318)—and to press his request for pity or "routhe." Behind these expressions of humility, however, he drives home the advantage that the magician's contrivances have offered him. "In a garden yond"—the garden in which the reality and the illusion of love were so complexly interwoven—Dorigen made him what was, in her mind, a "pleye," a distraction. It now returns to her as a promise solemn beyond her intention:

> Ye woot right wel what ye bihighten me;
> And in myn hand youre trouthe plighten ye
> To love me best—God woot, ye seyde so,
>
> (V. 1327–29)

and Aurelius, though he is ready to go through the form, which his situation as a lover imposes, of recognizing his unworthiness—"Al be that I unworthy am therto" (V. 1330)—is in effect ready to threaten Dorigen with the prospect of losing her "honour" if she refuses the bargain upon which she has so incautiously entered. Reality is reasserting itself, as it always will, against the efforts of those who, in one form or another, seek to base their lives impossibly upon "illusion." Its assertion takes the form of driving those who have sought to evade it beyond the limits that they set up for themselves in their original surrender to unreality. The terms of reawakening are painful for the simple reason that the abandonment of reality has its price, to which those who have fallen into this most enticing of temptations find themselves inexorably subject. It is a price that, if realistically, "patiently" paid, can lead to restored sanity; but it is in any event a condition of continuing to live in a human way and—as such—not to be evaded.

Dorigen, naturally, is horrified to hear the news that her unwelcome lover has brought to her. Her incautious indulgence of her forebodings has recoiled upon her in a way that has gone far beyond anything she can conceivably have imagined. "In al hir face nas a drope of blood" (V. 1340); and, even more significantly, "She wende nevere han come in swich a trappe" (V. 1341). Rightly enough, she feels that what has happened—this "monstre," or "merveille"—is "agayne the proces of nature"; but, although we feel sympathy for her when she complains against the trick that has been played upon her by an unkind fate—"'Allas,' quod she, 'on thee, Fortune, I pleyne'" (V. 1355)—the fact remains that the trap has been, however comprehensibly, of her own creation. By basing her original reaction on the suspicion that the ways of "Providence" in her regard were "cruel" or "unreasonable," she in effect placed herself in the position of hostage to chance, personified in the operations of a "Fortune" whose workings are, by definition, changeable and inconstant. Her plight has been the result of her original impulse to question the nature of reality, seeking to remold it to her desire; and now, as a result of this human but real error, she finds herself faced by a choice between the bleak alternatives, as the tale poses them, of "death" and "dishonour."

Her natural reaction is to prefer the alternative of death, which her declared fidelity to her marriage would seem to impose. This she supports in her "complaint" by what are, we may feel, an excessive number of noble "ensaumples." Such was the choice made by the daughters of "Phidon, in Athenes," who were made to dance "in hir fadres blood," by the "fifty maydens of Lacedomye," who chose death "with a good entente" rather than the surrender of their virtue: such also the result of the cruel importunity of

> the tiraunt Aristoclides,
> That loved a mayden, heet Stymphalides,
> (V. 1387–88)

and of a host of other victims:

> What shal I seyn of Hasdrubales wyf,
> That at Cartage birafte hirself hir lyf?
> (V. 1399–400)

What indeed? Knowing as much as we do of Chaucer's frequently disingenuous attitudes to reputable scholarly "authority," we shall not perhaps take all this learning at quite its surface estimate.[26] Dorigen's plight is genuinely pathetic, in terms of the tale, and we shall not deny her the sympathy that it demands of us; but, as we may after all reflect, it is still suicide, self-destruction, that she is contemplating, and perhaps we are not meant to load her dilemma with a harrowing content that would be foreign to the nature of her story.

At all events, since the tragedy may be said to be bound up with her husband's benign but imperfectly realistic view of the responsibility of marriage, it is logical that he should be brought back into the tale. We have been told that he was "out of toune" when his wife made her harrowing discovery. He now returns and Dorigen confesses to him the impossible position in which she has placed herself. Arveragus remains true to his values, expressing himself "with glad chiere, in freendly wyse" (V. 1467); perhaps we shall commend him for this tolerant understanding—which is the same as that which prompted his renunciation of "maistrie" at the beginning of the story—while reflecting that he may, by his initial evasion of his responsibilities in the matter of marriage, have ruled out for himself the possibility of any more forceful reaction.

The exchange in which husband and wife try to resolve their anguish is revealing in this respect. When Dorigan has finished telling him the disaster that has befallen her, Arveragus's reply is a mild "Is ther oght elles, Dorigen, but this?" (V. 1468). Dorigen seems to find this response to the urgency of her problem something less than adequate, as she implies when she says,

> "Nay, nay," quod she, "God helpe me so as wys!
> This is to muche, and it were Goddes wille."
>
> (V. 1470–71)

Arveragus's reply continues to reflect a certain complacency:

> "Ye, wyf," quod he, "lat slepen that is stille.
> It may be wel, paraventure, yet to day."
>
> (V. 1472–73)

Perhaps—Chaucer may be suggesting—the other face of Arveragus's civilized tolerance is a tendency to be determined to see only the bright side of things; possibly, in the last analysis, because to do otherwise would be disturbing to the equanimity of mind that he prizes. There seems, in short, to be a measure of complacency here that fits the note of unrealism which in so many different ways colors the whole story. Arveragus, too, may in his own fashion be ignoring the reality of the metaphorical rocks on which a human relationship that fails to take them into account may find itself in danger of foundering. This, however, should not lead us to underestimate the final seriousness of the conclusion, which is that Dorigen should keep her promise in recognition that "trouthe is the hyeste thyng that man may kepe" (V. 1479).

Here, at least, we have a positive point that the tale is concerned to make. By "trouthe" we are meant to understand nothing less than the trust upon which all valid relations between human beings must rest: the trust that is in general imperfectly manifested among men but that is the only serious answer to the assertions of "maistrie" which poison these relationships and which find in jealousy—the perverse determination to claim rights of property on another human being and so to limit his or her essential freedom—their absolute negation. In making this point Arveragus is being true to what is good and positive in the laws of "gentle" chivalry. We shall give him credit for this, while reflecting that he has perhaps been too ready to underestimate the real nature of the world in which these values are required to operate, too ready to believe that a statement of benevolent good intent can replace the need to make firm choices in relation to a hard, objective reality. The rocks are there, and no lastingly valid attitude to life can be built on a denial of their existence;[27] but it remains true that man is, by his nature, called upon to be something more than a realist, that he needs to allow free scope to the imaginative and civilizing instinct that expresses itself in his attitude to his most intimate human relationships and in which the virtue of tolerance or understanding needs to be combined with a firm and clear-sighted recognition of bedrock moral realities. The human "truth," which expresses itself in "trust," requires as its natural complement the recognition of another kind of truth, the acceptance of the permanent, unchanging reality of things as they are. Where this is absent no lasting relationship can exist; where it is present, it serves as a foundation upon which the other aspect of truth—that which is implied in the sense of "trust"—can profitably build.

In this spirit, Arveragus, having told his wife to cleave to the "truth" she has chosen, announces that he is ready to accept the unhappiness that this decision must bring him: "As I may best, I wol my wo endure" (V. 1484). The "wo" is real, and there is a sense in which he has brought it upon himself by his past complacencies; but to recognize this is in itself an aspect of the attitude that the tale seems concerned to advance. Prepared for in this way, we are brought to the conclusion that—in a manner perfectly true to the Chaucerian intuition of life—we are asked at once to accept and to treat with certain reservations. In anticiption of these, the Franklin begins by warning his hearers that to "an hepe of yow" Arveragus will seem "a lewd man" to place his wife in "jupartie." To such listeners, the values of the tale are likely to seem remote, inapplicable, and even finally absurd in their relation to what passes for normal, everyday reality. They are, indeed, values that belong to the imaginative order which tends to run contrary to that of real life; but, for all that, they answer to man's need to render his life civilized and tolerable and, as such, once the reservation has been firmly put forward, they are given their own measure of validity. Generosity, we like—or need—to feel, is capable of eliciting its appropriate positive response; and, in a tale, if not always in real life, it can be allowed to do so. Aurelius, faced by Arveragus's generosity, concedes that his own position is a shameful one and that he has acted on an impulse of

> cherlyssh wrecchednesse
> Agayns franchise and alle gentillesse.
>
> (V. 1523–24)

The terms of his avowal at once place them within a limited set of social and literary conventions and amount to a true assertion of necessary "gentility." In this spirit he answers "truth" with "truth" ("My trouthe I plighte"), releasing Dorigen from the rash promise she made in her hour of failing confidence and showing himself—by a stroke deeply indicative of the Franklin's social preoccupations—the equal of those who are, in the aristocratic terms that condition the tale, his "betters":

> Thus kan a squier doon a gentil dede
> As wel as kan a knyght, withouten drede.
>
> (V. 1543–44)

The satisfaction that this conclusion affords the Franklin is related, no doubt, to his own previous expression of disappointment in his son; and it adds an important element to the complete effect of his tale.

As a result of this renunciation, the proper and natural relationship of true marriage is restored. Husband and wife are able, at the end, to carry on their lives "in sovereyn blisse":

> Nevere eft ne was ther angre hem bitwene.
> He cherisseth hire as though she were a queene,
> And she was to hym trewe for everemoore.
>
> (V. 1553–55)

A fairy-tale ending, we may think, though one that answers—as fairy tales do—to some of man's deepest aspirations, and one to which the author adds his characteristically detaching comment: "Of thise two folk ye gete of me namoore" (V. 1556). Aurelius, for all his response to generosity, is left to consider that his passion has brought him to very concrete prospects of material ruin:

Myn heritage moot I nedes selle,
And been a beggere; heere may I nat dwelle.
(V. 1563–64)

Being what it is, however, the tale cannot be left to rest on
this note of bitterness. Aurelius has been brought to
realize where his ill-considered passions have led him; but
his recognition, which has borne fruit in the renunciation
of his claim over Dorigen, produces an answering generosity in the "magician" in whose hands he so rashly placed
himself. The "magician" is moved to release him from his
debt contracted in the process of "removing" the offending rocks that have meant something different to each
beholder as his own passionate or short-sighted needs
have prompted. He recognizes, as he does so, that "everich
of yow dide gentilly til oother" (V. 1608).

The question with which we are left at the end of the tale
is "Which was the mooste fre"—the most generous—"as
thynketh yow?" (V. 1622). Each of those who have heard
the tale is left to give his own answer. In view of this it
would be wrong to see in the story any formal or finished
answer to the so-called marriage debate. Chaucer's mind
does not seem to have moved in conclusive terms of this
kind. He is content to put forward different attitudes and
to see the "answers" to the problems raised as belonging, if
indeed they exist, as men must hope and believe, to an
order outside and beyond the tales themselves, in the true
and final reality that is the end of the "pilgrimage," but
which—in time—can only be, at best, intuited. If the
Franklin has given us an answer, of a kind, to the Wife of
Bath's insistence on domination, it is an answer clothed in
a certain irony, deliberately removed from too disturbing
a contact with the world of reality of which Chaucer was so
distinctively and subtly aware. The "answer" represents, at
best, a genuine human aspiration, expressed in terms of
"gentility" that constitute at once its attraction and its limitation. We shall give it the value it has but recognize at the
same time that it represents only one element in the com-

plete picture and that the true "solution"—should there be one—can only lie in another, a more inclusive and embracing order of the real.

NOTES

1. G. L. Kittredge, in "Chaucer's Discussion of Marriage" (*Modern Philology* 9 [1912]), was the first and most notable proponent of this point of view, which followed logically from his conception of the "marriage debate."

2. I. 43–78.

3. I. 331–60.

4. It is interesting to compare Arveragus's attitude to his marriage with the words of L'Ami in the *Roman de la Rose:*

> And he set himself up as lord over his wife, she who ought to be, not lady over him, but his equal and companion—this is the relationship in which they are joined together by law. And, in his turn, he ought to be her companion, not her lord and master. . . . The man who wants to be called master will never be loved by his wife: love dies when the lover wants to rule as lord. Love can only live and last in hearts that are generous and free. Therefore it happens to all those who begin as lovers that, when they embark on marriage, love is not an end. For the man who, while he was her lover, runs to be the servant of his lady, whom he desires to have as his mistress, now claims to be lord and master over one whom he called lady when he was her lover. (Ll. 9425–54)

5. III. 1109–206.

6. Compare *The Man of Law's Tale:* "Wher as they lyve in joye and in quiete" (II. 1131).

7. The relation of love to friendship has already been explored in the story of Palamon and Arcite in *The Knight's Tale.*

8. *Troilus and Criseyde* I. 15.

9. From the time of his earlier writings Chaucer shows himself concerned with the exercise of freedom of choice as a necessary element of marriage. In *The Parliament of Fowls* "the formel egle," faced with the conflicting claims of "aristocratic" suitors, requests of Nature the right to delay her final choice for a year:

> "Almighty quene! unto this yer be gone.
> I axe respit for to avise me,
> And after that to have my choice al fre:
>
> (Ll. 646–48)

a choice that is granted to her at the end of the poem.

10. More especially in relation to *The Clerk's Tale,* which deals with the theme of patience in a more artistic way.

11. V. 791.

12. For a statement of this view of the Franklin see D. W. Robertson, Jr. in *A Preface to Chaucer* (Princeton, N.J.: Princeton University Press, 1969), p. 276.

13. The point is well made by Paul G. Ruggiers in his *Art of the Canterbury Tales* (Madison: University of Wisconsin Press, 1965). See pp. 229–30.

14. See, for example, IV. 1267–73.

15. V. 781.

16. Compare Dante's use of the word *disio* throughout the *Commedia* and very notably in the Paolo and Francesca episode (*Inferno* 5).

17. We are reminded of the ladies who so reasonably, and so vainly, offered their consolations to the unresponsive Criseyde in her sorrow (*Troilus and Criseyde*, IV. 680–707).

18. The aged Januarius in *The Merchant's Tale* approaches his grotesque marriage in a mood of "heigh fantasye and curious bisynesse" (4. 1577) that reflects his determination to mold reality to his desire.

19. See Theseus's discourse on the "First Mover" and—more especially—l. 3004 and those which follow.

20. We are reminded of Pandarus's efforts to distract Troilus from his sorrow after the departure of Criseyde. See especially their visit to the palace of "King" Sarpedon and Troilus's inability to remain quietly there (*Troilus and Criseyde* V. 428–504).

21. I. 1051–55.

22. IV. 2029–41.

23. V. 682–86.

24. See IV. 1772–82. It may not be an accident that the adjective has been applied, in the lines just quoted, to the Franklin's "squire."

25. VIII. 720–1481.

26. It is, perhaps, not without relevance that *The Nun's Priest's Tale*, which comments pertinently on the excesses and absurdities revealed in so many of the other tales, should deal faithfully with this kind of preaching by rhetorical "example;" See VII. 3338–74.

27. It could be argued—and the argument would not be foreign to the spirit of the tale—that the "rocks" are, after all, a part of God's creative purpose, and that they are therefore not to be willed away but accepted even by those who are honestly unable to fathom the reason for their existence.

[4]

The Manciple's Tale

IN the present state of *The Canterbury Tales,* as given in the editions normally read, the last tale before the Parson's final sermon is told by the Manciple. We learn from the prologue to the tale that the pilgrimage has reached "a litel toun," which is given the name of "Bobbe-up-and-doun." This place has generally been identified with Harbledown, or occasionally with a certain Up-and-down Field in Thannington; both places are "under the Blee" (IX. 3), or Blea Forest, and are therefore beyond Broughton on the last lap of the pilgrim's route to Canterbury.[1] Moreover, in the manuscripts as they stand the tale told by the Manciple is connected by the first line of the prologue to *The Parson's Tale* with the sermon that winds up the whole pilgrimage. This last reading has, however, been questioned, both on grounds that concern the reliability of the text and because the indication in the Manciple's prologue (IX. 16) that the tale was told in the morning seems to imply that Chaucer may have meant to introduce other tales between it and the Parson's discourse, which began, we are told,[2] at four in the afternoon. It is impossible, in view of these uncertainties, to argue with complete conviction concerning *The Manciple's Tale* from its present position in the text; but it is attractive to think that Chaucer, however uncertain he may have been about the final order of the tales, and although he may have changed his mind concerning it or even left the matter finally undecided, at least considered

120

the possibility that this tale might provide a suitable round-
ing-off, previous to the Parson's concluding sermon, for
the series of pilgrim interventions that comprise the body
of the pilgrimage.

For the tale emerges, on careful consideration, as more
substantial than may immediately appear. It is characteristic of Chaucer to mask some of his more significant intentions under a guise of unemphatic, almost neutral presentation, as though to discourage any overly solemn or
simply one-sidedly committed interpretation. The Manciple does not strike us as one of the more interesting or
strongly defined members of the pilgrim company. Indeed, he is one of the characters who are thrown together
as a group at the end of the series of portraits in the
General Prologue;[3] but it is far from clear that the less
"gentle" or prestigious pilgrims are necessarily the least
perceptive, and we have to reflect that the Nun's Priest,
who tells one of the most subtle and variously relevant
tales in the whole collection, is not portrayed in the General Prologue at all, and our glimpse of him at a later stage,
through the eyes of the Host, seems almost to make him
interchangeable with the Monk.[4] The Manciple is at least
given a place in the initial rollcall of pilgrims. The emphasis there lies on his practical shrewdness, which is such that
he has been able to hold his own among the subtle and
learned lawyers whom he serves by purchasing their provi-
sions at the Inn of Court to which he is attached:

> Now is nat that of God a ful fair grace
> That swich a lewed mannes wit shal pace
> The wisdom of an heep of lerned men?
>
> (I. 573–75)

There is clearly an indication here, typically Chaucerian in
its unstressed irony, concerning the kind of pretension
that would lead that "heap" of learned men, the Manciple's employers, to see themselves on a superior level to
him; and with it a comment on the limitations of academic

learning and on the pretensions that are apt to accompany it when they are applied to the practical concerns of day-to-day living.

When the time comes for the Manciple to address himself to the telling of his tale, he stresses the unlettered, down-to-earth nature of his outlook upon life. He is, he says, no more than a "boystous"—that is to say, a rude, unlettered—man (IX. 211); but he is also—as he slyly implies—one who is capable of seeing the difference between fact, the plain reality of things as they present themselves to an ordinary, unpretentious man, and the embroidering devices that the imagination—or the vanity—of the literate is apt to impose upon those same facts in order to make them seem other, more gratifying, than in reality they are.

A man of this kind is not likely to stand out by obvious force of personality in a human group, in which he is more likely to occupy a marginal role of the kind that may have been congenial to his creator, observing and commenting on what he sees going on around him—not taken in by excessive pretension, to which he is indeed apt to reduce a great deal of human behavior, and always ready to insist upon what he sees as the way things actually and inescapably *are*. Given this point of view—which we need not identify with Chaucer's own, but which has with it enough points of contact to make of him a useful vehicle for some of the poet's purposes—the Manciple can become the instrument for expressing some of Chaucer's more insistent concerns in his portrayal of the human pilgrimage: so much so that it may well have seemed appropriate to place this intervention—deliberately played down, deprived as it is of surface emphasis or brilliance—just before the winding up of the entire undertaking.[5]

Something of this already begins to emerge in the exchange, in the prologue to the tale, that involves the drunken Cook,[6] the Host, and the Manciple himself. The Host, with his habitual bluntness, begins to "jape and pleye" at the Cook's expense and to call upon him, in spite

of his obvious incapacity, to fulfill his commitment by telling a tale:

> For he shal telle a tale, by my fey,
> Although it be nat worth a botel hey.
>
> (IX. 13–14)

When the Cook turns out to be manifestly in no state to do
any such thing, the Manciple intervenes to deflect the Host
from his intent, which he does with some diplomatic skill
of the kind that he has no doubt learned to apply in dealing with his employers and that he now displays in these
lesser circumstances:

> "Wel," quod the Maunciple, "if it may doon ese
> To thee, sire Cook, and to no wight displese,
> Which that heere rideth in this compaignye,
> And that oure Hoost wole, of his curteisye,
> I wol as now excuse thee of thy tale."
>
> (IX. 25–29)

The intervention is calculated to smoothe over what might
easily become troubled waters and to head off the danger
of an intolerably embarrassing performance by the Cook.
In the process the Manciple, by the carefully calculated
deference of his expression, allows himself a typically detached comment on the gap that habitually separates human pretension, the desire to appear well in the eyes of
others, from human reality. His effort is followed, again as
we may think very much in character, by a sharply visual
characterization of the drunken Cook (IX. 30–45) in
which the Manciple indulges a traditional rivalry between
those of his own profession and the cooks with whom they
were, by its very nature, in close and often competitive
contact. The picture drawn by the Manciple is one that
stresses, sharply and vividly, the displeasing aspects of
drunkenness. There are moments—like the reference to
the Cook's blurred eyes and sour breath—

Thyne eyen daswen eek, as that me thynketh,
And, wel I woot, thy breeth ful soure stynketh—
                                                    (IX. 31–32)

and the contemptuous lines that follow:

Hoold cloos thy mouth, man, by thy fader kyn!
The devel of helle sette his foot therin!
Thy cursed breeth infecte wole us alle.
Fy, stynkyng swyn! fy, foule moote thee falle!—
                                                    (IX. 37–40)

in which personal animus of a very different kind reminds us of certain of the effects achieved by the Pardoner in the denunciation of the sin of gluttony, which was a principal theme of his sermon.[7] Both contribute, each in its own way, to the "exemplary" function of "drunkenness," throughout the tales, as a sign of man's inability to keep to the "way" to which, in his reasonable humanity, he is committed.[8]

The Host declares himself sufficiently convinced by what the Manciple has said to recognize that the Cook is in no condition to tell a coherent tale. He accordingly calls on the Manciple to make his own contribution, while reproving him at the same time for having been too "nice" in the open reproof of his victim for his vice. After all, as he insinuates, the Manciple is not without faults of his own, less apparent perhaps, but not on that account less serious than those of the Cook, and the latter may well, under more favorable conditions, be able to raise these against him:

Another day he wole, peraventure,
Reclayme thee and brynge thee to lure;
I meene, he speke wole of smale thynges,
As for to pynchen at thy rekenynges,
That were nat honest, if it cam to preef.
                                                    (IX. 71–75)

To put the vagaries of human behavior "to preef"—to the test—is one of the main concerns of the pilgrimage; and the suggestion, here and elsewhere, is that few of the pilgrims will emerge with untouched consistency from this kind of scrutiny. This, it would seem, is something that men would do well to recognize if they wish to live tolerably in society.

The Manciple, at any rate, who is nothing if not a realist and whose view of human nature is dispassionate enough to include the recognition of his own weakness, is quick to recognize the truth contained in the Host's observation. "'No,' quod the Manciple, 'that were a greet mescheef!'" (IX. 76). He too is vulnerable to criticism, in a way, moreover, that might affect the material interests that are, no doubt, the real substance of life. "So myghte he lightly brynge me in the snare" (IX. 77): the snare in which, so he implies, all men are liable to fall and which the prudent man should seek to avoid:

> Yet hadde I levere payen for the mare
> Which he rit on, than he sholde with me stryve.
> (IX. 78–79)

"That that I spak, I seyde it in my bourde," in jest: the Manciple retires, with characteristic prudence, from the prospect of danger opening before him and in the process of so doing goes on to press his advantage over the drunken and incapacitated Cook, who is in no condition either to retreat or to reply, in the form of a further calculated jest. "And wite ye what?": one can sense in the apparently casual afterthought the speaker's dry sense of humor as he rises to the chance he sees before him both to turn the Cook's state into an opportunity for jest on behalf of the whole company and to press home, more consciously and coldly, the advantage that this gives him.

Encouraged in this way, the Cook takes the draft of ale offered him, and even thanks his rival, "in swich wise as he

koude" (IX. 93): a situation that gives the Host a good deal
of satisfaction. He began, we are told, "to laughen wonder
loude" (IX. 94) and to make a typically double-edged comment on the effects of drink in promoting human convi-
viality:

> I se wel it is necessarie,
> Where that we goon, good drynke with us carie;
> For that wol turne rancour and disese
> T'accord and love, and many a wrong apese.
>
> (IX. 95–98)

The comment, so ambivalent in its final sense, carries implications for the pilgrimage as a whole. As we have seen
from the outset, and as the Host more especially has been
concerned to stress, feasting—the establishment of human
sociability round a convivial table—has been an important
image in the social aspect of man's pilgrimage, and the
partaking in common of wine has had about it something
of a sacramental quality,[9] a shadow on the temporal plane
of the greater fulfillment in the "heavenly Jerusalem" that
is, as the Parson will shortly indicate,[10] the end of the
human journey. Under the influence cf this act of human
sociability it may be hoped that "rancour and disese,"
which so persistently affect the relationships between men
and which have by no means been absent from the pilgrimage, may turn to the "accord and love" that are their
opposites and in which human life as such aspires to fulfill
itself. The question remains whether this aspiration, the
product of human imagination in its moments of deepest
commitment, can rely on nothing more than "good
drynke" to maintain itself in the face of "real" facts as
more than a necessary delusion. The fact that the Host's
words are spoken in a situation of scarcely diguised rancor
and uncharity in which he himself has participated in his
treatment of the unhappy Cook, may seem to suggest
otherwise. There is a good deal of subtlety, in this respect,
in the Host's final address to the god of wine and convivial-
ity:

O thou Bacus, yblessed be thy name,
That so kanst turnen ernest into game!
Worshipe and thank be to thy deitee!

                                        (IX. 99–101)

The sociability that the Manciple has promoted, finally at
the expense of confirming his rival, the Cook, in his absurd vulnerability, is the product of man's innate, distinguishing gift of imagination; but this has been dedicated to
a god who is essentially other than the Christian deity proposed by the whole pilgrimage project: one who represents a reality marginal to the undertaking as strictly
defined but not on that account less attractive to many of
the pilgrims on their way.

   The effect is, as the Host puts it, to "turnen ernest into
game," which is precisely the reverse of the warning—"eek
men shal nat maken ernest of game"—that the poet himself, in his "apology" for *The Miller's Tale*,[11] had put before
his possibly censorious readers very near the outset of the
pilgrimage. It is, in other words, to react against what can
easily become false or self-congratulatory moralizing
seriousness (of the kind that Chaucer is constantly inclined
to reject) but to do so at the possible expense of turning
what can properly be considered "ernest"—the serious
business of living, which is not incompatible with and indeed requires a proper sense of humor and proportion—
into the shadow reality of "game." The turn of phrase is
one that Chaucer evidently found congenial. It is echoed,
to a different end, by the Pardoner in his reference to the
activity of the cooks engaged in a parody of the act of
consecration at the Mass by "turning substance into accident" (VI. 539) for the benefit of their gluttonous patrons.
The "substance" is the body and blood of Christ, as "ernest" a reality as any Christian orthodoxy can conceive; the
"accident" is the bread and wine that is transubstantiated
to the eye of faith but that retains its material appearance
to a more sceptical vision. In each case there is a similar
sense of the "serious" confounded with the "absurd," in a

reversal that touches the incongruous heart of the human situation. If it is clear that men do well to turn "rancour and disese" into the "accord and love" that is a principal goal of the pigrimage and by so doing to "apese" many a wrong (IX. 96–98), it is far from certain that the service of Bacchus, which has been so marked a feature of the journey, has always tended to that desirable end: or, indeed, that the Pardoner's powerful denunciation of drunkenness and its effects, suspect though it is coming from that particular exponent of morality, is not nearer the reality of things. It will be seen that the Manciple's prologue, beneath its surface of jest and normal human rivalry, raises—obliquely, indeed, as is so often the case when Chaucer follows his habitual urge to avoid undue pomposity or the absurd pretension that he regards, perhaps above everything else, as the ultimate human flaw—issues that touch some of the most real and serious concerns of the "pilgrimage" of life.

The tale to which this introduction leads is a typically unemphatic performance, as befits the dry, detached nature of the teller. Taken, like so many medieval stories, from Ovid's *Metamorphoses*,[12] it tells of what befell the god Apollo when he chose to assume human form and to sojourn on earth among men, exposing himself—as the classical sources so clearly stress on these occasions—to the dangers and absurdities that such a choice implies. The god who assumes human shape is liable to be deceived or subjected to ridiculous situations by the mortals among whom he finds himself; and this reality, which we may think is not unpleasing to the Manciple's turn of mind, is in fact central to the story. By becoming

> the mooste lusty bachiler
> In al this world,
>
> (IX. 107–8)

by being

                    fulfild of gentillesse,
        Of honour, and of parfit worthynesse,
                                    (IX. 123–24)

Phoebus exposes himself to the various misadventures that
this condition is likely to imply.

It is important, in connection with the tale, to note that
Phoebus had

                    in his hous a crowe
        Which in a cage he fostred many a day,
        And taughte it speken, as men teche a jay.
                                    (IX. 130–32)

Phoebus is among other things, the god of poetry, to
whom the classical poets (with Dante and other medieval
writers before and after him[13]) directed themselves as
source of inspiration. It is reasonable to think of the bird
as the poet's imagination, which he has sought to keep in a
"cage" and to which he has imparted the gift of expression. White as "a snow-whit swan" (IX. 133)—which, however, is what he is *not*—the crow has the capacity to
"countrefete" human speech and—as the Manciple dryly
observes—to transform human reality, making it appear
other and more attractive than what it is to the dispassionate eye of a detached observer:

        And countrefete the speche of every man
        He koude, whan he sholde telle a tale:
        Therwith in al this world no nyghtyngale
        Ne koude, by an hondred thousand deel,
        Syngen so wonder myrily and weel.
                                    (IX. 134–38)

It is not difficult to see here Chaucer reflecting on the
ambiguities and dangers of his art. He too has undertaken
to imitate—or is it to "counterfeit"?—the speech, if not of
"every man," of the considerable variety of those whom he

has chosen to include in his project; and the undertaking, as he has come increasingly to see and now indicates through the eyes of his latest narrator, is not without its dangers. The poet has at his disposal the gift of transposing or "counterfeiting,"[14] what presents itself to most men as plain "reality"; the effect is to make that "reality"—but only while the imaginative transformation lasts—more attractive than, essentially *other* than what it truly is. The gift is a fascinating, distinctively human one that confers a kind of "divinity" on the possessor. It enables him to transform the appearance of things—as Dorigen in *The Franklin's Tale* wished to do with the "grisly feendly rokkes blak"[15]—so as to make them conform more closely to his desire. The process, however, human, even necessary as it is, has its limitations. It bears within itself an element of self-deception, the danger implied in man's innate capacity to color the real with the exercise of his fancy and, in the particular case of the creative artist, to induce men to see it as otherwise than it actually is. The whole trend of the tale—one, we may think, congenial to this particular teller—may be seen as concerned with the uncomfortable process of awakening from this particular form of illusion.

Among the distinctively human attributes to which the god of the tale submitted himself by assuming human form is one that has played an important part throughout the pilgrimage and to which the Manciple now gives a distinctive turn of his own. He has in his house a wife whom—with a simplicity that perhaps befits a divinity but which is not characteristic of men, at any rate as this teller sees them—"he lovede moore than his lyf" (IX. 140). To love is to become vulnerable, to be subject to the possibility of betrayal—a theme that has already been touched upon, in a tone of comic uneasiness, by the Miller when he told his rival, the Reeve, that "who hath no wyf, he is no cokewold" (I. 3152), arriving at the essentially sceptical conclusion that

An housbonde shal nat been inquisityf

Of Goddes pryvetee, nor of his wyf.
So he may fynde Goddes foyson there,
Of the remenant nedeth nat enquere.

(I. 3163–66)

The Miller concludes, prudently, that he will "bileve wel"
that he has not been cuckolded, finding what comfort he
can in his belief; but the possibility of deception remains
and is only increased when the god in question is open to
the very human failing—one which, once again, has been
present in more than one of the previous tales—of jealous
possessiveness:

Jalous he was, and wolde have kept hire fayn.
For hym were looth byjaped for to be,
And so is every wight in swich degree.

(IX. 144–46)

This, we can hardly fail to remember, was also the aspiration of Januarius in *The Merchant's Tale:* though we may
also think that in his desire to "plese" his wife and to "doon
hire reverence" (IX. 142), Apollo was closer to the position
of Arveragus at the opening of *The Franklin's Tale.* However we may be meant to think of these parallels, the Manciple's conclusion reflects his particular brand of wry, unpretentious, slightly cynical commonsense. Having told us
what are the aspirations of "every man" in this delicate
matter, he goes on to make his own comment upon them,
suggesting that the destiny of all men—and of any "god"
who may be so incautious as to assume the burden that
goes with the human shape—is finally to come to terms
with a reality that tends to run counter to all forms of
idealism or excess.[16] To desire not to be "byjaped" may be
natural, but is not in the last resort always possible; for, as
the tale goes on to say, "al [is] in ydel, for it availleth noght"
(IX. 147). The real alternatives that face a man are likely to
be less absolute and less dramatic than those which a "god"
may be ready to contemplate. Commonsense tells us that

to keep a faithful wife in durance is both unnecessary and unreasonable:

> A good wyf, that is clene of werk and thoght,
> Sholde nat been kept in noon awayt, certayn;
>
> (IX. 148–49)

whereas, as it also tells us, on the other alternative,

> trewely, the labour is in vayn
> To kepe a shrewe, for it wol nat bee.
>
> (IX. 150–51)

To seek in either case "to kepe wyves" is to "spille labour," to waste effort in a "verray nycetee."[17] The best any man can hope to do is to adapt himself to reality and to make the best of what the Manciple sees as the necessity of the human condition. We should not—must not—go so far as to equate the Manciple's views with the poet's own. This is only one strand in the complex web of human attitudes and emotions that is being explored throughout; but, although men have other needs and other resources, though their lives are in part their own imaginative creation, they do well to remember that the claims of "experience," plain, commonsense fact, are not lightly to be set aside.

The "worthy Phebus," like many an ordinary man who lays no claim to his "divine" condition, is not willing to accept these limits, which he has none the less made his by his assumption of the human form. He sets out to do everything that he can to please the wife he loves and hopes, once again like the Arveragus who represented the Franklin's ideal of "gentility" in his tale, to maintain as a result a state agreeable "for his manhede and his governaunce" (IX. 158): that is, in the last resort, one that besides being natural, flatters his very masculine sense of his own dignity. To achieve this he keeps his wife—like his white bird—in the equivalent of a cage, which is in effect

the symbol of his conception of love, and which produces
only the result that she is impelled to seek her freedom:

> God it woot, ther may no man embrace
> As to destreyne a thyng which that nature
> Hath natureelly set in a creature.
>
> (IX. 160–62)

The Manciple may be, socially speaking, an inconspicuous
individual and one of no notable intellectual pretension,
but Chaucer is not above using such for some of his more
valid comments of life, and here the emphasis on what is
natural, what corresponds to the reality of things as seen
by an eye undistorted by prejudice, pretension, or imaginative self-indulgence, reads as an apt comment on attitudes that have been advanced in not a few of the preceding tales. The Manciple, we may think, would have found
the senile egoism of the Merchant's Januarius as absurd as
the courtly fantasies, touched as they were with social
snobbery, of the Franklin; and he would certainly have
been appreciative, in *The Miller's Tale,* of Alison's success in
freeing herself from the importunities of the carpenter-
husband who was "sely," innocently self-absorbed enough
to seek, in vain, to hold her "narwe in cage." His own view
might be seen as one that tends to deflation, even to a
somewhat bleak view of human realities; but it is one that
the poet is likely to have thought it desirable, even necessary, to take into account if the disappointment that at-
tends excessive pretension is to be avoided. It may even be
that a comment is implied, as we approach the end of the
pilgrimage, on the limitations of "tale-telling," with its implication that the "real" can be subjected to imaginative
transformation, as an approach to the "truth." It will not
be before the poet, stepping as it were out of his creation
and leaving his pilgrims conspicuously short of their destination, assumes his personal responsibility for what he
has written, that he recognizes the final subjection of his
art to an order that, if it exists (a question that, within the

limits of "tale-telling," has been left conspicuously open), must necessarily be thought of as implying a final act of renunciation.

The lines that follow (IX. 163–74) stress the natural desire of all creatures to escape the "cages" that their circumstance seems to have contrived for them in such a way as to achieve their natural condition of "liberty":

> For evere this brid wol doon his bisynesse
> To escape out of his cage, yif he may.
> His libertee this brid desireth ay.
>
> (IX. 172–74)

The same, he goes on to say, is true of the cat who is fostered "wel with milk" and "tendre flessh," and given a "couche of silk." He too, as soon as he sees "a mous go by the wal,"

> weyveth milk and flessh and al,
> And every dayntee that is in that hous,
> Swich appetit hath he to ete a mous.
>
> (IX. 178–80)

Applied to men, this situation leads to a revealing comment that amounts yet again, to an exposure of human and more specifically male vanity. God that he was, it was rash of Apollo, having renounced his divinity, to take it for granted that his human wife—or his bird—would be content to live in the gilded "cage" that he had contrived for them. The observation has a bearing on not a few of the attitudes of presumption and self-esteem reflected in the tales, and especially on those that have to do with the relationship between men and women. These "examples," the Manciple says, are spoken

> by thise men
> That been untrewe, and nothyng by wommen:
>
> (IX. 187–88)

a comment that, in the process of conveying a necessary redress of the common balance, manages to read remarkably like the Nun's Priest's disclaimer of any intention to speak or think ill of any member of the opposite sex.[18] The comment is very characteristically double in its intention. Chaucer makes his character disclaim an opinion in such a way as to reinforce the effect that it leaves upon the mind of the reader; but when this has been said there can be no doubt that the final emphasis lies in a place that will offer little support to the cruder forms of masculine self-esteem. "For men," as the Manciple concludes,

> han evere a likerous appetit
> On lower thyng to parfourne hire delit
> Than on hire wyves, be they never so faire,
> Ne never so trewe, ne so debonaire.
>
> (IX. 189–92)

The conclusion is one that moralists may find discouraging but that—so the implication runs—they will do well to consider if they wish their precepts to remain in useful contact with reality: for

> Flessh is so newefangel,[19] with meschaunce,
> That we ne konne in nothyng han plesaunce,
> That sowneth unto vertu any while.
>
> (IX. 193–95)

This—we must repeat—is the Manciple's conclusion, not necessarily to be equated with Chaucer's own; but men are well advised to consider it as a possibility, and the same applies to those gods who are so rash as to assume human form and the burden of human obligations:

> This Phebus, which that thoghte upon no gile,
> Deceyved was, for all his jolitee.
>
> (IX. 196–97)

As we know, on what Chaucer would no doubt have considered excellent authority, the children of this world are wiser, at least in their own generation, than those of light.[20] What may be true in the "divine" order of the imagination when it operates in freedom from the limitations imposed by the nature of sublunary reality becomes suspect when required to deal with the more devious aspects of human nature. The fact is that "whan Phebus was absent," his wife "for hir lemman sent" (IX. 204). In revealing this inconvenient but "true" development, the Manciple, not without irony, excuses himself for his plain statement of the fact—"Hir lemman? Certes, this is a knavyssh speche!" (IX. 205)—without in any way disguising the reality that the *truth* of his tale imposes.

At this point, interestingly, Chaucer returns to what has been throughout a principal underlying theme of the *Tales*—the obligation that the poet's art imposes upon him to declare the truth of things as they are, even when they may appear unpleasing to morally or socially sophisticated members of his audience. The words that convey this echo very closely Chaucer's self-justification, spoken as narrator in the General Prologue:

> The wise Plato seith, as ye may rede,
> The word moot nede accorde with the dede.
> If men shall telle proprely a thing,
> The word moot cosyn be to the werkyng.[21]
> (IX. 207–10)

The problem so presented is indeed less Plato's than Chaucer's; but it is one that seems to be inseparable from his conception of his function as a poet, and there is certainly a sense in which it is one of the main questions—less directly stated than hinted at, or assumed to exist—behind the whole undertaking. The Manciple, having raised the issue, tries to evade responsibility for what he has said by referring to himself as a plain, unlettered ("boystous") man; but, having uttered this apparent disclaimer, he goes on to advance conclusions that are destructive of not a few of the pretensions upon which a great part of human life in society rests.

We shall, perhaps, be in danger of failing to see how far the Manciple's argument in the next few lines leads when pressed to its logical conclusion:

> Ther nys no difference, trewely,
> Bitwixe a wyf that is of heigh degree,
> If of hir body dishonest she bee,
> And a povre wenche, oother than this—
> If it so be they werke bothe amys—
> But that the gentile, in estaat above,
> She shal be cleped his lady, as in love;
> And for that oother is a povre woman,
> She shal be cleped his wenche or his lemman.
> And, God it woot, myn owene deere brother,
> Men leyn that oon as lowe as lith that oother.
>
> (IX. 212–22)

At this point, evidently, we are dealing not with gods, who operate in the "imaginative" order, but with very human issues. Life in society, it would seem, consists in giving realities the names that it is convenient to give them and then in establishing these distinctions as real differences. In the relationship between the sexes, which has been considered under different lights in so many of the preceding tales, a single bodily reality is given a different name when it concerns a woman of "heigh degree," of the kind with whom the poets prefer to concern themselves in their writings dealing with what they choose to dignify by calling it "love," and when a "povre wenche" is in question. For those who like to think of themselves as "gentils"—once more, the word has appeared with various resonances in the course of the pilgrimage[22]—and as enjoying a social position "in estaat above," the simple facts are disguised, made socially more acceptable and personally flattering, by being seen in terms of the fiction that passes for love. Poetry dignifies them under this light, presenting them in a manner that can be—where moral principle and practice do not go hand in hand—a deceptive fiction. The fiction, however, is not only or necessarily deceptive. It may indeed be that some measure of acceptance of it is indispensable for a tolerable human life; but the process has its dangers inasmuch as it can induce a surrender to willed self-deception. When exactly the same reality presents itself without the covering of social pretense that seeks to dignify it the woman who, in respectable, "gentil" society, is the mistress, the object of adoring devotion celebrated by the poets, is given the plain name of "wench" or "lemman" that in reason belongs to both.

The same finally disturbing principle is also applied by the Manciple to a wider range of realities; for there appears—again in the light of dispassionate reason—to be no real distinction between a "tiraunt" who is "titlelees," who has achieved power outside the due processes of law, and an "outlaw" or a base highway robber, "a theef erraunt." Once more it is a question of using names to disguise uncomfortable realities:

> To Alisaundre was toold this sentence,
> That, for the tirant is of gretter myght,
> By force of meynee, for to sleen dounright,
> And brennen hous and hoom, and make al playn,
> Lo, therfore is he cleped a capitayn;
> And for the outlawe hath but smal meynee,
> And may nat doon so greet an harme as he,
> Ne brynge a contree to so greet mescheef,
> Men clepen hym an outlawe or a theef.
>
> (IX. 226–34)

"Men clepen hym": in that phrase lies the heart of the Manciple's contention, one full of disturbing possibilities for what men like to think of as the convenient ordering of society. In it Chaucer seems to be pressing to disquieting conclusions the initial assertion, advanced by the poet-narrator—who has perhaps not considered the full implications of his statement—that the writer or the teller of a tale is bound by the nature of his undertaking to be true to what he sees as reality.[23] The apparently innocent assertion can, it seems, lead to conclusions that tend to the destruction of the moral distinctions upon which the order of society rests. Having brought himself to the border of these dangerous assertions, the Manciple once more takes refuge in his posture of a plain men without literary or philosophical pretensions—"for I am a man noght textueel" (IX. 235)—and returns to the plain surface of his story.

The tale, however, is full of insinuated implications. It is relevant, as we have seen, that Phebus, or Apollo, is the god of poetry. His crow, we may reasonably think, is the poet, or "maker" of fictions, who has the obligation of relating truly what in his fiction he sees. The obligation is one that can lead to uncomfortable conclusions, both for the god who rashly proposed to fashion a cage for his bird, from which it might conveniently and decoratively sing for his delectation, and for the bird itself. The bird is driven by its nature to declare the "truth" of things as it presents itself under his eyes: "the truth" that the god finds it intolerable to hear. Struck by the difference between the bird's former songs—

> Ne were thow wont so myrily to synge
> That to myn herte it was a rejoysynge
> To heere thy voys—
>
> (IX. 245–47)

and the present tone of disillusionment implied in its harsh "Cokkow!" Apollo rashly inquires into the meaning of the new song. Thus challenged, the crow is bleakly faithful to his truth-telling vocation:

> "By God!" quod he, "I synge nat amys.
> Phebus," quod he, "for all thy worthynesse,
> For al thy beautee and thy gentillesse,
> For al thy song and all thy mynstralcye,
> For all thy waityng, blered is thyn ye

With oon of litel reputacioun,
Noght worthy to thee, as in comparisoun,
The montance of a gnat, so moote I thryve!
For on thy bed thy wyf I saugh hym swyve."
(IX. 248–56)

The final theme is that of the imagination and its relationship to "plain reality." Apollo is possessed, in his divinity, of all the civilizing graces—"worthynesse," "beautee," and "gentillesse"—which pertain to his status and shine through his human form. Above all, he is the god of poetry, whose gift of "song" and "minstralcy" enables him to effect an imaginative transformation of the real world that is, as we may think (and as a poet may above all be presumed to think), the highest of the distinctively human faculties. The poet, however, caught in the "cage" that his god has contrived for him, finds himself in the position of having to reconcile these gifts with adherence to the often incompatible reality of things. The crow brings out the true basis of fact as it has presented itself to him. Apollo's graces do not protect him from deception. He may be a god, but once he has exposed himself to the condition of a mortal man, he is, however incongruously, subject to all the contradictions which that state implies. His eye is "blered" by one of inferior standing, one no more worthy to stand in comparison with him than a "gnat": one, however, who has been capable of the base achievement that the bird puts bluntly, without advantage of poetic adornment or social fiction, before his master: "on thy bed"—where else, indeed?—"thy wyf I saugh hym swyve."

It is as difficult as it is important to try to determine the exact tone that underlies these words. The Manciple is clearly something of a cynic, or one at least whose self-professed devotion to plain realism is apt to lead to a cynical view of life. We need not—indeed, should not—believe that Chaucer asks us to share the point of view that the tale seems to advance, but he certainly saw in it something that needed to be taken into account in any rendering of human reality that aspires to completeness; for the distinction between realism and cynicism, essential though it is, is not always clear or absolute. It is not an accident perhaps that the later stages of the pilgrimage, in its progress from the springtime morning of its inception to the darkening tones of evening that introduce the Parson's final move beyond the order of "tale-telling,"[24] are marked by a growing sense of strain that seems at times to threaten the "fellowship" with dissolution, and by an increasing number of tales—*The Pardoner's Tale, The Canon Yeoman's Tale,* and the Manciple's own contribution—that tend to expose dark and potentially disruptive drives in human nature.

The crow in the tale, at any rate, has been faithful to its truth-telling vocation. It is significant and necessary to the point that the tale is concerned to make that he suffers for his truthfulness. After Phebus has been reduced to exacting an all-too-human vengeance upon his wife, he renounces the symbols of his imaginative vocation:

> This is th'effect, ther is namoore to sayn;
> For sorwe of which he brak his mynstralcie,
> Bothe harpe, and lute, and gyterne, and sautrie,
> And eek he brok his arwes and his bowe.
> (IX. 266–69)

Having done so, he turns to his reckoning with the crow, whom he denounces as "traitour" (IX. 271) and accuses him of having brought him to a very un-godlike "confusioun." The wife whom, in his human form, he loved, seeing in her a "gemme of lustiheed" (IX. 274), has been slain by his own hand; and, having slain her, he has come to think that she was, in the event, "giltelees" (IX. 277)— because that is how, very humanly, he *needs* to think of her—and that his imagination has led him into "wantrust" or "fals suspicioun" (IX. 281). In this conviction—which we know, in terms of the tale's fact, to be a delusion—the god accuses the crow of having practiced deception upon him and punishes him by turning his feathers from white to black:

> And to the crowe, "O false theef!" seyde he,
> "I wol thee quite anon thy false tale.
> Thou songe whilom lyk a nyghtyngale;
> Now shaltow, false theef, thy song forgon,
> And eek thy white fetheres everichon."
>
> (IX. 292–96)

He deprives him, further, of the gift of song and turns his voice into one of foreboding before casting him "out at dore" and consigning him to the devil (IX. 307). The reference to the gift of imaginative creation and its ambiguous relation to the reality of things is apparent and is placed appropriately, in this deliberately unemphatic way, at this late stage in the pilgrimage. It reflects some of Chaucer's deepest considerations about the nature of his art and helps to prepare us, in no simple or one-sided way, for the spirit of the final retraction,[25] at the same time as it stresses the intractable nature of the issues with which the decision to make the retraction is obstinately confronted.

The Manciple in his tale has raised a number of themes that go notably beyond what the tale itself, on its plain, unvarnished surface, seems to imply. He has been anxious throughout to deny any pretension to subtlety or learning; and now, at the end of the tale, he retires into a series of proverbial reflections—taught him, as he says, by "my dame" (IX. 317)—that come naturally to a man who has declared himself to be "noght textueel" (IX. 316). Like the tavern boy in *The Pardoner's Tale*,[26] the Manciple, faced by the unspoken challenges implied in the fable he has chosen to tell, disclaims any intention of pursuing them further and falls back on the teachings of common experience mediated to him from childhood at his mother's knees or at that of his first teacher: for therein—and in the limitation that the conclusion implies—lies a kind of safety. The immediate lesson is the prudent one that should induce a man to keep a close guard on what he speaks for fear of the consequences. It has, of course, universal application, but it applies not least to the poet who has been, as he may now feel, rash enough to commit himself to declaring the *truth* of what he sees, however unflattering or socially inconvenient it may be. As the last words of the tale, he leaves us with this:

> "My sone, be war, and be noon auctour newe
> Of tidynges, wheither they been false or trewe.
> Whereso thou come, amonges hye or lowe,
> Kepe wel thy tonge, and thenk upon the crowe."
>
> (IX. 359–62)

They are not, indeed, words that we need be tempted to think of as Chaucer's final conclusion in this matter. No artist of his caliber could remain content with them; but we may feel that they do contain matter that we are invited to reflect upon and which a dispassionate attitude to the creative process—insofar as one is conceivable or desirable—will do well to incorporate into its final picture of the human pilgrimage.

NOTES

1. For a convenient summary of the present state of the discussion in respect of the tale and its position in the plan of the pilgrimage, see F. N. Robinson's notes on p. 762 of his edition (*Works* [Boston: Houghton Mifflin, 1957]).

2. See X. 5.

3. See I. 542–44.

4. See VII. 3450–60, and compare VII. 1937–62.

5. Donald Howard, in his important study of *The Canterbury Tales* (Berkeley and Los Angeles: University of California Press, 1976), pp. 304–6, tends to see the tale as an example of Chaucer's deliberate use of "bad art." This is an argument that throws light upon some aspects of the tale and its place in the general plan of the pilgrimage but which seems to me to do less than complete justice to the poet's conception.

6. The fact that the Cook has already been introduced and has even begun the fragment of a tale, in I. 4325–422, has suggested to some students that

Chaucer intended to cancel the earlier intervention and to introduce him here for the first time. But there are other possibilities, such as that he may have written the sequence represented by *The Miller's Tale, The Reeve's Tale,* and *The Cook's Tale* after *The Manciple's Tale* and then, for whatever reason, failed to make the necessary amendment. In any case, as we shall argue here, the exchange between the Host, the Manciple, and the Cook is not without relevance to important themes developed in the course of the pilgrimage.

7. Compare VI. 517–28, 534–36; 551–59.

8. This theme was first raised by Arcite in *The Knight's Tale,* I. 1361–65. The comparison originated with Boethius.

9. Something of this is implied, however indirectly, in the Host's arrangement of hospitality for the company at the outset of the journey. See I. 749–50.

10. See X. 50–51.

11. I. 3186.

12. *Metamorphoses* 2. 531–632.

13. See especially *Paradiso* 1. 13–15.

14. Chaucer has used the word elsewhere in the *Tales,* notably in the prologue to *The Pardoner's Tale* (VI. 447), where it carries similar implications.

15. V. 868.

16. We may recall the somewhat similar conclusions reached by the Miller, in the prologue to his tale, concerning the possibility that his wife is deceiving him (I. 3158–66).

17. IX. 152.

18. VII. 3266.

19. For the use of the word *newefangel* with similar implications, see V. 618–20.

20. *Luke* 16:8.

21. Compare I. 741–42.

22. Compare, more particularly, the attitude of "thise gentils" to the tale about to be told by the Pardoner in VI. 318.

23. See I. 730–38.

24. "Thou getest fable noon ytoold for me" (X. 31).

25. X. 1081–92.

26. VI. 684.

"Unaccommodated Man" in *King Lear*

THE third act of *King Lear,* which covers Lear's exposure
to the storm, is the keystone upon which the whole elaborate construction of the play rests. It is, above all, a marvelous example of poetic elaboration for dramatic purposes.
At the center of the action, at once the main protagonist
and symbol of a humanity wrenched out of its "fixed
place" in "the frame of nature,"[1] provoking our wonder
and inviting our compassion, stands the figure of the aged
king. The intimate fusion of inner conflict and external
convulsion has often been noted and is indeed an essential
part of the entire conception. The "storm" that has broken
out in Lear's mind, the result of his rejection by his children, is intimately fused with the evocation of the warring
elements mainly entrusted to his lips; and the external
storm, which exercises upon his aging physique the intolerable strain under which it finally breaks, is in turn a
projection of his inner state. Related in this way to the
action of the elements—which, as it were, he draws upon
himself in the process of reacting to it—Lear assumes a
stature more than merely personal, becomes not merely *a*
man, but *man,* the microcosm of a problematic universe,
exposed to an ordeal to which the frame of things contributes but which finds its most acute expression in the intimate disunion that the earlier action has introduced into
the family bond.

The opening dialogue between the disguised Kent and a

gentleman, as they meet on the bare stage that represents the wind-swept heath, makes this connection explicit. Kent's challenge, "Who's there, besides foul weather?" (3. 1. 1), is answered by "One minded like the weather, most unquietly": from the first the personal disorder and its external projection are united in a single process, of much the same kind as that by which the witches, in the opening scene of *Macbeth,* establish the spiritual climate of the tragedy—"Fair is foul, and foul is fair"[2]—and indicate the confusion of moral categories with which it is to be concerned.

From this opening it is only a step to pass to the picture, which immediately follows, of the king "contending with the fretful elements" and striving—most significantly of all—"in his little world of man" to

outscorn
The to-and-fro-conflicting wind and rain.
(4. 1. 10–11)

The fact, established immediately after, that this is a night in which even the lion, "the cub-drawn bear" (1. 12) deprived of its offspring, and the "belly-pinched wolf" (1. 13) driven by need to prey upon its fellow victims—and it is worth observing that Lear has himself "lost" his children and is about to be exposed to hunger—would seek for shelter is a measure of the strength of the contending passions by which he is torn and which compel him in his agony to contemplate the advent of universal chaos, bidding "what will take all" (1. 15). From the first there is something precarious, even overweening, in the pretension that a mere human being, reduced to the basic elements of his unsupported humanity, can aspire to "outscorn" or affirm his superiority against the action of the elements.

Against the background so established, a Kent under sentence of banishment and driven to conceal his identity by the most elementary need of self-preservation brings news of a world dedicated to covert rivalry and ultimate self-destruction. The reports from the world of power and self-assertion are of "division," "covered/ With mutual cunning" (1. 19–21), between Cornwall and Albany, whom we last saw with their respective consorts, exercising the mastery that their assumption of authority has given them over the public situation. Like others "throned and set high" by their "great stars" (1. 22–23)—the seemingly favorable operations of a Fortune that appears in its inscrutable course to favor the advance of the ruthless and the powerful—these great personages are attended by "servants,"[3] who "seem" to be faithful executors of their purposes but who act in reality as "spies" bringing to the opposed realm of France "intelligence" of hidden intrigues—"snuffs and packings of the Dukes" (1. 26), as Kent's phrase, reflecting urgency and concealment, puts it—that underlie the public appearance of purposeful harmony. Against this "scattered kingdom" (1. 31), united in appearance but torn by covert rivalries and conflicting "appetites," a "power" is gathering across the sea: a "power" still hidden in secrecy but preparing to reveal itself with "open banner" (1. 31) to advance its restoring aims. All this is declared in enigmatic form by a Kent who is not yet ready to reveal himself as "much more/ Than my out-wall" (1. 44–45), and who proposes to leave it to Cordelia—absent from this central part of the action but hauntingly present in our thoughts—to reveal in the fullness of time "who that fellow is/ That yet you do not know" (1. 48–49). Darkness, enigmatic uncertainty, and the first intimations of an obscure, almost an apocalyptic revelation to come set the tone for the excruciating descent into pain and cruelty that follows.

Such a conception, stated generally in this way, presents problems of presentation that Shakespeare is seen, throughout this central part of his play, in the process of transforming into dramatic assets. To do this, to turn the obstinate limitations imposed by his medium into opportunities for the unfolding of his art, is a distinguishing sign of the great dramatist. If Lear has become, in a phrase that he will soon make his own,[4] a mirror for the state of "unaccommodated man," which it is the play's concern to explore, it is evident that he cannot bear alone the entire weight for which the tragic conception has destined him. He is, therefore, by a superb exercise of dramatic tact, surrounded during his exposure to the elements by a series of supporting characters whom we have already met and who are now introduced in carefully established succession: characters who are called upon to serve, as it were, as the external buttresses of a great architectural construction,[5] to take from his dangerously isolated presence some of the strain to which he would otherwise be subjected.

The success in *Lear* of these "buttresses" as conditioning elements in the dramatic structure may best be measured by a comparison with a play—*Timon of Athens*—that sometimes suggests a partial coincidence of mood and that must have been conceived at a point not very distant in time. In point of fact the comparison, stated in these terms, is in important respects misleading. There is evidence of a textual kind to support the view that *Timon* may have been an experiment on Shakespeare's part that he found unsatisfactory and left in an unrevised state.[6] As such, it is perhaps more usefully approached as a play essentially different in kind from *Lear,* rather than as a one-sided or unsuccessful version of the greater work. *Timon* may show us a Shakespeare engaged in trying to write a very personal kind of morality play in which elements of deliberate exaggeration and sardonic farce[7] have a large and—paradoxically—serious part to play. Nonetheless, while recognizing the essential difference, the comparison may be useful, if only because an element of disenchanted comedy—what we have just called "farce"—is present as a powerful thematic element in the complex effect that Lear's tragedy produces in us.[8] If *Timon* were—as I believe he essentially is not—what we normally understand by a "tragic" character, he would be too isolated in his suffering, too sweeping and too savagely generalized in his denunciations of his human environment, to carry complete conviction. His exaggerated and hysterical outbursts of misanthropy become significant when we see in them the obverse of his equally exaggerated, prodigal, and finally self-flattering gestures of generosity. Rather than morally opposed attributes, these are finally two sides of a single coin, excesses that derive, beneath the appearance of opposition, from a single foundation in egoism. The result is to make Timon, at least in part, ridiculous in a way in which Lear, for all the elements of absurdity and vain self-will that shadow his tragic self-projections, is *not*.

For Lear's situation is essentially different in terms of its dramatic projection from that of Timon. Although he bears throughout the storm the main weight of suffering, and although he is given a very considerable measure of presumption and vain self-commiseration, he does not—like Timon—stand *alone* in his predicament. He is surrounded by beings who, in varying degrees and distinct ways, suffer with him and who serve to illuminate some aspect of his central situation: the fool, who has been from the first a voice of unrecognized realism uttering unwelcome truths, operating on the margin of his master's awareness; Kent, who combined loyalty with frankness and who has taken both with him into exile; Edgar, who has been driven by the half-brother who operates upon his trusting nature into a situation that parallels that of Cordelia. All these characters, by being brought successively into the action and exposed with Lear to the action of the elements, bear some fraction of his tragic burden and show an insight into some aspect of its "meaning," and before the storm ends they are further joined by Gloucester, whose fortunes have been from the first parallel to Lear's own. The result is an intricate and progressive dovetailing of characters and situations that lead step by step into an understanding of the full implications of the central tragic theme embodied in Lear's outraged fatherhood and shattered royalty.

Lear's first appearance in the storm act (act 3, scene 2)

shows him in the state of resentful denunciation that reflects outraged egoism in the form of natural resentment. Once more, the theatrical circumstances are important. Given the bare stage for which Shakespeare wrote and the exigencies of which invariably underlie his dramatic conceptions,[9] it was necessary that the illusion of the storm should be created through words put into the mouth of the central character. As always, the apparent limitation is turned into a crowning asset. It enables us to see that there are, at this moment, *two* storms converging upon Lear's person in a mutually heightening effect. The external storm, conveyed through the words in which he expresses his outraged reaction to it, presses upon his faltering physique with a force that will end by breaking it; and to it there corresponds the internal "tempest" that proceeds from the old man's outrage at his treatment by his daughters and that, in the process of seeking an impassioned outlet, becomes one with the outer commotion. The two storms, brought into being through words spoken by a single individual, reinforce one another, converge to produce the central situation of the entire drama by concentrating their effect upon the broken figure of the old man whose plight dominates the stage under our eyes.

Lear's first words show him in the extremity of his outraged incomprehension, calling upon the elements to execute upon nature the curse of sterility that, in a shocking reversal of the "natural," he has already called upon his own children:[10]

> Crack Nature's moulds, all germains spill at once,
> That makes ingrateful man.
>
> (3. 2. 8–9)

The pathetic response that these words invite in Lear's new situation should not blind us to a sense of unreality and to the reversal of natural feeling implied in them. The content of his prayer, like the curse that preceded it, is perverse, the expression of a willed negation that—

however understandably—involves the rejection of life it-self. Moreover, by calling on the elements to carry out his curse, the old man seems to be seeking to involve nature, the very frame of things, in his resentment. Since the play offers few signs, here or elsewhere, that nature is likely to prove accommodating to so large and self-centered a claim—Lear's microcosmic status in relation to his world, which we have already discussed, is alternately tragic and deflating in its implications—there is something dispro-portionate about his attempt to involve the universe ver-bally in his predicament. His tirade, in fact, is swallowed up in the storm and evokes—both here and later—no re-sponse from the indifferent reality it addresses.

The failure of Lear's attempt to involve the frame of things in his problem serves, accordingly, to bring out what is still his impossibly self-centred understanding of his predicament. His indignation is both natural, having regard to its human causes and ultimately self-defeating. His sense of outrage at an "unkindness" (2. 16), rejection of kinship, which he rightly feels to be contrary to any tolerable conception of what is natural, moves us properly to sympathy; but it is balanced as yet by no glimmer of understanding for the elements of blindness and self-will, the obstinate rejection of the conditions—call them "love," "giving," what you will—that initially prompted the excess-es from which he now suffers. The only new element so far introduced into Lear's mind by exposure to the storm is the clearer realization of a truth already born in him as a result of his encounters with his "unnatural" daughters: the truth that he has reduced himself to the status of a "poor, infirm, weak, and despised old man" (2. 20) who is driven, in the absence of any comforting human response, to look for redress to the elements that press so feelingly upon his unprotected humanity. What responses he will receive, other than the reverberation of his own voice raised in outraged pain, remains to be seen.

The beginnings of at least a possible answer to this ques-tion start to emerge—dimly and uncertainly, indeed—in what follows, as we share the stages of Lear's involvement with his companions in misfortune. Through his interchange with them, if at all, he will arrive at some prospect of breaking the circle of self-imprisoning resentment in which he finds himself. The first step in this process is taken when he becomes aware of the presence of the fool. In the relationship during the tempest between the king and his fool we begin to perceive an extreme case of those inverted relationships upon which the play so persistently relies in its exploration of the deeper senses of the bond that unites human beings in the face of a seemingly indifferent world and by clinging to which their lives acquire some semblance, real or illusory, of meaning. Through the early scenes of the play, prior to the storm, the fool's relationship to the king has rested, generally speaking, on the traditional conception of his office. He has been the licensed speaker of inconvenient truths: truths that are apparent to his wry and disillusioned perception of the ways of the world and that tend increasingly to bring to the surface unrecognized, because unwelcome, thoughts that Lear has preferred to ignore. The intimacy of this relationship between the fool and his master, which increasingly makes of him something very like a projection of Lear's unconscious thoughts, distinguishes him from all his predecessors in Shakespeare's work in ways that only become apparent during the storm scenes. Under the pressure of the elements, which brings them increasingly together in their shared misfortune, the "bond" between king and fool grows over closer; and, in the inversion of Lear's mind through which the exposure to adversity brings him to see himself "upside-down," reflected in the comments of his creature, we become aware of a relation of contraries, deeper than any so far envisaged, between the "wise man" and the "fool."

The paradox, indeed, probes deeply into the realities of the human situation. It consists of a reversal of the accepted values that distinguish the "wise" man from the "fool" and leads to the question, "Which is which?" The

supposedly "wise" man of the opening scenes, the Lear
who was in a position to have his slave whipped[11] and to
exercise his will without fear of contradiction, has become
as a result of his own acts of "unwisdom" the "fool," and
his former creature is now in a position to offer the comments of a practical, largely disillusioned "wisdom" that his
master can no longer ignore. Yet the full sense of the
conception does not end here. The contrast between the
fool's realism and the king's folly does not exhaust the
relationship as it is now perceived to exist between them.
Both, like separated fragments of a single mind, turn out
to have something in common. The fool has come to represent for "royal" Lear the voice of a reality that, to his
own ruin, he has sought to ignore, but that has been somewhere present, rejected but continually inserting itself, beneath his favorable estimate of himself; while Lear, in
turn, continues to be "king" for the fool, retains for him
even in his misfortune some part of that compelling "authority"[12] that humanity in its desire for certainty insistently craves and that draws from him a loyalty which his
disenchanted realism can hardly justify. As the fool has
already put it, explicitly rejecting the "truth" of his own
reason and of the self-interest that it seems to justify:

> The knave turns fool that runs away;
> The fool no knave, perdy.[13]

And both, in their divided unity, are bound together by
common exposure to an external force that would seem to
pity neither "wise man nor fool" (2. 10–13).
    The fool's instinctive and, as it were, unwilling concern
for his master does not prevent him from responding to
Lear's impassioned conjuring of the elements with a recall
to reality. By so doing he cuts the ground from under the
old king's attempts to cast himself as the central actor in a
drama of cosmic proportions. In response to Lear's grandiloquent rhetoric, he stresses in bare prose the reality of
their common situation and implies the futility, which

Lear would no doubt prefer not to recognize, of attempting to read nature in the light of his own concerns. "Court holy-water" (2. 10)—flattery of the kind accepted and indeed invited by Lear from his daughters—is, he says, more conducive to material comfort or even to survival than exposure to the elements: Lear has lost through his folly the "dry house" that gave him protection against the action of an inclement world, and whether he will learn wisdom from the sincerity of "rain water out o' door" (2. 11) remains to be seen. When he advises his master to follow the dictates of worldly prudence by seeking his daughters' blessing (which they have shown themselves indisposed to grant him and which implies a reversal of the normal pattern, in which the act of blessing proceeds from the father to his children), the fool is at once reminding Lear of the "natural" understanding of paternity, which his own folly has reversed, and looking forward to the later scenes in which the full significance of that blessing is restored by Lear's reconciliation to Cordelia.[14] It is interesting to note, in this last connection, that when the time comes for Cordelia to return to the action, the gentleman who describes the royal quality of her grief will speak of her as shaking "the holy water from her heavenly eyes."[15] The verbal texture of the play, as closely woven as any in Shakespeare, allows us to find meaning in the echo.

The fool's contribution at this point, moreover, begins to go notably beyond mere realism or unprejudiced commonsense, though it certainly includes these necessary tools for survival in a harsh and indifferent world. As he begins to touch more closely upon the emotional aspects of the situation that has brought his master to his present state of collapsing identity, he enters directly into what we may call the subconscious ground of the play. The contrast between the "wise man" and the "fool," between the man who "has a house to put's head in" (like a snail whose shell protects it from the inclemency of the elements) and a "good headpiece" (2. 25–26) and he who has come to lack both, evidently touches closely upon Lear's situation. It is now seen in terms of a deeper conflict between controlling reason and a passionate drive toward self-assertion, the roots of which are, as always, ultimately sexual.

The importunity of "blood," sexual appetite, has indeed played a large part in bringing the tragic situation into being. It led to the birth of Edmund, whose "unpre-judiced" reading of "nature," the result of his own concep-tion outside the "bond," inspired him to turn against his father and his brother. Channeled into less direct forms of self-assertion, it drove Lear, in his unawareness of his true nature, to demand flattery—"court holy-water"—from his daughters and so to expose himself to be repudiated by them in the name of an unbridled craving for power that itself has implications in terms of "appetite." In general, it has led to a reversal of the state of nature, in its distinc-tively human form, by replacing the "heart" of due affec-tion by the "toe" of an undue craving for empty forms of flattery. The fool's perception of the situation, as reflected in his riddling snatches of song, is complex, even to the point of deliberate ambiguity. From the early stages of Lear's decline, the fool's reason has told him that the rela-tionship between "head" and "heart" is understood by the world in terms of a contrast between thrift, an economic foresight that is essentially self-regarding, and thriftless improvidence. The poor man who allows himself to follow the promptings of "natural" instinct, symbolized in the "codpiece"—a euphemism for the male sexual organ, and therefore for the drive to domination that is associated with it—before he has made due provision against an evil day, is likely to find his whole being, "head" and "heart" alike, involved in a catastrophe that his rational faculties had no part in willing:

> The codpiece that will house
> Before the head has any,
> The head and he shall louse:
> So beggars marry many.

> (2. 27–30)

The saying extends to the social sphere that preoccupation with a "dry house," as a protection against the inclement elements, which the fool has already urged upon his master. It reflects an ethic to which an acquisitive society gives tacit assent; and, in the eyes of such a society, it justifies the exclusion of compassion for those who are held—conveniently from the point of view of those who are concerned to justify their selfish actions—to have brought their misfortunes on themselves by their improvidence.

This affirmation of a prudence thriftily and parsimoniously exercised does not, however, represent the full range of the fool's thought. A careful reading of this, one of the most many-sided of all his comments, will show that he is not prepared to accept his own statement as all the truth. We have already seen him rejecting the dictates of his own reason, which prompts him to abandon the declining fortunes of his lord, in the interest of preserving the "bond" of loyalty that unites him, even beyond the limits of his "realistic" understanding, to Lear in the hour of misfortune. Part at least of his nature recognizes the existence and reality of Cordelia's "bond," which cannot be verbally exalted or rhetorically affirmed because it lies as a norm, a basic and unargued assumption that supports any distinctively human life that is worth living. The recognition leads him, dimly and in defiance of the dictates of his own "reason," to reject thrift, the prudent refusal to "give," as an ultimate virtue; and so, in the second part of his rhyme, he almost imperceptibly shifts his ground, substituting for the contrast between calculating "head" and impulsive "codpiece" another, not less fundamental to human nature, between "heart" and "toe," between the proper recognition of natural feeling and its unworthy caricature in unchecked indulgence:

> The man that makes his toe
>   What he his heart should make
> Shall of a corn cry woe,
>   And turn his sleep to wake.

(2. 31–34)

Beneath this play of shifting opposites the fool's riddling catch is leading to a consideration of what is perceived in the play as a central—perhaps *the* central—human paradox. The "toe"—a further euphemism for the penis—continues to stand at the opposite extreme from the reasoning, self-sufficient "head." Between the opposed extremes of "head" and "toe" there lies, or *should* lie, the "heart" to serve, in distinctively human terms, as a mediator between what becomes, in its absence, the clash between the pitiless rationality of the one and the animal incontinence of the other. It is the "heart," however, that seems to be entirely absent from the ferocious world to which both Lear and the fool find themselves subjected: a world in which the fool sees men and women reducing the claims of the "heart"—those of compassion, natural feeling—to the level of an unworthy "toe" and the trivial inconvenience of a "corn."[16] "Head," "heart," and "codpiece" (or "toe") represent, in fact, an endlessly shifting triangle of relationships that replaces the more direct one between control and indiscipline, thrift and improvidence as a possible reflection of the human situation. It is very largely with the various relationships contained in this triangle that the tragedy of *King Lear* is concerned.

The evident contradictions in the behavior, personal and social, of men are only to be understood, if indeed we are willing to suppose that the innate human craving for "understanding" can be satisfied, in the light of a distinction more penetrating, more indicative of the central tragic dilemma, than any so far indicated. Possession and poverty, self-control and indulgence are, after all, relative categories, capable of interpretation by each individual in the light of his own situation and fortunes, and therefore, in the last resort, not in themselves revealing. What is needed is a reading of human nature that will carry us beyond the fool's vision, including what in it is "true" to experience, but without being bounded by its limitations. This is connected, in the long run, with the return of Cordelia, in whom the claims of the "heart" are supported by a full understanding of the nature and necessity of the "bond." The fool's "reason" does not extend to this affirmation, which belongs to a later stage in the development of the tragedy; but in the meantime his words, reaching out beyond his normal disillusioned realism, occasionally point to the existence in him of a first, dim, broken indication of the truth that exceeds his reasoned understanding.

One such indication occurs precisely at this point when he greets the entry of Kent, and with it an extension of the developing dramatic pattern, with the words: "Here's grace and a codpiece; that's a wise man and a fool" (2. 40–41). The contrast between wisdom and folly which the fool has already considered in relation to the conflict between reason and passion, or between saving and spending, now merges into a deeper antithesis, which in turn illuminates the others, between "grace," expressive of the state of harmony in accordance with a "natural" sanction, and the continually rebellious "codpiece." The word "grace," which will become increasingly significant in Shakespeare's late work,[17] here assumes—perhaps for the first time—something of its full range of meanings. It is necessary to stress that these are not limited to any single sense, religious or secular. Inclusive of, though not necessarily endorsing, the full range of traditional associations in terms of a supernaturally sanctioned gift of spiritual life, it also builds upon its sense of the truly courtly, the humanly enhancing virtue summed up in the idea of "graciousness," to indicate a vision of life lived on a level of human fulfillment, personally fruitful and socially integrated. In the world of *King Lear,* this harmony—or the possibility of its as yet unfulfilled attainment—has been broken up by the operation of the "codpiece," uncontrolled instinct operating through the drive for power to destroy the balanced order of nature and lead to the opposed extremes of inhuman acquisitiveness and improvident poverty. "Grace" stands for the sum of human qualities that Lear and his world have so far conspicuously ignored. Whether he and it will in due course arrive at some measure of achievement of them stands at this point in a state of dramatic suspense.

At this stage, then, and before the end of the scene, Kent enters to make his contribution in the light of the fool's greeting. His renewed evocation of the dreadful reality of the storm serves, of course, the immediate dramatic purpose of taking some of the burden of its necessary recreation in poetry from Lear; but, in the act of doing this, it also does more. Expressed in terms that recall in their dramatic function the storm described by Lennox that coincided with Duncan's murder in *Macbeth*,[18] it leads into an indication of intolerable pressures directed against the false, shallow homogeneity of man's appearance or "nature":

> Man's nature cannot carry
> Th' affliction nor the fear.
>
> (2. 48–49)

It is not Kent, however, but Lear who takes the step of relating this "fear," this "affliction," to his own need to find compensation for the woes that have fallen upon him by invoking a conception of supernatural judgment. The "dreadful pudder" (2. 50) of the storm is, for him, the work of the "great gods," and its purpose is—or so he proposes—to allow them" to find out their enemies" in the shape of sin and sinners:

> Tremble, thou wretch,
> That hast within thee undivulged crimes
> Unwhipped of justice. Hide thee, thou bloody hand,
> Thou perjured, and thou simular of virtue
> That art incestuous. Caitiff, to pieces shake,
> That under covert and convenient seeming
> Has practiced on man's life. Close pent-up guilts,
> Rive your concealing continents and cry
> These dreadful summoners grace.
>
> (2. 51–59)

The fear felt by a helpless humanity in the presence of the unleashed elements is seen—by Lear—as proceeding from a general consciousness of hidden guilt. By a kind of celestial whipping (justice and the whip are repeatedly connected in the course of the play, not necessarily to consoling ends[19]), the storm is summoned by the outraged Lear to bring to the surface the "undivulged crimes" that are normally concealed under the decent "seeming" of man's behavior in society. The emphasis rests upon deceptive appearances and hidden corruption, upon the "*simular* of virtue": upon "*covert* and convenient *seeming*," upon "concealing continents" and "*close pent-up* guilts." The storm, it seems, has come to prise out, to "rive open" the "concealing continents" of man's deceiving sophistication, to act—in Lear's mind—as a "summoner" to justice, before which the sins so disclosed may be compelled to cry "grace"—"grace" this time in the sense of "pardon" for admitted wrong-doing—as a first step in the restoration of spiritual health.

I have insisted, with good reason, that these are *Lear's* words. They represent *his* particular reaction at a moment of special stress in his progress. Neither here nor elsewhere should one be tempted to read into words spoken by a character within a Shakespearean play the statement of a "philosophy" that might confer "meaning" upon or otherwise "justify" the events enacted. Whether Lear, in making these grandiloquent statements and in requiring collaboration from whatever "justice" may be presumed to govern the universe, sees as much or as clearly as he seems to claim remains, at best, an open question. His referring of the elemental commotion around him as the action of the "great gods" (2. 49)—who or whatever they may be—remains a projection of what he desires or *needs* to "see," and there is nothing in his words to encourage us to find in it more than the expression of an old man's outrage and bewilderment breaking violently through the restraints that he has been accustomed to impose upon his passionately self-centered nature. Once more his reactions are an extreme example of a state common to all men. The gods we invoke are, in the first instance and whatever else they may be, the projection of our own perceived needs, of the compelling human desire to see the course of our lives as justified, made plain, in relation to some larger purpose. Whether this aspiration is a pathetic fallacy or whether our imaginative projections reflect some corresponding "reality" remains, at most, an open question, the expression of an unrealized possibility. It is also a question that a dramatist, by the very nature of his endeavor as a creator of theatrical illusion, is likely to find himself particularly engaged to answer.

There is meaning, in this connection, in the fact that at the end of Lear's outburst, denunciation collapses into a broken plea for sympathy, as the plain "truth" of his condition returns to occupy the forefront of his mind:

> I am a man
> More sinned against than sinning.
>
> (2. 59–60)

True as the statement is, we may feel that it represents a retreat, a pathetic falling-away from the preceding invocation of an avenging divine action. It is one thing to assert a belief in the existence of a universal justice, another to be led by the sense of one's own pitiful predicament to plead with that justice to collaborate in rendering it tolerable to our sense of outrage. Once more, however, this is not all the truth. Lear's utterances thus far have been marked by an element of self-projection that stands between him and the complete reality of his situation. He must go further and descend lower—from "sanity" to "madness"—before he can begin to "understand." He needs, in other words, to divest himself or to be stripped of these judgmental pretensions and to return to a truer sense of his basic, unadorned humanity. This need, connected with the sense, which is beginning to impose itself upon him, of his failing grip on "reason"—"My wits begin to turn" (2. 67)—has to be seen in relation to the original causes of his downfall. By his initial abdication Lear surrendered his sense of his identity, which was bound up with his conception of himself as king and projected in the trappings of his office. To be Lear and to be king have been, for Lear, two ways of saying the same thing: that is why, having willfully renounced the reality of "kingship," he was so concerned to maintain his grasp upon the external signs of "authority." The consequences of an unreal decision have involved Lear in a progressive descent into unreality: in this sense, there was more meaning than he could have begun to realize in the warning he directed at Cordelia but which applied in truth, bleakly and desolately, to himself: "Nothing will come of nothing."[20] "Nothingness," indeed, has now become, through the successive stages of a process of reduction, the description of his own condition. The process of self-negation, once embarked upon, has to be painfully followed to its final consequences before any possible restoration, in the form of a restored and more adequate selfhood, can begin to take shape. Whether any such reversal is finally possible or whether we can see in Lear's gropings towards it anything more than a projection of our need to deceive ourselves in order to render the reality of our situation tolerable is a question that remains inescapably open. Indeed, the dramatist is careful to leave it so, requiring each spectator to arrive at his own answer, and this—if then—only at the end of the action.

For the moment we are required to witness the demolition of the flattering self-image upon which Lear has so far rested his life. In pursuit of this necessary process of "stripping" he will have to lose such precarious control as he retains over his wits in order to become—in the fool's terminology—himself a "fool," before he can emerge, in whatever shape, on the far side of his ordeal. Meanwhile, as has often been noted, his sufferings have made him more aware than ever before of the plight of others and he is concerned that his companions in distress should find shelter. Kent's description of the hovel before them stresses its harsh, unaccommodating reality, the fitting response to Lear's own situation: "this hard house"; "more harder than the stones whereof 'tis raised" (2. 63–64). We are being brought, with Lear, to contemplate life on the margin of subsistence and to consider the unrelentingly stony face[21] that it presents to the innate and pathetic desire of men to find refuge in extremity from the pressure of a cold and indifferent reality.

It remains true that the theme of poverty is forcing its way to the fore in Lear's mind, as it slips into incoherence, to become an integral part of his growing experience. Seeing before him the fool, whom he calls for the first time in a gesture that implies community and concern "My boy" (2. 68), he is led to make the fateful connection established in the simple, direct recognition "I am cold myself" (2. 69). The possibility of a common destiny is established in a way that looks beyond the self-centered railings and presumptuous identification with the action of the gods that marked his first reaction to the storm. The effect is to raise, however tentatively and uncertainly, the possibility of a learning process arising from the extremity of his situation. "Necessity," in spite of and beyond the cruelty with which it imposes itself, is perceived by Lear, who scarcely knows what he is saying, to possess the mysterious "art" of making "vile things precious" (2. 70–1). His speech, having been pushed into this unaccustomed direction, concludes with a direct affirmation that implies solidarity in affliction:

> Poor fool and knave, I have one part in my heart
> That's sorry yet for thee.
>
> (2. 72–73)

The fool, in his responding catch, salutes this first stirring of the heart in Lear as the birth of "a little tiny wit" (2. 74), a glimpse of understanding to set against his master's related recognition of failing self-control.

Once more we need to know exactly where and how far

we are being taken. The relation between "madness" and "understanding" or the willingness to see in "madness" the price to be paid for "understanding" is indeed a theme that will be increasingly explored in the coming action; but the fact remains that there is nothing in the fool's brief song to encourage any belief that Lear's new perceptions can in any way alter the "hard" reality that faces them both. The "rain raineth every day" (2. 77) at the heart of the *Lear* world, as it had already done at the end of *Twelfth Night*,[22] when the audience was required by Feste the Clown to relinquish the comic illusion and prepare itself for a return to the real world beyond the play and outside the theater. Inevitably and necessarily, "The words of Mercury are harsh after the songs of Apollo";[23] the rain continues to rain and the man exposed to its action must learn to "make content with his fortunes fit" (2. 76), accepting what he cannot change and renouncing the temptation to believe that the way of a harsh world can readily be accommodated to the requirements of his imagination. The fool's next utterance, "This is a brave night to cool a courtesan" (2. 79) leads, as the scene ends, into a doggerel (2. 81–94) that subjects the present state of "the realm of Albion" to riddling inversion in which the normal perception of time (2. 95) is included.[24] The effect is to take up Lear's previous emphasis on the "cold" and to bring us back once more, through the mention of the "courtesan" to the theme of passion and to the chastening influence upon it of the action of the elements.

After a short scene (act 3, scene 3) designed to remind us of the continued existence of a "real" world beyond the storm and to present a Gloucester who is beginning to be moved by pity for the plight of his king, Lear's next appearance (act 3, scene 4) takes us, at the very center of the play, to the heart of his human predicament. As the scene opens, Kent emphasizes, more urgently than before, the inability of man's "natural" defenses to endure the action of the elements. Lear in his response at once stresses his sense of a fundamental unity encompassing the external and the internal storm and shows further signs of a break-ing coherence:

> The tempest in my mind
> Doth from my senses take all feeling else
> Save what beats there.
>
> (3. 4. 12–14)

The inner tempest, in the very act of becoming fused with the exterior commotion, takes precedence over it, asserts its total dominion over the old man's mind. By so doing, it confirms and advances his growing "madness" and the connection between this and his increasing withdrawal from the world around him; for such withdrawal, carried to the extreme, is itself a measure of insanity. Lear, in fact, is now engaged in projecting his personal situation on a world that he perceives only as a reflection of it. "Filial ingratitude" he conceives in terms of a bestial struggle between the different parts of a single body:

> Is it not as this mouth should tear this hand
> For lifting food to 't?
>
> (4. 15–16)

From now on the imagery of beasts in conflict, of the ten-der human organism torn remorselessly by fang or claw or separated by the pitiless action of the rack will play an increasing part in the play. All this, in effect, is the accen-tuation of a process initiated by Lear's words in the pre-ceding scene. The "concealing continents" of man's na-ture, already invoked by him,[25] are being violently prised open by a process that is at once revealing and insane; and the state of disruption so revealed to Lear's failing mind represents itself to him as no more than a physical pro-jection of the "close pent-up guilts" that they normally cover. Under the strain that these thoughts impose upon him, Lear's own mental state continues to break down into an incoherence that removes from him the last traces of royal dignity. Threats of undetermined future actions that might have befitted a king but that he is now in no position to undertake ("I will punish home": 4. 16) alternate with assertions of his readiness to "endure" (4. 17). These in turn lead to increasingly broken expressions of pathetic self-commiseration ("In such a night as this! . . . Your old kind father": 4. 18–20); and beneath these fragments of a once-unified intelligence, present as an approaching threat against which he vainly struggles, lies the intolerable shadow of coming madness: "O, that way madness lies . . . No more of that" (4. 21–22).

Once more, however, we need to recognize that disintegration is only one aspect of Lear's development at this stage. Not all that is coming to the surface under the pressure of the elements is negative. The distinctive human solicitude that is in Kent a natural extension of loyalty communicates itself to his king, to reinforce and render more explicit the sympathy already noted in the previous scene. The two aspects—that of shattered coherence and that of glimmering perception—vie with one another in his thoughts, and we are required to hold a precarious balance in their regard, neither rejecting nor one-sidedly emphasizing their relevance to the whole. After he has invited the fool—whom he addresses for the second time as "boy"[26] and refers to as "houseless poverty" (4. 26)—to precede him in taking shelter, Lear declares his intention to remain in the open, exposed to the action of the elements, and adds: "I'll pray, and then I'll sleep" (4. 27). Whether we are to believe that his words reflect real concern for the fool as a fellow human being or whether his determination to remain outside the hovel points simply to a state of self-isolation that amounts to madness and that makes any sustaining human gesture finally meaningless remains—as always—impenetrably obscure.

None the less, the resolution to pray and the reference coupled with it to sleep represent new developments in the old king's hitherto self-centered attitudes. More particularly, the mention of "sleep," with its healing connections,

both physical and moral,[27] looks forward for the first time
to the reunion with Cordelia, which will follow the storm
and be accompanied by insistent references to the restoring virtues of repose.[28] Moreover, the content of Lear's
"prayer" is new, confirms the extension of his understanding—even at the price of sanity—to new areas of life.
These concern the speaker as king rather than as father,
his responsibilities to society rather than his position as
head of a family. The starting-point of the "prayer" is the
new concern with "houseless poverty," already inspired in
Lear by the contemplation of his fool and now extended to
new areas of compassion. As Lear considers, perhaps for
the first time in his long and selfish life, the state of those
whose heads are "houseless" and whose "sides" are "un-
fed" (4. 29), he is brought to declare his own previous lack
of understanding—

> O, I have ta'en
> Too little care of this!—
>
> (4. 32–33)

and, as a reaction against his past indifference, to introduce more specifically than ever before the concern for
"justice" that befits a king. The elemental equity invoked
in the previous scene gives way to a more explicit social
criterion. The visibly breaking Lear now proposes to see in
the contemplation of misery a "physic" in redress of the
"pomp" that he has regarded as a simple extension of his
"royal" status, the world of appearances that has so far
supported his sense of identity and to which he has been
clinging since he so shortsightedly renounced the reality in
his initial gesture of theatrical divestment. A new
awareness born of rejection has led Lear to a desire to
redress the balance upset by what he now perceives as the
superfluous wellbeing ("the superflux": 4. 35) of the
privileged, and so—with tremendous, perhaps even presumptuous daring—"to show the heavens more just" (4.
36). Whether men and women have any reason to postu-

late in the heavens an inclination to respond to their innate craving for justice remains, here and throughout the play, unclear.

At this point, and as if in response to Lear's expanding range of awareness, the scope of the action is still further enlarged by the entry of the fugitive Edgar, in whose pitiful disguise the state of "houseless poverty" becomes a visible reality. The connection with Lear's preoccupation with nakedness is apparent. He is being brought to "see" himself in Edgar, just as in the previous scene he had begun to "see" certain aspects of his own predicament in the fool. In the fortunes of "poor Tom," as related by Edgar, the personal and social issues that are in the process of coming to the surface of his breaking mind are presented as related symptoms of a single disorder. The connection eventually penetrates Lear's consciousness and leads to the next stage in his tragic progress.

Seen from this point of view, Edgar's description of "poor Tom's" descent into poverty is much more than the raving utterance of a supposedly mad creature. When he projects himself as a "servingman, proud in heart and mind" (4. 81), he focuses attention upon a contradiction that is at once personal, a consequence of the ambiguous part, alternately dominating and enslaving, played by the passions in human behavior, and social, a reflection of the mixture of servility and ferocious pride produced by the pursuit of worldly advancement. A "servingman" may be either, in the idiom of the day, a courtier who has obtained advancement and the power that goes with it by rendering obsequious service to his lord, or the slave, in a less public sphere, of his mistress, to whose favor, again, he may owe his social position and so, ultimately, his pride; but the fact that he is "proud in heart" may, in turn, indicate not only the satisfaction he feels in the position he has attained but the passionate intensity that has led him, again in Edgar's words, to serve "the lust of my mistress' heart" by doing "the act of darkness with her" (4. 82–83).

"Poor Tom's" "mad" evocations of a disordered and

predatory world need to be seen against the intimations of
a "natural" human order that have immediately preceded
them:

> Take heed o' th' foul fiend; obey thy parents; keep thy
> words' justice; swear not; commit not with man's sworn
> spouse; set not thy sweet heart on proud array. (4. 76–
> 79)

These are the "natural" values, recognizing and respecting
the existence of fundamental "bonds," which the personages of the *Lear* world from the king downward have rejected or ignored. Their rejection has led to the chaos that
Lear, having glimpsed it obscurely in himself, now sees
projected upon the grotesque figure before him. The ambivalent relationship, social and personal, between pride
and servitude in a distorted world is illustrated by the essentially commonplace, "exemplary" story of the fine courtier's downward progress to "Bedlam," the madhouse; for
private lust and public ambition are connected links in the
chain of egoistic determinations by which the "servingman" has been led to break the "bonds" of "nature" by
following his unrestrained appetites. Alternately arrogant
and servile, free from all traditional restraints and yet the
slave to his passions, "poor Tom's" history is the reflection
of a society that has given free rein to its dark and finally
sex-inspired urge for domination to the extent of setting
its "toe" in the place where its "heart" should be and thus
producing a state of affairs psychologically mirrored in
"madness." Led by his baser instincts and "pride of heart"
(4. 54) to follow "through ford and whirlpool," "bog and
quagmire" (4. 52), the delusions reflected in his night-
mares: driven "to course his own shadow for a traitor" (4.
56), consumed by fear of the envy and intrigues of those
whom he has displaced and those who covet his position:
condemned to "ride on a bay trotting horse" like any successful man of the world, but over bottomless gulfs peril-
ously spanned by "four-inched bridges" (4. 55), he has

lived in a state of frantic unreality that fittingly mirrors the precarious state of Lear's wits and is finally reduced, after exposure to the prevailing "cold" to the awakened condition of "unaccommodated man."

It is as such that Lear, in his newborn desire to penetrate to the bedrock "truth" of human nature, proposes to see him. For the old king, as he gropes toward his first glimpses of understanding and as the storm continues to rage around his shattered person, the appearance of "poor Tom" presents itself as a revelation of what he perceives to be the basic, unadorned human condition:

> Why, thou wert better in a grave than to answer with thy uncovered body this extremity of the skies. Is man no more than this? Consider him well. Thou ow'st the worm no silk, the beast no hide, the sheep no wool, the cat no perfume. Ha! here's three on's are sophisticated. Thou art the thing itself; unaccommodated man is no more but such a poor, bare, forked animal as thou art. (4. 96–102)

Once more we are confronted with a series of commonplaces, familiar in the mouths of generations of preachers and the writing of endless moralists. Shakespeare is inventing nothing, expressing no novel view of the wretchedness of the human condition. He is merely exploring what is already known, extracting its significance for his theme. With his nakedness confronted by that of Edgar and both subjected to the action of the elements, Lear's awakening concern for justice shows signs of shading into something deeper, more universal than itself. That "poor Tom," who—in Edgar's fictitious presentation—had formerly "three suits to his back, six shirts to his body, horse to ride and weapon to wear" (4. 127–29), but who finds himself "whipped from tithing to tithing," "stock-punished and imprisoned" (4. 125–27), is the embodiment of a cruel and unstable social order is clear enough; but it is not the whole or even the most important part of the

picture. *King Lear* is a great tragedy because it looks beyond these issues—important, even central as they are—in
the process of including them in its wider range of vision
and because it is a play about human nature before being a
play about the abuses of government or social injustice. It
is this nature that is being revealed at this turning-point in
the action, exposed to the prevailing cold and stripped for
our consideration.

The process of stripping, indeed, to which both Lear
and "poor Tom" are being painfully subjected, has already
been prepared for in Lear's earlier utterances. More particularly, in a speech that touches upon themes central to
the play, he has had occasion to consider the problem
posed by the craving for "superfluity" that looms so large
in human conduct. His plea to Regan and Goneril, when
faced with their reasoned, mathematical whittling down of
his request to be allowed to retain his royal retinue of one
hundred knights, contained these words:

> O, reason not the need! Our basest beggars
> Are in the poorest thing superfluous.
> Allow not nature more than nature needs,
> Man's life is cheap as beast's. Thou art a lady;
> If only to go warm were gorgeous,
> Why, nature needs not what thou gorgeous wear'st,
> Which scarcely keeps thee warm.[29]

From the point of view of "reason," as the world conceives
it, the sisters' position is unquestionably valid. Lear, as an
old man who has chosen to relinquish the obligations of
kingship, *can* be fittingly provided for by the servants
under their authority. Their "houses" *are,* no doubt, "too
small" to accommodate his unruly retinue of a hundred
followers;[30] and the presence of so many, which served a
purpose in the days of Lear's effective exercise of rule but
which serves none now that he has divested himself of the
reality, as distinct from the appearance of royalty, *is* bound
to lead to riot and drunken disorder on the part of those
who have no necessary duties to perform:

How in one house
Should many people, under two commands,
Hold amity? 'Tis hard, almost impossible.[31]

"Hard," "almost impossible," indeed, in terms of bare fact;
but Lear's mind, in its moment of bewildered disorienta-
tion, is occupied with "realities" of another order: realities
that Cordelia will recognize and place at the heart of any
livable human order but that his elder daughters find
neither comprehensible nor convenient to the ends they
have in view. The logical progression of their utilitarian,
practical argument leads to an essentially reductive conclusion: from "fifty" to "five-and-twenty," from there to "ten,
or five," and—finally—to the stripping away of any remaining element of illusion in the question "What need
one?"[32]

The unspoken but required answer to that question is,
of course, "None," and it brings us back to that misguided
choice of "nothing"[33] that has determined Lear's descend-
ing course from the outset. Lear, however, has been
driven by the very extent of his self-inflicted misfortunes
to concern himself with "truths" of quite another kind.
The question of what it is that men and women truly need
forces itself upon his attention and produces his anguished response. The state of "sophistication," through
and beyond which he now desires to penetrate, is seen to
involve more than the pride of external position or the
lavish consumption that goes with it. Both these things
answer, beyond the obvious realities of greed and domination that constitute their immediate attraction, to a deeper,
more universal "need"—the need that, however disguised
or degenerate the manifestations which accompany it,
finally distinguishes *human* nature from nature in its raw
state.

Once again we return to Lear's perverse or unrealistic
action that set the tragedy in motion. When, by his own
choice, he ceased to exercise the reality of kingship while
proposing, unrealistically and impossibly, to cling to the

trappings—the crown, the "gorgeous" robes of office, the impressive retinue—that seemed to confirm him in what had come to be his sense of himself, Lear embarked upon the course that led him, through a process of "stripping," of successive eliminations, to the condition that now confronts him, mirror-like, in the visible shape of a naked "madman." The plight he has brought upon himself has led him to glimpses of a new understanding of what it truly means to be human. He is beginning to understand that to be human is, among other things, to aspire to the "superfluous," that the desire for something beyond the strictly necessary may be what distinguishes a man from the condition of the "beast," whose only concern, in the words of Hamlet's last soliloquy, is with the satisfaction of the immediate need to "sleep and feed."[34] The qualities of which I have spoken—pride of position, abuse of power, greed for possessions—have become in Lear's consideration the perverse manifestations of attributes that, considered in a different context, are normal to human nature. They belong to the conventional superstructure on which men depend to affirm their selfhood and to hide even—perhaps especially—from themselves the naked and unacceptable truth of their undisguised natures. They represent a reality as inescapable from the human nature we perceive and admire in society as the garments that men and women owe to the brute creation and that they use to protect their otherwise pitifully "uncovered" bodies from the extremity of the skies.

It is man's unique dilemma, as we are now being brought to see it, that his distinctive humanizing need is also his intractable problem. Fine clothes and an unchecked desire for the status that they symbolize are connected attributes of Lear's "unnatural" daughters that were not, in the past, foreign to his own concerns. In defending the "superfluous" claims even of the "basest beggar" against Regan's reductive conception of "need," he refers bitterly to the "gorgeous" apparel that contrasts so sharply with their advocacy of austerity for others. To this state of false pretension the storm has come as a harsh recall to reality. It has brought those exposed to it back to the familiar truth, ceaselessly advanced by the moralists and preachers but always forgotten, always in need of restatement, that "unaccommodated man," stripped of the conventional attributes that alternately support his humanity and lead to its perversion, is no more than "such a bare forked animal" as the disguised Edgar. This is the reality with which Lear, in his new state of crazed understanding, is in process of coming to terms. The pitiable human object of his present contemplation has become, by his own confession, at once a "serving-man," a courtly aspirant "proud in heart and mind," and a miserable slave to his own lust and ambition: one who has had occasion to learn from the bitter experience of his downward progress that it is a "poor heart" (4. 91) that betrays itself to the passing satisfactions of the flesh, only to find itself enveloped at the last in the "cold" to which this order of aspiration returns.

Lear, meanwhile, remains too tied to the contemplation of his own predicament to respond to the full implications of Edgar's transformation into "Tom o' Bedlam." For him, it is axiomatic that the pitiful creature before him can only have been deprived of his saving human attributes by the agency of "unkind"—unnatural—daughters. After visiting his own curse upon them (4. 65–66), he brushes aside Kent's patient recall to reality—"He hath no daughters, sir" (4. 67)—and goes on to project his own pain and resentment at having been reduced to the position of a "discarded father" in the strange reversal of a familiar figure:

> 'Twas this flesh begot
> Those pelican daughters.
>
> (4. 72–73)

The emphasis on the flesh and on the intimate process of begetting reinforces the instinctual and *feeling* sources of Lear's outrage: an effect that is carried further by his reference to his "pelican" daughters. The pelican, according to an ancient tradition familiar in Shakespeare's age and turned to iconographical use in much religious art, gives of its own blood to nourish its offspring. The bird becomes in this way a figure for the saving action of Christ, who also gave his "blood" in a sacrifice on behalf of mankind. It is typical of Lear, however, that in having recourse to this idea to give expression to his own sense of outrage, he subjects it to a strange inversion: for it is not the wounded father who is associated with the pelican's generous and unappreciated sacrifice, but the "unnatural" daughters who have turned against their loving parent to tear his flesh and to nourish themselves cannibalistically, as it were, in his blood. In Lear's use of it the image emerges as both painful and grotesque in ways that are close to the heart of the experience which the play offers: nor is his attempt to express (albeit in this strangely inverted form) the pathos associated with the original reference allowed to pass unchallenged. "Poor Tom's" echoing of Lear's words in a crazed snatch of nursery doggerel—"Pillicock sat on Pillicock Hill" (4. 74)[35]—has the effect of reducing his outburst and the agonizing question implied in it to the status of a nonsense rhyme, devoid of dignity or meaning of any kind. Having achieved this demolishing effect, he lapses into an incoherent conclusion—"Alow, alow, loo, loo!" (4. 74)—that further involves the whole exchange in the prevailing descent into chaos and unreason.

Confronted with what he perceives, albeit dimly and through the curtain of approaching "madness" as a mirror of his own condition, Lear is ready to move into the heart, the central turning-point of his own predicament. To bring this about a new meeting in the storm is required: a meeting for which "poor Tom's" crazed inversions of normal "sanity" have prepared, and which now brings together the two fathers whose initial misconceptions have set the tragedy in motion. Once again the fool, whose role has become less prominent as the number of characters and situations projected upon Lear's central presence has multiplied, intervenes with one of his most penetrating comments. The occasion is in part Lear's move towards divesting himself of the remaining "lendings" that differentiate him from the final reality embodied in the nakedness of "poor Tom" and in part the entry of Gloucester, newly moved to compassion and a sense of the duty that loyalty—the bond that unites king and subject in any tolerable polity—imposes. Once again his words point in more than one direction. The comment on Lear's gesture of disrobing—"Prithee, nuncle, be contented; 'tis a naughty night to swim in" (4. 104–5)—amounts to a recall to reality, reminding us that what remains of Lear's imperious and dominating self-projection in the opening scene has been reduced to the condition of a broken old man, who can be addressed with a mixture of sarcasm and concern as "nuncle," and whose palpable descent into madness and incoherence qualifies any temptation we may feel to ascribe deep moral significance to words and actions that hover on the edge of absurdity. As always in *King Lear,* the tragic and the comic, the anguished movement toward understanding and the rejection of any easy human claim to have achieved it, stand in the closest relationship.

In what remains of his speech, the fool turns his attention to the approaching Gloucester, whose past complacencies in the matter of Edmund's begetting are—like Lear's own follies—in the process of returning to him upon the whirlwind. The effect of the fool's greeting is to unite the two tragedies in a common perspective. Taking up the contrast, already developed by Edgar, between the brief fire of lust and the "cold" that surrounds it (4. 86–94), he is moved to see in the old courtier's entry with a torch an image for the flame of life flaring up, briefly and ineffectively, in the surrounding desolation:

Now a little fire in a wide field were like an old lecher's heart—a small spark, all the rest on's body cold. (4. 105–6)

The "old lecher" already points to Gloucester himself and

the "little fire" to the smoldering remains of the sexual energy that once bore fruit in his "unnatural" child. The "little fire" corresponds further and beyond this to the redeeming spark of life that is impelling him, in his old age, to risk his life and well-being by extending compassionate support to his broken king: a gesture that sheds, however briefly and ineffectively, a little light to illuminate the surrounding darkness.

Throughout these exchanges the fool's comments have answered to our awareness of standing at the frontiers of "sane" human affirmation, beyond which—it would seem—there is nowhere to go: "This cold night will turn us all to fools and madmen" (4. 75). As sympathetic spectators of the action being dreadfully unfolded before us, we share in, feel ourselves crushed by, the necessary desolation of Lear's situation, but we are also aware, however dimly and uncertainly, that it is no longer unique or entirely unsupported. It is now balanced by that of Gloucester; and though the sharing of grief can afford no measure of physical relief to those who suffer from it, it brings an increase in compassion upon which a humanly positive reaction may conceivably be built. Gloucester is not yet in a position to realize that the past sin of his own flesh has turned, brutally and savagely, against himself. It is doubtful, in any case, whether he would be willing to accept the dark "morality" implied as relevant to his case; but he does "see" sufficiently to be able to relate the disorders so rampant in the world of men to a corruption, a flaw in the fleshly fabric of man's nature. That nature, like the strangely inverted "pelican" of Lear's imagining, seems to stand at the limit beyond which there is only self-annihilation:

> Our flesh and blood, my lords, is grown so vile
> That it doth hate what gets it.
>
> (4. 136–37)

When Gloucester refers to the "son now outlaw'd from my

blood" (4. 158), he continues to lay the blame for the breaking of the family bond mistakenly upon Edgar, and not where it lies, upon Edmund and, ultimately, upon the manner of his begetting. That is his error and he will pay for his lack of "vision" with nothing less than his "eyes" and eventually with his life. In the harsh world of *Lear* such errors have consequences that may not be reversed or evaded and which need to work themselves out to and perhaps beyond the limits of what can be endured; but, in the new anguish of Gloucester's utterance, we find him for the first time ready to contemplate the reality of the "embossed carbuncle" conceived in the sinister darkness of his "corrupted blood."[36]

Against these dark imaginings, indeed, a counterbalancing development of the kind already enigmatically declared by the fool, is taking shape. Gloucester's new sense of the depths of human "unkindness" issues in a saving reaction, a return to the natural concept of "duty" (4. 139) that, in his own words, "cannot suffer" to obey commands themselves unnatural. Edgar, in turn, touched by the appearance of his father and aware, as Gloucester is not, of the circumstances that led to his tragedy, can only repeat his sense of the cold that envelops human helplessness in the face of an unnatural and menacing world: "Poor Tom's acold" (4. 138). Lear, meanwhile, absorbed in the contemplate of his own misery and only intermittently aware of the presence of those around him, is visibly losing his hold upon "reality," slipping into the dream-world of inverted fantasies that leads him to hail the naked madman before him as a "philosopher" and to inquire of him in his nakedness "the cause of thunder" (4. 145–46): the "cause," if any there be, and if indeed it makes any sort of sense to speak of "causes," of the pitiless process to which all the actors in the human tragedy, sinned against and sinning, are equally exposed.

Once again we are reminded by the very facts of the situation, and in case we should be tempted to expect some comforting revelation of "meaning," of the kind that the play consistently refuses to advance, that whatever "philosophy" we may be inclined to extract from the contemplation of so much suffering reduces itself, in the last analysis, to an elemental instinct for survival. Lear's evident loss of his wits and his increasing abstraction from reality of any kind confers upon his choice of a "philosopher" a note of absurdity that borders, beyond the evident and recognized pathos, upon the farcical. When he asks his "learned Theban" (4. 148) to declare the object of his "study," Edgar's reply—"How to prevent the fiend, and to kill vermin" (4. 150)—amounts to a recall to the reality of a situation that seems to defy any attempt to dignify it by imposing upon it any comforting illusion of significance. The elemental disorder that produces the thunder is not readily reducible to consoling human terms, and any temptation we may feel to relate it to our own situation seems likely to end in disillusionment. Any insight that these elemental catastrophes may seem to offer to our innate craving for "meaning" finds its bitter counterpart in the dissolution of sanity. In accordance with this sense, the scene ends with Kent referring to the oncoming of Lear's madness—"His wits begin t' unsettle" (4. 153)—and Gloucester's parallel recognition of the state to which his son's "outlawing" has brought him: "I am almost mad myself. . . . The grief hath crazed my wits" (4. 157–161).

After another brief return (act 3, scene 5) to the "real" world and to an Edmund whose services to the new order have been rewarded by the enjoyment of his father's title, Lear's next appearance (act 3, scene 6) brings the play's concern with the intricate balance of "sanity" and "madness" to a head. This affects him both as father and as king. It is significant that he replies to the fool's question about "whether a madman be a gentleman or a yeoman" with the words "A king, a king" (6. 11). The exchange between them turns upon the idea that personal lunacy has a counterpart, at once its background and its projection, in terms of social behavior. The "unnatural" relationship between the yeoman and his socially ambitious son, who feels no compunction in pushing his parent aside to achieve the status of a "gentleman," is one more instance of the inversion of societal roles with which the whole tragedy is concerned. The king, who has conferred authority irrationally and—in traditional terms—contrary to natural order upon his children, is in the position of the yeoman "that has a gentleman to his son": for it is "a mad yeoman that sees his son a gentleman before him" (6. 12–14). Once again, the fool's reproaches are expressed in terms of cautious self-interest. The "yeoman" who acquiesces in the reversal of the established order is procuring his own downfall, participating in the reversal of a "natural" situation that is assumed to be the foundation of ordered stability. That this reversal of social roles, by the substitution of one generation by its successor is also—as Edmund would no doubt plausibly argue—part of the order of things is no doubt true and relevant; but, in the *Lear* world at least, the consequences are pitiless and extreme. Kent in the stocks, Edgar in disguise as "poor Tom," Lear excluded from his own hearth, are all victims of the ruthless pursuit of the acquisitive instinct engaged in breaking the bonds of "nature" and custom in the satisfaction of its unlimited craving for power.

These points having been made, the scene passes to a consideration of the nature of "justice." Lear's crazed imaginings lead him to invert the conventional values of his social world by raising the poor and the outcast, victims of an inhuman conception of justice, to the position of avenging ministers. The naked Edgar, haunted by the "foul fiend" he is struggling to subdue (and which he associates grotesquely with the vermin that plague his naked body), becomes "Thou, robed man of justice" (6. 36); and the fool, the living incarnation of subjection to irresponsible power, emerges as his "yokefellow of equity" (6. 37). Together, these extreme examples of an unjust order are called upon by the "mad" king to judge those who have risen, like Goneril and Regan, to the exercise of authority and who now, stripped in Lear's imagination of the "gorgeous" clothes that conceal their subsistent animality, are revealed to the penetrating eye of "madness" in their true nature as so many "she-foxes" (6. 22). The "madman," it may be, is less the victim of his delusions than one who suffers the consequences of "seeing" too clearly, of concentrating on one object of "seeing," obsessively and exclusively, to the exclusion of everything else that offers itself to his "vision."

In assessing these matters and in defining their significance for the total experience offered by the play, we need to reject the temptation to read into Lear's intolerably one-sided clarity of "vision" any simple statement of humanly comforting insights. *King Lear,* like all Shakespeare's plays, *explores* human situations; it does not make statements *about* them. The continuing presence of the fool, with his deflating comments so consistently anti-tragic, even farcical in their prevailing tone, reminds us of this truth by recalling us from crazed and hysterical delusions to the diminished reality of things. What Lear, in his fancied "arraignment," sees as a Goneril brought to justice is nothing more than a "joint-stool" (6. 51), a vulgar and unlovely chattel; and what is set up in his mind as a formal action of "justice" implies, as Kent observes, an abandonment of the saving quality of "patience" (6. 57)—realism, acceptance of what reason tells us cannot be altered to accommodate our desire to see things as other than they are—to which a "sane" human understanding must necessarily return.

The point made in this way touches closely upon whatever perception we may achieve of the play as a whole. We are required, indeed, to be "sane," but the cost of what we choose to call "sanity" is grievous. More than any other of Shakespeare's plays, *Lear* proceeds by way of paradox, by the bringing together of contraries. Repeatedly in the course of the action, and at many of its most intense moments of emotion, a positive statement seems to be made, a consoling action undertaken, and then immediately, in the very act of its assertion, is cut down to size or deliberately reversed. To enter the *Lear* world is to see human life as precariously structured upon contradictions and endlessly exposed to reversal.

The play, indeed, abounds throughout its course in examples of the kind of reversal that it seems to raise to the status of a dramatic "method." Two examples, both from the latter part of the action, will serve to illustrate this. When Edgar, immediately after the storm and the cruel blinding of his father (which we have just witnessed, but of which he is still unaware), seeks at the beginning of the fourth act to find some measure of comfort for his plight in the thought that he has suffered the worst that can conceivably befall him, he generalizes his experience in the following terms:

> To be worst,
> The lowest and most dejected thing of fortune,
> Stands still in esperance.[37]

The attempt is being made, evidently, to assert the speaker's arrival at an ultimate position, from which nothing but a positive reaction, as yet unformed, can conceivably follow. It is not allowed to stand unqualified. It is necessary in terms of the play's conception that Edgar's statement of hope—"esperance"—for the future should immediately be followed by the entry to him of his newly blinded father led by an old man, in visible proof that the "worst" is always, in the order of the obscurely ambivalent "fortune" that governs human life in time, still to come. An even more chilling instance occurs at the very end of the play. When Albany hears from the lips of the dying Edmund that orders have been given for the hanging of Cordelia, his immediate reaction is to express the hope, which must be that of the audience following the action, that there may still be time to reverse a decision that offends our deepest instinct for "justice." Where men have proved so consistently heartless, Albany calls upon the gods to "defend" Cordelia. The reply comes at once, with appalling directness, in the form of a bare stage direction—"Enter Lear, with Cordelia in his arms"—that says more than the words can indicate, and in the old king's desolate and uncomprehending cry of blind reiteration as he bursts upon the stage: "Howl, howl, howl! O, you are men of stones!"[38]

Modern readers reacting to this scene, and to others in the play, are apt to find a certain complacency or a lack of understanding of the nature of tragedy in Johnson's well-known confession that he had been "so shocked by Cordelia's death" that he did not know whether he ever "endured to read again the last scenes of the play till he revised them for his edition."[39] If so, they may be unwise or themselves complacent. It may be that Shakespeare intended his audience to be shocked, and that if we take for granted this outrage to our instinctive craving for justice or try in one way or another to make it part of some kind of redemptive process, it is we and not Johnson who are being in some sense insensitive to the play's intention. The *method,* so to call it, followed in the play seems to support this contention. It rests very largely on the powerful and disconcerting juxtapositions we have been considering and seems designed to advance a distinctive vision of human life, a vision that concerns the nature and the limitation of our efforts to impose "order" upon or to discern "meaning" in our experience of it. The exercise of the imagination by which our lives are rendered, however precariously, tolerable prompts us to interpret events in ways that seem to bring out some measure of "meaning" in them, some sense of distinctively human significance. The process is necessary inasmuch as without it our lives would become simply unlivable; but in *Lear* at least, this consoling process is both affirmed and consistently shadowed by the countering possibility of illusion. Most of us would like to believe that suffering in some way ennobles the sufferer; but the reality is that most often it brutalizes and annihilates him. The life we bring into being by exercising the imaginative faculty is challenged by awareness of a "reality" which it seems that no creative effort can finally modify or lastingly transform. The balance that holds these two forces in necessary relationship, alternately transforming the "real" in the light of the "imaginative" and recalling the "imaginative" to the intractably "real," touches the heart of the Shakespearean intuition of life; and none of his plays more consistently mirrors it than *King Lear*.

Lear's situation at the point we have reached, then, is one in which delusion and truth, insanity and the glimmerings of "vision," stand in the closest relationship. Once more, it is not intended that our sense of what we see and hear should be limited to an inversion of the normal social categories. Beneath the reversals of justice so common among men, inspiring and obscurely supporting them, there lies an intractable, irradicable element of evil with which justice itself is required in the long run to deal." Let them anatomize Regan. See what breeds about her heart. Is there any cause in nature that makes these hard hearts?" (6. 74–76). This is a question less about the nature of justice or its application than about human nature; and it lies at the heart both of Lear's "madness" and of any "redemption" that may conceivably prove to be open to him. The problem raised differs from even the most insistent that the tragedy has so far raised by admitting of no solution; it is, indeed, rather the sense of its existence than of any possible resolution that emerges from this moment in the play. It creates a tension so deep that the only possible transition from it is into repose, the sleep that is so frequently in Shakespeare the resolving agent of intimate tragic conflicts; and so it is at this point, in the presence of excruciating pain and with even more intolerable pain to come, that Kent calls upon the exhausted Lear to "lie here and rest awhile" (6. 80). Lear's last phrase in the scene— "We'll go to supper i' th' morning" (6. 82)—and the fool's response (the final word he speaks in the play), "And I'll go to bed at noon" (6. 83), emphasize between them how complete is the reversal that has brought them at this, the play's point of balance, to their present state. To Lear's agonized questionings, stated and implied, the fool has no answer to offer. Having accompanied his master to the lowest point in his downward progress, he drops— enigmatic as ever—out of the action.

The last part of the scene, as befits a turning point (real or illusory? the question remains teasingly open), contains features that further develop the tragedy. Gloucester enters once more to warn Kent of the impending threat against Lear's life. The news he brings serves, typically, to destroy our hopes that Lear may at this point be allowed to find relief in sleep. It also bears upon Gloucester's disinterested gesture and upon the abandonment of worldly prudence and the exposure to mortal danger that he is now ready to contemplate. *This*—the brutal renewal of their exposure to pain—is the answer that the "world" offers to those who seek relief from its intolerable pressures. The fact that Lear is in the pitiful state of one whose "wits are gone" (6. 85) and who stands, both physically and morally, in urgent need of "rest" does not, and in the *Lear* world cannot, save him from further exposure to "a plot of death" (6. 87) against his person.

Once again, however, there is a more positive side to this new development that concerns the human rehabilitation of Gloucester. By accepting the risk involved in his decision, he confirms the step tentatively taken at his previous meeting with the king, a step which seems to indicate that he is on the point of assuming, by his conscious recognition of the claims of common humanity, his part in the developing tragic pattern. Hitherto a time-serving man of the world (a "servingman" in "poor Tom's" vocabulary), he allows natural feeling to lead him into an abandonment of his previous "neutrality." His choice will not save him from exile, blindness, and death—there can be no short cuts to salvation in *Lear*—but it will bring him to the possibility of whatever redemption the play allows us, in its austere and unflinching realism, to contemplate. Kent, for his part, stresses once again the healing properties of sleep. His concern, which will find no immediate response in the action, looks forward to what will be, in due course, Lear's awakening in the restored presence of Cordelia:

> Oppressed nature sleeps.
> This rest might yet have balmed thy broken sinews.
>
> (6. 95–96)

"*Might* yet": the repose of which the broken old man is at this point so brutally deprived will only be his when the time has come for him to be restored to the love of the daughter whom he wronged.

The rhyming speech with which Edgar brings the scene to an end is a first example of the oracular comments that will become from now on a prominent feature of his utterances and that will serve to separate him, in his successive transformations, from the other characters in whose tragic fortunes he is involved. Suffering, he proposes, can bring with it a sense of human solidarity and the contemplation of misery can become paradoxically a source of relief:

> Who alone suffers suffers most i' th' mind,
> Leaving free things and happy shows behind;
> But then the mind much sufferance doth o'erskip
> When grief hath mates, and bearing fellowship.
> How light and portable my pain seems now,
> When that which makes me bend makes the king bow,
> He childed as I fathered.
>
> (6. 102–8)

The rhyming artificiality and the deliberate triteness of the content have the effect of a comment standing out from the surrounding action. Lear has been denied by his children and Edgar rejected by his father; upon that central knot of "unnatural" situations the play builds its complex layers of experience. There is nothing in Edgar's words to suggest that the harsh, intolerable reality of these situations can be transformed to answer more closely to our desires. Such relief as can be conceived is confined to the "mind" and to its sense of community, of possible "fellow-ship." Edgar feels that his own private and personal grief has become, or may become, more bearable—"portable"—when related to the sorrow that "makes the king bow." By a strangely vital paradox which points beyond any "truth" that reason may discern, it can even—or so he proposes—come to be regarded as "light." The justification for this assertion lies in the recognition of interchangeable and related human destinies that underlies it. "Grief," it seems, becomes more supportable when it has "mates" and when the inescapable human condition of "bearing" is perceived (as Edgar's assimilation to the state of "poor Tom" has taught him to see it) in the light of "fellowship." Finally, real as grief is in its call to leave behind "free things," these are seen in turn, in the light it sheds upon them, as "happy *shows*," in a certain sense as delusions. The Stoic insistence upon freedom from slavery to external circumstance, though not an ultimate positive utterance—if any such is indeed conceivable—is one of the elements without which no such statement would be possible.

The scene that follows (act 3, scene 7), the last in this central part of the play, represents a brutal counterpart to these assertions of moral insight. In it the full effects of the savagery unleashed in human nature by the blind follow-ing of passionate self-interest are revealed in an ultimate act of physical cruelty. For some time past we have been aware of an accumulation of images that relates the behav-ior of human beings to that of fanged and devouring beasts. The wolf, the lion, and the fox—alternately preda-tory, crafty, and overweening—have been constantly pres-ent in the words of the human actors, reflecting the dis-ruption of "natural" order and restraint. What is humanly "natural," distinctive to the fulfilled lives of men and women, tends inexorably to fall back into the sphere of animal savagery from which it has so precariously emerged. Side by side with those references have been others, equally insistent, to "sight," its relativity and its

possible loss. The two lines now converge upon the bound
and helpless figure of Gloucester, accused of treason
against the new order and surrounded by Regan, Goneril,
and Cornwall moving round him with a passionate intensity that culminates in the visible blinding of their helpless
victim. Characteristically, Gloucester's words in the face of
his ordeal emphasize that this is a crime doubly unnatural
because it is committed not merely by men against a fellow
being but by guests against their host (6. 38–40).[40] Equally
characteristically, he ends, when he sees that his fate is not
to be avoided, by denouncing the "cruel nails" and "boar-
ish fangs" of his torturers, who would have been ready to
"pluck out" Lear's "poor old eyes" and to tear his
"anointed flesh" (6. 56–58), and who are prepared, in his
absence, to wreak their vengeance upon Gloucester's person.

Side by side with these savageries, the parallel preoccupation with "sight," with eyes and their loss, which has run
like a hidden thread through the earlier part of the play,
comes to the surface in a palpable dramatic form. The
blinding of Gloucester, indeed, has more than a factual
meaning in the structure of the play. The moment when
he loses his physical sight, the victim of a gratuitous act of
cruelty, coincides with the birth in him of a certain moral,
or human, understanding. This new development is at
once passively induced, the product of circumstances beyond the old man's control, and the occasion for a personal response. "I am tied to th' stake, and I must stand the
course" (7. 54)[41] he affirms, helplessly bound as he is to his
chair and with his torturers before him, the last "human"
beings whom he will see. This affirmation corresponds to
the only choice—if choice we can call it—open to him; and,
having made it and been reduced to blindness, he learns—
in what is at once a final blow of ironic sarcasm and a first
faint illumination—of the treachery of Edmund:

O my follies! Then Edgar was abused.

Kind gods, forgive me that, and prosper him.

(7. 91–92)

The moment in which Gloucester's past "follies" come home to him is also, enigmatically enough, the occasion for a first declaration of the restored, "natural" bond uniting tortured father and misunderstood son in a common destiny.

One short but pregnant word in Gloucester's speech of recognition—his reference to the "gods" as "kind"—must come to us, at this moment, with the force of something like a moral blow. The adjective has already appeared, also in the mouth of Gloucester, in the earlier part of the scene (7. 34), and the effect of the repetition, falling immediately after the act of savagery committed upon his helpless person, represents a challenge to our reasonable understanding. We shall not easily be tempted to read into it any easy "providential" or "redemptive" meaning that would be foreign to any honest reponse to what the play offers. Shakespeare, it would seem, is requiring us, as spectators to these horrors, to face squarely the implications of any optimistic assumptions that, in our craving for "meaning," we may be inclined to impose upon the bare reality we have just witnessed. Men and women *need*, it seems, to believe that whatever "gods" they may conceive— whatever, indeed, the very word may be held to mean-- are in some sense "kind"; but it is far from clear that the need is sufficient to create a corresponding truth, and Gloucester's pain is *there*, palpably inflicted under our eyes, to promote an intractable question in the face of any such consoling belief.

That the "gods" whom we, in our extremity, desire to think of as "kind" are in fact to be so described seems to be, in terms of what we see in the play, an insult upon our intelligence. The implications of the epithet, indeed, are not consistently maintained in the course of the action. The same Gloucester who invokes the kindness of the gods will speak of them, in the very next scene, in very different terms:

> As flies to wanton boys are we to th' gods;
> They kill us for their sport.[42]

Other statements toward the end of the tragedy seem calculated to raise questions concerning the very affirmations they seem to advance. When Edgar says to Edmund, whom he has just mortally wounded in single combat,

> The gods are just, and of our pleasant vices
> Make instruments to plague us.
> The dark and vicious place where thee he got
> Cost him his eyes,[43]

we find ourselves—as is surely intended—asking what kind of savage and revengeful "morality" is being proposed. That Gloucester's sin in the matter of Edmund's conception should be spoken of in terms of "*pleasant* vices" is appropriate enough having regard to the attitude of cynical worldliness that emerges for a moment in the conversation with Kent that opens the play.[44] That it "cost him" his eyes may even seem a justifiable balancing of the "sin" and its consequence; but, if it is "just" on these terms, the "justice" invoked is one that seems to ignore the disproportion between the act and its consequences and to exclude any saving consideration of human "charity."

That the questions raised are fundamental to the play becomes clear when we relate these dark sayings to others concerning the gods that play an equally important part in the tragedy,[45] without however dispelling the sense of obscurity that they have left with us. The challenge—for such it surely is—represented by Gloucester's disconcerting choice of adjective is underlined by the fact that Cordelia will echo it, when she is restored to the father whom she lost, by referring to her gods in the same way:

> O you kind gods,
> Cure this great breach in his abused nature!
> Th' untuned and jarring senses, O, wind up
> Of this child-changed father![46]

Finally, the claim concerning the gods that arises from Gloucester's anguished understanding of his situation is connected with the central paradox we have discovered in Shakespeare's use throughout the play of the image of *sight*. In *King Lear* those who most confidently claim to "see," who pride themselves on their clear-sighted appraisal of the ways of the world and on their ability to turn what they "see" to their own ends, find themselves betrayed by their "sight" and prove to be, in a very real sense, "blind"; while those who "stumbled when they saw"[47] and who have lost even the use of their eyes may, in the very moment of losing them, receive a flash of moral illumination and in fact "see." Gloucester's achievement of this kind of "sight" at the moment of his blinding—imperfect and questionable though it is in relation to the reality of his pain—corresponds to the deepest and most inclusive of all the paradoxical inversions used in the play to penetrate the deeper realities of the human condition. It is balanced by the growth in understanding, in his sense of the true human situation, that accompanies—again, however, obscurely and questionably—Lear's collapse into madness. In *King Lear,* the blind *see,* the *mad* understand. Their blindness and their madness represent the cost, almost intolerable in its extremity, of such vision and such comprehension as they achieve.

One final incident—brief and seemingly ineffective in its consequences—stands out against the prevailing inhumanity. Natural human feeling reasserts itself in the servants who accompany Cornwall and who are called upon to be instrumental to his act of savagery; affirms itself, in the face of all the odds, in a protest against what seems to be an unmitigated cruelty at the very heart of things. "If she live long," one of them says, speaking of Regan,

And in the end meet the old course of death,
Women will all turn monsters.

(7. 101–2)

There *is* "an old course of death," a way of dying that
answers to the natural rhythms of life and is not offensive
to our sense of what is acceptable, even appropriate. Death
is, in this sense, a reality that men are required to accept as
inseparable from their understanding of their humanity.
Were Regan to be granted an end of this kind, the speaker's rough instinct for "justice" would be violated, his belief
in his own particular "gods"—to whom he does *not* refer—
called into question. This is, at the extreme limit of moral
endurance, the reaction of normal humanity to a world in
which the most intimate ties of nature seem to be on the
point of dissolution and in which the condition of "unaccommodated man" has been reduced to that of the fox
and the wolf, a being condemned to destroy till he himself
meets destruction. Against the finality of such a view of life
Cornwall's servant reacts instinctively, without appealing
to a "philosophy" of any kind. It may be that his reaction
offers as much in the way of positive statement as the
author, in this play, cares or is able to make.

It is typical of *Lear* that, on a short-term point of view at
least, the reaction seems to end only in defeat. The servant
who follows up his protest by drawing his sword and
wounding Cornwall is himself stabbed in the back by Regan and his body is callously thrown on the "dunghill" (7.
97) by his master's orders. Once more the striking of a
note of hopeful humanity has been answered by its opposite. Yet the fact remains that the protest *has* been made
and that it has borne fruit in the "untimely hurt" (7. 98) of
which Cornwall complains. Other plays by Shakespeare
offer parallels which suggest that the introduction of this
brief episode has a meaning in relation to the author's
understanding of life. When, at the end of *Othello*, Emilia
awakes finally to the truth of her husband's nature and the
enormity of his contrivings,[48] she asserts herself against

him for the first time and refuses to obey his command to stand by in silence. A point is reached, it seems, beyond which human nature cannot be pushed in acquiescence to the inhuman. In the case of Emilia, as in that of Cornwall's anonymous servant, a disinterested gesture of human solidarity has been offered—against all the odds—in mitigation of the appalling reality under our eyes; and in both cases—more effectively, indeed, in *Othello* than in *Lear*—the progress of inhuman evil has been checked in the name of a reality that it has failed to take into account, that indeed it has dismissed as irrelevant, but upon which—immediately in the one case, more remotely and uncertainly in the other—its mastery of the situation founders.

The importance of the episode for *King Lear* is out of proportion to its appearance and tells us something about the sense that we can derive from the play as a whole. Whatever the difficulties may be—and no one will accuse Shakespeare of concealing or underestimating them—men *need* to believe in the "kindness" of whatever "gods" they set up for themselves in their effort to make sense of the world in which they are so mysteriously placed. In this sense at least, to recognize *no* "gods" is finally intolerable. Yet in saying this, one should be clear as to exactly what it is that is being asserted. Some readers of *King Lear* have been tempted to take what we might call a "redemptive" view of the play and especially of Lear's alleged growth in moral understanding that they perceive as taking place in the course of it. Such a view often leads them to impose upon what they see or read a "Christian" or otherwise "transcendental" conclusion that projects their own beliefs—or, it may be, their will to believe—upon what the play offers. It seems unlikely that the tragedy, objectively considered, can support such a conclusion. Those who are tempted to find it attractive may do well to consider the reaction, already quoted, of Dr. Johnson, himself a believing Christian concerned to find a firm ground for his own conviction of "meaning" but unwilling to confuse the "truth" of this conviction with his own will to believe.

Whatever idea Shakespeare may be pursuing in *King Lear,* it can hardly be the comforting illusion that suffering necessarily or often ennobles or humanizes the sufferer.

The rejection of any easily "redemptive" reading of the play should not, on the other hand, tempt us into an opposite extreme, which has also been frequently proposed, with the effect of turning what Shakespeare wrote into a seventeenth-century anticipation of Samuel Beckett's *Endgame.*[49] This too, it seems, will hardly serve. For all the desolation of its perspectives, the play has an expanding humanity that reflects a vision vastly richer and more complex than that honestly available to the twentieth-century playwright. No doubt *King Lear* contains *Endgame* as an ever-present possibility in human experience; but, if so, it refuses to be limited by this presence. In the light of *King Lear,* we understand that to be human is to ask reasonable questions and to ask them—again reasonably—without the expectation of finding, in time, final or inclusive answers; but it is also human to refuse to conclude, in spite of and at times in the face of contrary evidence, that the asking of the questions is pointless or without value. It seems that a certain act of faith—not in a theological or philosophical but in a simple human sense—is required if the business of living is to be carried on at all. After our sense of the justice of the order of nature seems to have been called into question by the horrors we have witnessed, it can be no accident that the last word of this central stage in the tragedy, entrusted once again to a humble servant moved to sympathy by the spectacle of Gloucester's suffering, is an expression of simple human concern: "Heaven help him!" (7. 107). The very simplicity of the phrase, set against the intolerable savagery we have witnessed, serves as a prologue to the developments that follow.

NOTES

1. 1. 4. 259–60.

2. *Macbeth* 1. 1. 10–11.

3. Compare Edgar's "servingman" at 3. 4. 81. In both cases, the word has to do with a dweller in the courtly world of power and intrigue.

4. 3. 4. 101.

5. The comparison was made by H. Granville Barker in the study of the play included in the first volume of his *Prefaces to Shakespeare* (Princeton, N.J.: Princeton University Press, 1946).

6. See Una Ellis-Fermor, *"Timon of Athens": An Unfinished Play* (*Review of English Studies* 18 [1942]: 270–83).

7. I use the word in the sense in which it is used by T.S. Eliot in his essays on Marlowe and Ben Jonson.

8. G. Wilson Knight's essay on the play in *The Wheel of Fire* (Oxford: Clarenton Press, 1930) was perhaps the first study to deal extensively with the element of grotesque comedy in the play.

9. I am thinking, of course, of conditions at the Globe Theatre, for which most of the plays were written. Some of them, particularly those of a late date, are likely to have been written with different conditions in mind; but the idea of a bare stage is surely a fundamental presupposition of Shakespeare's art, which remained unaffected by these changes.

10. 1. 4. 266–80.

11. 1. 4. 104–7.

12. 1. 4. 26–29.

13. 2. 4. 80–81.

14. 4. 7. 57–59.

15. 4. 3. 30.

16. In *The Tempest*, Antonio reduces "conscience" to an inconvenient "kibe," or "corn," which has no restraining effect upon his actions. See 2. 1. 269–71.

17. The word *grace* plays a particularly important part in the last plays, and particularly in *The Winter's Tale*. See, among other instances, 1. 2. 99, 105: 2. 1. 121–22.

18. *Macbeth* 2. 3. 50–57.

19. 4. 6. 157–60.

20. 1. 1. 90.

21. Compare 5. 3. 258.

22. *Twelfth Night* 5. 1. 381.

23. *Love's Labour's Lost* 5. 2. 919–20.

24. 3. 2. 95–96.

25. 3. 2. 58.

26. The first use of the word was at 3. 2. 68.

27. Compare *Macbeth* 3. 2. 34–39.

28. 4. 7. 12–20.

29. 2. 4. 259–65.

30. There is no reason to doubt the essential truth of the picture conveyed by Goneril at 1. 4. 231–36.

31. 2. 4. 235–37.

32. 2. 4. 258.

33. 1. 1. 87–90.

34. *Hamlet* 4. 4. 33–35.

35. Once again there is a sexual implication in the refrain.

36. 2. 4. 219–20.

37. 4. 1. 2–4.

38. 5. 3. 258.

39. Johnson's note to his edition of 1763.

40. The sense of a crime committed against the mutual trust that should unite a host and his guest is, of course, powerfully expressed in *Macbeth.* See 1. 7. 12–16.

41. We are reminded of *Macbeth* 5. 7. 1–2:

> They have tied me to a stake. I cannot fly,
> But bear-like I must fight the course.

42. 4. 1. 36–37.

43. 5. 3. 171–74.

44. 1. 1. 7–23.

45. A full treatment of the subject of the "gods" in the play will be found in W. R. Elton's *King Lear and the Gods* (San Marino, Calif.: Huntington Library, 1966).

46. 4. 7. 14–17.

47. 4. 1. 19.

48. *Othello* 5. 2. 219–24.

49. Some such idea seems to have inspired in great part Peter Brook's impressive film version of the play.

[6]

The Imaginative and the Real in *Antony and Cleopatra*

NONE of Shakespeare's plays has proved more elusive to the defining ambition of critics than *Antony and Cleopatra*. That the play is one of his greatest few would deny: the quality and range of the poetry, hardly surpassed for scope and imaginative power in all the dramatist's work, is such as to compel acceptance. When it comes, however, to defining the nature of the achievement, we find ourselves faced with a problem of approach, of the reading of the author's intention, which has given rise to remarkably contradictory solutions. Sooner or later we are faced by two possible readings, each strongly defended and each based on elements demonstrably present in the text,[1] whose only disadvantage is that they seem to exclude one another. Is *Antony and Cleopatra* a tragedy of lyrical inspiration, justifying love in the romantic manner as affirming its value triumphantly over death and circumstance (Dryden seems to have favored this interpretation when he chose to call his re-creation of Shakespeare's play *All for Love: or The World Well Lost*); or is it rather a ruthless exposure of personal frailties leading to foreseen disaster, a presentation of human possibilities senselessly squandered? *Both* interpretations can be and have been defended, but neither—taken by itself—seems adequate as an account of the effect that the play makes upon us.

It may be important to note that these mutually exclusive readings tend to agree in attempting to extract from Shakespeare's play something in the nature of a moral judgment: and that may not be the best way, here or elsewhere, to approach his work. Certainly, when we allow ourselves to experience the play immediately, either in reading or in stage production, we do not, it seems, find ourselves under constraint to resolve these contradictions. This suggests strongly that what we may come to see in the process of analysis or dissection as disparate or conflicting elements are in fact the product of a unified and coherent vision. In what follows I am going to propose that a solution to the vital dichotomy that seems to emerge so persistently from critical consideration may be found in Shakespeare's lifelong concern with the deeper implications of the dramatic illusion: that the theme of the play is the relationship of the imaginatively *creative* to the obstinately *real,* of the "reality" that, following an inherent compulsion of our natures, we "make" for ourselves to the ineluctable "reality" with which that "making" is required to come to terms. For Shakespeare, who was in this as in other respects a uniquely self-conscious artist,[2] these are questions involved in the very decision to set up a group of actors to present "characters" to an audience in the interlocking and developing action of a play: and they are, perhaps, as subtly addressed in *Antony and Cleopatra* as anywhere in his work.

The short opening scene of the tragedy, which serves as a kind of "overture" to introduce the main themes for future development, turns very precisely upon a contrast between the subjectively *theatrical* and the objectively *real*. The opening speech by Antony's officer and companion in arms Philo—the first words of the play—leaves us in no doubt of the estimate that we are bound, on any realistic view, to form of his general's infatuation:

> Nay, but this dotage of our general's
> O'erflows the measure.

(1. 1. 1–2)

"Dotage": the word implies, on the one hand, the diminished faculties associated with senility and, on the other, the degree of self-infatuation that is so often implied in Shakespeare's use of the word to describe the absurd behavior of lovers in his comedies.[3] Antony's heart has become "the bellows and the fan/ To cool a gypsy's lust" (1. 9–10): a "gypsy," an "Egyptian," a person outside the accepted limits of society, approaching the condition of a "strumpet" (1. 13). The judgment is firm, uncompromising, and—from its "Roman" point of view—final. It rests on a plain, simple evaluation of the reality we see before us, and no amount of poetical elaboration can—on its own terms—evade it.

There are, however, for what they are worth (and just what *are* they worth? this is the question that the play insistently poses) other possible terms and people who are willing to commit their lives to an affirmation of them. The entry of Antony and Cleopatra, which follows immediately on these bleak considerations, is an invitation to enter a different world, one that exists primarily in the minds of the protagonists. The tone becomes, by contrast, theatrical and almost operatic in its effect as the dramatist begins to work deliberately on different planes of dramatic reality. The words of the central pair come to us, as it were, from an elevated platform set up within the limits of the larger stage. They address one another antiphonally, voice responding to voice, emotion challenging emotion in a mutual heightening, a progressive accumulation of intensities; and the effect, a cunning combination of lyric spontaneity and conscious self-projection, of passionate dedication and the deliberate stimulation of feeling, is to show us characters engaged in a powerful effort to convince one another and themselves that the sentiments they express are true. To Cleopatra's request that Antony should tell her "how much" he loves her,[4] he replies "There's beggary in the love that can be reckoned" (1. 15); and to her further statement, made to lead him on, that she will "set a bourn how far to be beloved," he answers with a lyrical declaration that suggests infinity, transcendance in emotion: "Then must thou needs find out new heaven, new earth" (1. 17).

These rapt exchanges give us, as spectators, the sense of a duet, of two consummate tragic actors playing to the limit the roles that convey their sense of themselves for the benefit of a listening public in which admiration and skepticism are oddly balanced: the audience of Romans and Egyptians on stage, of which we, as spectators in the theater, form a kind of extension. The little "play"— a "play" inside the greater play, as it were—is being acted out at a remove from reality, as the nature of the dramatic illusion imposes; we are all the time aware that Antony and Cleopatra are *actors* speaking the parts assigned to them. No sooner, however, have the words been spoken, the appropriate gestures (a little larger than life) made, than the play's "real" world asserts itself in the person of a messenger from Rome. Antony, resenting this inconvenient intrusion as an interruption of the game in which he is engaged, thrusts the newcomer aside with a petulant gesture of impatience ("Grates me! The sum"); but Cleopatra, playing on the dependency that draws him to her, is quick to chide him with the scolding of his "shrill-tongued" wife (but may not Cleopatra be described, here and elsewhere, as "shrill-tongued" too?) and with that inferiority to "the scarce-bearded Caesar" (1. 21) whose youth and competence inspire him throughout the play with a galling sense of inferiority.[5] For the entire course of the scene we are required to balance the theatrical against the real, giving to each its due (the theatrical is not necessarily spurious nor the real unequivocally admirable) while maintaining a necessary detachment in regard of both. On the one hand the poetry may persuade us, while its effect lasts, to identify with Antony in his first gesture of triumphant passion: on the other, and at the same time (since we are conscious of our status as spectators), that gesture is—for us— deliberately distanced, seen as resting, beneath the appeal of its rhetorical splendor, on foundations of willed and sustained self-deception.

Antony's first full declaration of the emotion that moves him—the opening tenor aria, so to call it, which sets the tone for the action to follow—contributes to the same effect:

> Let Rome in Tiber melt and the wide arch
> Of the ranged empire fall! Here is my space,
> Kingdoms are clay: our dungy earth alike
> Feeds beast as man! The nobleness of life
> Is to do thus; when such a mutual pair
> And such a twain can do't, in which I bind,
> On pain of punishment, the world to weet
> We stand up peerless.
>
> (1. 1. 33–40)

The poetry here is designed to move an audience; to move it rhetorically, indeed, but in a way that contributes to the effect of the whole. The vast spaciousness of the evoked background, the sense that a world order rests as upon its keystone on the individuals whose tragedy we are to witness, is conveyed by reference to the "wide arch" of the "ranged empire." That Antony is ready to turn aside from issues so vast, so world-encompassing, gives us a sense of the weight, the presumption of value that he attaches to his emotion. Against this background of a world dismissed as paltry, Antony emphasizes the "nobleness" of life: a nobility to which Shakespeare's great tragic characters aspire, which they are engaged in creating for themselves, and which is to be presented, for exaltation *and* criticism, in the story of his lovers.

For if there is exaltation, indeed, there is also criticism. To be ready to "let Rome in Tiber melt" amounts, for a man in Antony's position, to something very like a dereliction of duty: a dereliction, we cannot help asking ourselves (for the play persistently asks it for us), in the name of what? Antony, after all, *is* a Roman; by declining to be what this implies, he is, in effect, surrendering his identity, the *only* identity he can have. He will recognize as much, very little later (act 1, scene 3), by announcing his decision to return to Rome. Meanwhile, his essentially theatrical gesture is at once reduced, cut down to size, by the realism of Cleopatra's comment:

> Excellent falsehood!
> Why did he marry Fulvia, and not love her?
> I'll seem the fool I am not. Antony
> Will be himself.
>
> (1. 1. 40–43)

The words amount to a recognition, on Cleopatra's part, that the game of "noble" passion in which she and Antony are engaged is based on self-deception. She will play it knowing it to be such: Antony will play it as "himself," as the "fool" she recognizes him to be in this matter. Antony's next words confirm her estimate. From the high-flown expressions of "nobility," he passes at a stroke to the clinging, "doting" sensuality that is equally a part of his nature. He exhorts Cleopatra for "the love of love and her soft hours" to set aside the thought of the disagreeable reality that threatens to interrupt their dream:

> There's not a minute of our lives should stretch
> Without some pleasure now. What sport to-night?
>
> (1. 1. 46–47)

"Sport" and "pleasure": these turn out, when we pass from the universally lyrical to prose reality, to be the true objects of Antony's devotion. The "sport" he proposes to obtain by neglecting the obligations of his state: the seizing of the "pleasure" of the moment and the desire to endow it with a spurious "eternity" represent the real content of his generalized expressions of "nobility." The working out of the contrast so presented, and the bringing together of its elements into a single range of dramatic emotion in which the comic and the tragic, the desolately "real" and the poetically "aspiring" are inextricably interwoven, is the central theme of the tragedy.

The working out of this theme depends in great part upon a contrast between the two realities represented by Rome and Egypt. This has sometimes been seen as a contrast between two worlds, each with its appropriate character and poetic expression; but it is important to understand that in reality, in the tangible and objective truth of things, there its in the play only one world; its name is Rome, and its representative, whether we respond to him or not, is Octavius Caesar. Politically speaking, Egypt is no more than a province of Rome, Cleopatra its queen by Roman sufferance. Her affair with Antony is, among other things, a move in the game of survival, an attempt to secure for herself and eventually for her heirs some measure of independence within the all-embracing Roman order of things.

Two scenes—perhaps the finest "political" scenes that Shakespeare conceived—show us what this, the play's "real" world, is like. The first presents his prophetic vision of what, in modern terms, we have become used to calling "a meeting at the summit": one of those meetings at which, supposedly, a great deal is discussed but little that is either useful or creditable decided. Octavius and Antony, "pillars of the world" (and very fallible human beings), have been brought together by the only thing that can, however momentarily, unite them: fear of their common rival, Pompey. They meet in Rome to find some way of sinking their differences in the face of a common threat. The meeting opens, as such occasions are apt to do, on a note of deep-seated mutual distrust. The two "pillars," each accompanied by his train of obsequious advisers, greet one another warily, with oblique gestures of mistrust, as they enter from opposite sides of the stage:

Flourish
CAESAR: Welcome to Rome.
ANTONY: Thank you.

CAESAR: Sit.
ANTONY: Sit, sir.
CAESAR: Nay then.   *(They sit.)*

                                                (2. 2. 28)

With these uneasy preliminaries disposed of, Antony
opens the discussion on an aggressive note, with the determination of a man who has reason to doubt the validity of
his position and who therefore feels that he must be the
first to take offense:

> I learn you take things ill which are not so,
> Or being, concern you not.

                                                (2. 2. 29–30)

After some recrimination in which Caesar's rather frigid
disdain for a rival whom he has already described as
tumbling "on the bed of Ptolemy" and keeping "the turn
of tippling with a slave" (1. 4. 17–19) and Antony's studied
posture of carelessness display themselves to the worst
possible advantage, the trend of the argument is changed
by one of those sudden, theatrical shifts of mood for which
Antony is notable throughout. Caesar accuses him bluntly
of breaking his pledged word: he replies with a gesture to
"honor"—"the honor is sacred which he talks on now" (2.
85)[6]—followed by a show of self-exculpation that reflects
his underlying insecurity. His oath to come to Caesar's aid
was, he says, "neglected" rather than denied. The request
for support came to him while he was "feasting three
kings," and at a time when

> poisoned hours had bound me up
> From mine own knowledge.

                                                (2. 2. 90–91)

Having thus shifted the blame, to his own satisfaction,
upon Fulvia, upon Cleopatra, upon anyone but himself,
what Antony is pleased to call his "honor" is satisfied and
he is ready to make a deal. To lend a hand in arriving at an

agreement there is Caesar's serviceable instrument, "Secretary of State" Agrippa, ever ready to insinuate a "realistic" proposition into his master's ear:

> Thou hast a sister by the mother's side,
> Admired Octavia: great Mark Antony
> Is now a widower.
>
> (2. 118–20)

The irony, bordering on sarcasm, implicit in the reference to Antony's marital status, produces the parody of self-respect implied in Antony's stiff rejoinder, "I am not married, Caesar," where a false dignity covers a false situation and leads to a bargain as callous and calculating as it is clearly destined to be impermanent.

Even more beautifully constructed in its wealth of underlying motives is the great drunken scene on Pompey's barge in Alexandria harbor (2. 7) where the "pillars of the world" have met to celebrate their show of reconciliation. Antony, who carries his drink well and knows it, is in his "Egyptian" element: the life and soul, as they say, of the party, explaining to the befuddled Lepidus the marvels of Egypt—the Nile, the pyramids, the serpents, and so forth: all the wonders that so enticingly appear on colorful posters in the travel agencies of Rome:

LEPIDUS: What manner o' thing is your crocodile?
ANTONY: It is shaped, sir, like itself, and it is as broad as it hath breadth; it is just so high as it is, and moves with its own organs. It lives by that which nourisheth it, and the elements once out of it, it transmigrates.
LEPIDUS: What color is it of?
ANTONY: Of its own color too.
LEPIDUS: 'Tis a strange serpent.
ANTONY: 'Tis so, and the tears of it are wet.

> (7. 39–48)

The whole scene conveys marvelously the sense of conversation carried on at a remove from reality, of perceptions obscured by a drink-imposed cloud of comforting illusion. Reality, however, is still there, and we are reminded of it by Antony's reference to "crocodile's tears": tears of hypocrisy and double-dealing pointing to the underlying content of the occasion. As the conversation takes us at each moment further from common reality, it culminates in Antony's warning, which says so much more than he knows:

> These quicksands, Lepidus,
> Keep off them, for you sink.
>
> (7. 58–59)

The "quicksands," of course, belong to the marvels of Egypt, which Antony is concerned to expound for the benefit of his Roman audience: but he mentions them just as Pompey's lieutenant, Menas, on another part of the stage, is trying to catch his master's ear, urging him to seize the offered opportunity to cut the throats of his guests and so to make himself "lord of all the world" (7. 60).

Pompey's reply adds one more to those comments on the concept of "honor" in which the "political" action of the play abounds:

> Ah, this thou shouldst have done,
> And not have spoken on't. In me 'tis villainy,
> In thee 't had been good service. Thou must know,
> 'Tis not my profit that does lead mine honor;
> My honor, it.
>
> (7. 72–76)

A strange notion of "honor," indeed, and one that fails to strike Menas as either convincing or practical: as he puts it, in a comment delivered in an aside,

> Who seeks, and will not take when once 'tis offered,
> Shall never find it more.
>
> (7. 82–83)

This is Menas's version of a truth repeatedly recognized by Shakespeare's "political" figures, who invariably see success in the ends they propose to themselves as dependent on their ability to seize the opportunity that, if rejected, will scarcely present itself again.[7] In Pompey's case, events confirm the truth of his lieutenant's observation: when we next hear of him, it is to learn that he has been assassinated, stabbed in the back by one of Antony's "officers" (3. 5. 17–18). For the moment the scene ends with a general surrender to dissipation, as the drunken pace quickens and as Lepidus, "third part of the world" (7. 90), is carried off drunk to the tune of the remaining "pillars" and their associates carousing in tipsy celebration of their shadowy reconciliaton:

> Come, thou monarch of the vine,
> Plumpy Bacchus with pink eyne!
> In thy fats our cares be drowned,
> With thy grapes our hairs be crowned.
> > Cup us till the world go round,
> > Cup us till the world go round!
>
> (7. 112–17)

However, one man on Pompey's barge has been notably unwilling to join the general rush into inebriation: as Caesar puts it, in the act of turning rather self-consciously aside from his colleagues:

> 'Tis monstrous labor when I wash my brain
> And it grows fouler.
>
> (7. 98–99)

lines that may, incidentally, be one of the best descriptions of the effects of a hangover to be found in literature. It may be that, in this typical gesture by which the young Caesar places a distance between himself and his fellow revelers, he presents himself in a light that is not particularly attractive: but it is because he can make it, and live up to it, that he becomes master of the world: of the only "real" world, as the play conceives it. To understand Octavius without falling into the temptation to underestimate him is to respond to an essential part of the play's conception. We can think of him as the last of Shakespeare's great series of "public" men, the successor, on a vastly more ample and less patriotically conditioned stage, of Henry IV and his supremely efficient son: men whose acceptance of their necessary, their indispensable vocation conditions them to think of moral issues in Machiavellian terms of effectiveness and practical success. It would be profoundly wrong to underestimate them on that account. Political success is a necessary, an indispensable part of life that, in its absence, is apt to be reduced to a brutal struggle for survival in a world dominated by conflicting appetites. We may, indeed *should*, recognize that it is not the whole of it. That, it seems, is what this play finally insinuates: but it does not, in the process of so doing, ask us to depreciate Caesar's victory or to sentimentalize Antony's defeat. From first to last Octavius is conscious of himself as the instrument of "strong necessities" in relation to which personal considerations count for little. As he puts it,

> let determined things to destiny
> Hold unbewailed their way.
>
> (3. 6. 84–85)

Shakespeare's successful public men are those who know this, who choose to act in accordance with their knowledge, and who show the limitations that their choice implies. In the struggle with Antony, Caesar prevails, and—in the public order of things—we would not have it otherwise. His are the ends of empire, firm rule and universal order, ends necessary and indispensable if civilized and humane living is to remain possible in a world that desperately needs them: as again Caesar says, at the turning point of his fortunes:

The time of universal peace is near:

Prove this a prosp'rous day, the three-nooked world
Shall bear the olive freely.

(4. 6. 5–7)

"Universal peace" and its classic symbol, the olive: no
mean things to depend upon one man's conscientious and
effective choices. Even so, on the smaller stage of English
history did the clear, practical competence of Bolingbroke
overcame the forces of chaos implied in Richard II's legiti-
mate, poetical, but irresponsible kingship. The cause of
victorious empire—the vision, so compelling to Renaissance minds, of the *pax Romana,* the universal Roman
peace celebrated by Virgil in his great poem—wins the day
and wins it justly in the interests of humanity; but because
in human affairs, personal and public alike, every victory
has its price, its cost in terms of other possibilities rejected,
fatally destroyed, the fall of Antony is there to remind us,
beneath the squalor, the degradation, and the self-
deception, of what was left out, what might have been. For
the successful practical men, the Octavius Caesars of this
world, what might have been is finally irrelevant, only
what *is* counts; but for a poet, engaged in the contemplation of a wider range of human possibilities,

> What might have been and what has been
> Point to one end, which is always present.[8]

From this point of view, if from no other, the rejection of
Falstaff at the end of *Henry IV,* Part II, and the death of
Cleopatra answer, each in its entirely different way, to a
common intuition of life. To live is, for human beings, to
make choices, and to choose one thing is to will the exclusion of another, to leave something out. Shakespeare is
always concerned with the *cost* of choosing, aware of what
the success in achieving one set of ends (in this case necessary political mastery) implies in terms of the exclusion of
other possibilities of life.

Accordingly, if Caesar's successful pursuit of his public

ends leaves us asking questions about his private humanity, Antony's failure reflects personal weaknesses that the
play stresses with remorseless realism. At Actium, where
his own fortunes and those of the world are at stake, he
leaves the battle to follow the fleeing Cleopatra: acting, in
the judgment of one of his own followers, "like a doting
mallard" (3. 10–20), a lovesick duck. The same soldier
compares Cleopatra to "a cow in June": not a very romantic view of the Egyptian queen of "infinite variety." In the
face of his ruin, Antony shows the cruel and incalculable
side of his nature when he turns on Caesar's helpless messenger in a sadistic frenzy that covers the intolerable
awareness of personal shame:

> Take hence this Jack and whip him. . . .
>   Whip him, fellows,
> Till like a boy you see him cringe his face
> And whine aloud for mercy. . . .
>   Is he whipped? . . .
> Cried he? And begged 'a pardon?
>   (3. 13. 93; 99–101; 132–34)

For all its poetry, no play of Shakespeare's is more unspar-
ing in its moral realism than *Antony and Cleopatra*. This is
"the old lion dying," botched in the teeth, ready to cover
the reality of failure and betrayal by alternating between
bouts of hysterical rage and self-dramatizing gestures of
generosity that are intended to distract from but can never
annul the bleak, unconfessable reality that underlies them.

Yet true as all this is, it is not all the truth about Antony.
He is also the man who can on occasions inspire a personal
loyalty in his followers that "reason" can hardly justify and
Caesar barely inspire. Enobarbus, the hard-headed Roman whose reason tells him that his master's cause is beyond remedy, deserts him; but he dies in a ditch, broken
by his sense of betrayal and having—in the "real" world—
gained nothing by his act of shame. Above all Antony
shows an intermittent capacity for seeing himself as he is,

honestly, in recognition of what, desolately, he has become:

> when we in our viciousness grow hard
> (O misery on't!) the wise gods seel our eyes,
> In our own filth drop our clear judgments, make us
> Adore our errors, laugh at's while we strut
> To our confusion.
>
> (3. 13. 111–15)

It is the business of a great writer not to impose moral
judgments but to reveal moral realities: and this is what
Antony's words at this point unerringly achieve. For once
he is allowing himself to contemplate the reverse side of
the coin, which the nature of his choices has habitually led
him to conceal even from himself. He is, perhaps, one of
the greatest of those Shakespearean characters who, each
in his respective way, chooses to live by the imagination
and who follow their choice even at the expense of reality.
Shakespeare, it seems, requires of us, both in his comedies
and in his tragedies, to consider the proposition that to live
imaginatively is the same thing as, quite simply, to be alive.
To live is to be imaginative, to follow the distinctively human compulsion to create our own reality by making the
choices appropriate to our sense of ourselves; but, on the
other hand, to insist on remaking the world in our own
image is to run the risk, which is equally inherent in the
human situation, of living at the expense of reality, in self-
dedication to an illusion. The truth about Antony's
tragedy, like that of all human lives, lies, creatively and
humanly speaking, somewhere between these alternatives.

The tragedy, however, is not Antony's alone. It concerns
two central figures and involves, uniquely for Shakespeare, two separate tragic climaxes.[9] We need, therefore,
to give some thought to Cleopatra, whose tragedy is more
than an aspect of Antony's, by considering one of the
play's most memorable passages—the description, closely
adapted from Plutarch, of the queen of Egypt floating

down the river Cydnus on her ceremonial barge to meet
Mark Antony for the first time:

> The barge she sat in, like a burnished throne,
> Burned on the water.

(2. 2. 192–93)

The words are something more than a setpiece of bravura
writing, though that effect too contributes to the total impression they make. The words are spoken by Enobarbus,
the experienced and somewhat cynical Roman officer who
has accompanied Antony to Egypt, who has seen the famous Cleopatra in her native element, and who has come
back to Rome to tell a fascinating tall tale about the things
he saw and took part in there. Egypt offers a welcome
release from the hard-headed, practical commonsense
that prevails so weightily at home: a sort of travel-poster
Paradise in "glorious technicolor": a Hawaii or a Bermuda
where Romans go—or where they like to think that they
could go—to spend their hard-earned *sesterces* and to find
release from the dull, prosaic plod of day-to-day living in
the real world: a place where every kind of exotic thing is
to be seen and wondered at—"strange serpents," a magic-
ally beautiful and fascinating queen, Pyramids, twelve people eating eight wild boars at a breakfast: all too good to be
quite true, perhaps, and surely too good to last, but the
aspiration nonetheless of a plain-spoken level-headed soldier in his occasional flights of imaginative fantasy.

Of this fairyland—fascinating, endlessly elusive, and
suspiciously larger than life—Cleopatra is the embodiment. Her barge, with its "purple sails"

> so perfumed that
> The winds were lovesick with them,

is unlike any real boat that ever sailed on a real river:
certainly unlike any to be seen by a Roman on the swift-

flowing, uncomfortable Tiber. Its oars of "silver" that made

> The water which they beat to follow faster,
> As amorous of their strokes:

its contrived, "seeming" mermaid at the helm, its "silken tackle" swelling "with the touch of those flower-soft hands": the "strange invisible perfume" that "hit the sense/ Of the adjacent wharves": all these things represent a triumph of artifice over plain Roman reality. The memory, relived (and perhaps improved) in the telling, tickles the erotic fantasy of a sober Roman and moves him, for as long as the impression lasts, to very un-Roman poetry. What moves Enobarbus, beyond his own typically detached amusement at the conduct of "our courteous Antony," is the limitless volubility, the fascinating freedom from constraint that is summed up in his haunting, almost wistful phrase:

> Age cannot wither her, nor custom stale
> Her infinite variety:
>
> (2. 236–37)

the remembered vision of a queen whom he saw (and the memory lingers in his mind with the force of an alternative vision of life: a life that sober Rome never saw)

> Hop forty forty paces through the public street;
> And having lost her breath, she spoke, and panted,
> That she did make defect perfection
> And, breathless, pow'r breathe forth.
>
> (2. 230–33)

The presentation of this evasive and endlessly fascinating being by various characters in the course of the tragedy gives substance to the poetry of wish-fulfilment that plays so large and so necessary a part in human lives that would, in its absence, be simply intolerable. Cleopatra's words and actions exercise their fascination by embracing the whole immense range that separates high tragedy, consciously and deliberately staged, from broad farce, holding alternatives apparently incompatible together within the limits of a single experience. Her vitality is incongruously reflected in her treatment of Antony by contraries:

> If you find him sad,
> Say I am dancing; if in mirth, report
> That I am sudden sick. . . .
>
> (1. 3. 3–5)

and in her reception of the messengers who bring the unwelcome news of his marriage to "the still Octavia" (2. 6. 120). It is a vitality in which powerful emotion exists—as it does, on a lesser scale, in most human lives—side by side with the quixotic, the corrupt, and the plainly, broadly farcical. Shakespeare's acceptance of the real incongruities of human nature, together with his ability to make us believe in the transformation that the imaginative energy of his character operates upon the "reality" of their situation, constitutes a large part of the measure of the play's achievement.

For the final transformation, not less than the absurdity, has after all been there from the first. Antony's opening gesture of passionate, self-conscious dedication—"Let Rome in Tiber melt"—is matched, also early in the action, by Cleopatra's re-creation of a (no doubt largely imaginary) past when she hears from his own lips his decision to leave her for Rome. "Bid farewell and go," she tells him, meaning of course the opposite:

> when you sued staying,
> Then was the time for words: no going then,
> Eternity was in our lips and eyes,
> Bliss in our brows' bent, none our parts so poor

But was a race of heaven.

(1. 3. 33–37)

"The nobleness of life/ Is to do thus," "none our parts so poor/ But was a race of heaven": phrases such as these tend to a reshaping of reality in the image of desire: and, as such, they both carry us with them (inasmuch as the reshaping of reality is a condition of living) and lead us to ask necessary questions. No moralist can convince us, under the immediate impression of such phrases, that no more is involved at this point than a shadow triumph, an exposure of self-indulgent and self-destroying passions: but equally, no poet will persuade us that this mood can be affirmed, permanently held, in the face of the obstinately real. For these are words spoken on a stage, with an effect that is theatrically self-conscious: spoken in the presence of a tongue-tied, finally comic Antony who is uncomfortably trying to tell Cleopatra that he intends to leave her and who fails very conspicuously to get his word in edgeways:

> Now, my dearest queen. . . .
> The gods best know. . . .
> Cleopatra. . . .
> Most sweet queen. . . .
> Hear me, Queen.

(1. 3. 17–42)

words that remind us of nothing so much as a guilty adolescent caught in the act by his tormentor. It is of some significance that this, supposedly the greatest of romantic love tragedies, *never*—except perhaps fleetingly, uncertainly, at the moment of their last meeting on Cleopatra's monument (4. 15)—shows us the protagonists joining one another in mutually responsive declarations of passion. What we are nearly always given is Antony in pursuit of an evasive Cleopatra, or Cleopatra seeking to entice a bashfully retreating Antony. Evidently the play requires from us a creative balance of sympathy and detachment. We are to see this love, indeed, as realistically absurd, necessarily impermanent, but, equally, we are to conceive of it as something that can exalt, can give to those who are ready to accept involvement in it the power that derives from the strength of their imaginative commitment: the power to make themselves, in classical terms—illusory, no doubt in the cold light of objective truth, but while they last capable of imposing their own validity—*divine*.

The final test of this validity is provided by death. The confrontation with this, the play's one incontrovertible reality, is, not accidentally, double: for there are aspects of Antony's end that the presence of Cleopatra undercuts and things asserted by Cleopatra concerning him that only his removal can render plausible. Antony approaches his end under the sign of a dissolution of personality that his own words hauntingly convey:

ANTONY: Eros, thou yet behold'st me?

("Yet": the reality of his state is slipping away, inexorably fading into the insubstantiality and shadow that, at heart, he now desires for himself.)

EROS: Ay, noble lord.
ANTONY: Sometime we see a cloud that's dragonish;
         A vapor sometime like a bear or lion,
         A towered citadel, a pendant rock,
         A forked mountain, or blue promontory
         With trees upon't that nod unto the world
         And mock our eyes with air. Thou hast seen
            these signs;
         They are black Vesper's pageants.
EROS: Ay, my lord.
ANTONY: That which is now a horse, even with a
            thought
         The rack dislimns, and makes it indistinct
         As water is in water.
                                        (4. 14. 1–11)

"Here I am Antony,/ Yet cannot hold this visible shape" (14. 13–14). As we respond to these final speeches in which the sense of recognized failure, the loss of his "real," his Roman identity, is so poignantly balanced against a desire for liberation, we sense the presence of tragic emotion of a unique kind. In the movement of the poetry, "labor"—the sense of a man tied up, engaged in the final stages of a struggle to come to terms with what he understands to be "the heart of loss" (4. 12. 29), the recognition of intimate failure—and its opposite—the craving, intensely desired for release—are marvelously fused in what is at the same time weakness, exhausted renunciation of all effort, and an intuition of peace:

> now all labor
> Mars what it does; yea, very force entangles
> Itself with strength.
>
> (14. 47–49)

The very falling rhythm of the expression, the carryover from "labor" to what it "mars," and the separation of "entangles" from "itself," answers to the mood of slipping, dissolving identity. In the face of an inevitable, indeed necessary death, the contrary judgments that this tragedy so consistently invites and that answer to its special "metaphysical" inspiration, remain inextricably fused. The tragic hero, as he contemplates the resolution that he has brought upon himself, incorporates expressions that proceed from his human weakness into an effect that, up to a point—and it can only be so far—seeks to look beyond them.

Antony's last scene with Cleopatra confirms what the entire action has insinuated. He is carried to her dying—"I am dying, Egypt, dying" (15. 18,41): the phrase, twice repeated, comes to us with the sense of a tragic refrain—to act out his last moments with her on the elevated platform that is her monument. This is to be, in his conception, the final affirmation of the Roman identity with which his self-respect has been bound up and to which, at this final moment of truth, he needs to cling:

> The miserable change now at my end
> Lament nor sorrow at; but please your thoughts
> In feeding them with those my former fortunes,
> Wherein I lived the greatest prince o' th' world,
> The noblest: and do now not basely die,
> Not cowardly put off my helmet to
> My countryman. A Roman, by a Roman
> Valiantly vanquished.
>
> (15. 51–58)

A last expression of recovered *Romanitas*, spoken by one who is conscious of having renounced the reality, and addressed—perhaps—less to Cleopatra than to the theater audience and, through them, to the world. Antony's final concern is with the nobility that he needs to assert to make the prospect of his otherwise "miserable" end tolerable. We sympathize and respond to a speech that has, we recognize, a "theatrical" design upon us: but we can hardly fail to remember the series of events that has brought him to the necessity of speaking them. He is there because Cleopatra has *lied* to him, sending false news of her own death to draw him to her; and now that he is there, dying, she holds back from giving him the last kiss that he asks of her because she is aware of the need to keep open what options she has in respect of the victorious Caesar: "I dare not, . . . Lest I be taken" (15. 21–23). He, for his part, is still alive—barely—because he failed to carry out the Roman act of suicide and was left—by a devastating stroke of realism—to grope helplessly on the ground in self-inflicted pain, surrounded by "Romans" more concerned to secure their future with the victor than to afford their wounded leader the mercy of release. In no play of Shakespeare's is the ultimate sin of *betrayal*—both self-betrayal and betrayal of mutual trust—more intimately woven into the action. None is more unflinching in its estimate of human possibilities, its recognition of the frailties that we seek to cover—from others and, most of all perhaps, from ourselves—by our acts of comforting self-dramatization: and precisely because this is so, because the emotional buildup is called upon to justify itself in the face of uncompromising realism, none achieves greater heights of poetry.

The tragedy, however, we remind ourselves again, has a double peak: Cleopatra's death follows on, and is conditioned by, that of Antony. Already her final words on the monument—words, once again, *theatrically* conceived—have assumed a note (new for her) of "Roman" magniloquence:

> We'll bury him; and then, what's brave, what's noble,
> Let's do't after the high Roman fashion,
> And make death proud to take us.
>
> (15. 89–91)

Now, with Antony dead, Cleopatra is free to express her imaginative recreation of the heroic image she has made for herself out of his reality: free, because he is no longer there to force, by his physical presence, a sobering contrast with the truth.

To the last—or almost to the last—Cleopatra's attitudes fluctuate in a way that answers to the prevailing rhythms of the entire action. The last scene opens with an expression of her determination to follow Antony in his death and so to assert her own share of tragic nobility. Her mood carries on that expressed at the end of the monument scene:

> it is great
> To do that thing that ends all other deeds,
> Which shackles accidents and bolts up change;
> Which sleeps, and never palates more the dung,
> The beggar's nurse and Caesar's.[10]
>
> (5. 2. 4–8)

Once more, however, the note of high resolve is not left

unqualified. When Caesar's envoy Proculeius appears (the man whom the dying Antony advised her to "trust" [4. 15. 48] and who, as it turns out, is instrumental in her betrayal), she is Egyptian queen enough to request from the victor "conquered Egypt for my son" (2. 18) and to offer to kneel to him "with thanks" (2.21) if the request should be granted. Evidently the resolve to die "nobly" has not entirely obscured the instinct that moves her to explore the terms on which something might be salvaged from disaster. We are left unsure whether Cleopatra is playing for time to carry out her purpose or, once again, is keeping her options open; and this ambivalence, which answers to the sense of fluctuating human purposes that prevails throughout, is maintained for a long time before the final resolution ends it.

By now, however, every wish of Cleopatra's that evades the contemplation of death is based on illusion. Proculeius, after tricking her with fair words concerning his master's purposes in her regard,

> Have comfort, for I know your plight is pitied
> Of him that caused it.
>
> (2. 33–34)

has her surprised and seized to prevent her from frustrating Caesar's intention that she should grace his triumph in Rome. Alone with Dolabella and faced with the bleak reality of her situation, Cleopatra is left to express her imaginative re-creation of the dead Antony in one of the play's supreme poetic moments:

> I dreamt there was an Emperor Antony.
> O, such another sleep, that I might see
> But such another man. . . .
> His face was as the heav'ns, and therein stuck
> A sun and moon, which kept their course and lighted
> The little O, th' earth. . . .
> His legs bestrid the ocean: his reared arm

Crested the world: his voice was propertied
As all the tuned spheres, and that to friends;
But when he meant to quail and shake the orb,
He was as rattling thunder. For his bounty,
There was no winter in't: an autumn 'twas
That grew the more by reaping: his delights
Were dolphin-like, they showed his back above
The element they lived in: in his livery
Walked crowns and crownets: realms and islands were
As plates dropped from his pocket.

(2. 76–81; 82–92)

This is the reflection of a process by which Cleopatra *creates* an Antony in tune with her emotional need. The images flow together from the most varied sources to compose a compelling dream sequence. The Colossus whose "legs bestrid the ocean" becomes one with the heraldic device implied in the "reared arm" that "crested the world," and both merge into the evocation of a supernatural "bounty" immune to the action of the seasons (it had "no winter in't") and into the strange folk- or fairy-tale quality suggested by those two eyes, like a "sun and moon" adorning the "heaven" of their owner's face, and confirmed by the effect of the two final lines.[11] That an apostrophe of this scope and splendor can be accepted as natural, unstrained, and that images so diverse and so intensely conceived can come together to produce a sense of superhuman magnificence is a sign that Cleopatra, while she speaks, is *living* her dream and carrying us to live it with her; but that it *is* a dream, that there never was an *emperor* Antony (that place of eminence is occupied in the "real" world by his rival), and that she must sleep to keep it in being, is a sign that warns us to maintain a necessary measure of detachment in its regard. When she challenges Dolabella to confirm the reality of her vision—

Think you there was or might be such a man
As this I dreamt of?

(2. 93–94)

—the "might be" tells us that Cleopatra is, in spite of herself, aware of the limits of her dream: and indeed the Roman's reply, at once sympathetic and gently deflating, as befits one used to living in the real world and limited by the very fact, warns us against making excessive claims upon it. "Gentle madam, no". Cleopatra is living, or seeking to live, in a world that is the projection of her own emotions. That world, as she creates it, is splendidly valid in the effect that it works upon the Roman, who feels himself, almost in his own despite, fascinated by it, and through him upon us in the theater; but the fact remains that in the real world only death can prevent an awakening from it. For that reason, if for no other, Cleopatra is resolved to die.

"Reality," indeed, makes its immediate return in the self-contained, chilly person of Caesar. It is his first and last meeting with Cleopatra, and his first question—brief, detached, and to the point—indicates the spirit in which he approaches it: "Which is the Queen of Egypt?" (2. 113). Faced by a man who holds the fate of the world in his competent hands and who does not care enough to distinguish a "royal" queen from her attendant maids, Cleopatra knows that she has nowhere to go: that any hope she might still harbor of repeating with this man her successes with Julius Caesar and Antony are vain. The real world remains, as it has always been, Roman, and she has by now no living place in it.

Given this reality and aware that even her power to dispose of her own life is likely to be taken from her, Cleopatra plays for time. There follows the disconcerting exchange with the eunuch Seleucus, from which it emerges that she has kept back "some lady trifles" for purposes never clearly defined: an embarrassing revelation witnessed by Caesar with the detachment habitual in one who rarely allows himself to be surprised by the incongruity and weakness of human conduct:

Nay, blush not, Cleopatra, I approve

Your wisdom in the deed.

(2. 149–50)

Yet whatever reason she may have had for this action—
and Shakespeare chooses to keep us very effectively in the
dark at this point—Cleopatra knows what Caesar's intentions are and that they run contrary to her own resolution:

He words me, girls, he words me, that I shall not
Be noble to myself!

(2. 191–92)

and she proposes to assert her "nobility" in the only way
left open to her: by dying. The words of the clown (2. 243–
48) as he brings in his basket with the instruments of release, announce by their comic misuse the fusion of metaphysical contraries—life and death, reality and deception,
mortality and the "immortal"—to which the entire action
now tends. He warns her that the "biting" of the serpent—
bearer of poison and instrument of death—is "immortal:
those that do die of it do seldom or never recover" (2. 247).

An ambiguous immortality, indeed, is the content of
Cleopatra's culminating contrivance. She will stage her
own death because that is the one act by which she can,
however paradoxically, assert control over her desolate
circumstance. Her last great speech, steeped in consciousness of the theatrical, opens with a gesture of immortal aspiration:

Give me my robe, put on my crown, I have
Immortal longings in me.

(2. 279–80)

Conscious of being on a stage and in the presence of an
audience—both that of her fellow Egyptians and, as an
actress playing her role, of the theater public beyond
them—Cleopatra disposes herself to act out her last part in
what has become for her the self-created and self-

projecting drama of life. The "immortality" she evokes has a "noble" content that memory supplies. It is the final assertion of her love for the dead Antony, whom she is now free to call, for the first time in the play and because his living presence can no longer negate her claim, "Husband" (2. 286). In the light of this affirmation of "immortality," death becomes a dissolution, a purging of the earthly elements—the "dungy earth," we remember, of Antony's first speech—upon which love had been based and which now—so Cleopatra asserts, and so, while the impression lasts, we are persuaded to believe—it aspires to transcend:

> I am fire, and air; my other elements
> I give to baser life.
>
> (2. 288–89)

On the verge of dying, of the final untying of that "knot intrinsicate" (2. 303) of body and soul, death and life, which constitutes the "metaphysical" heart of our human reality, only the purest elements of feeling remain in Cleopatra: those, by a paradox now particularly meaningful, which are most fully, most intensely alive. An emotion founded upon the sensuous, unashamedly and often debasingly physical in kind, has become, in the light of her transforming imagination, something more: a taking up of the sensible into a "dream" that shadows permanence. That it *is* a dream, of course, that it can have no exclusive or lasting claim to be real, remains true. Cleopatra implies as much when she, whom we have seen in the play as "serpent of old Nile" (1. 5. 25), asks her audience and through them ourselves to see the self-chosen instrument of her release as

> my baby at my breast,
> That sucks the nurse asleep.
>
> (2. 309–10)

Reason, which our distancing as a theater audience from the stage allows us to assert, tells us that it is not new life, but poison, death, that she has taken to herself. The poetry affirms one thing, which she needs to believe, and which we—or one part of us—want to believe with her; the reality of the situation says another. By holding the two "realities" in balance, by asserting the creative power of the imagination without diminishing or ignoring the real and tangible foundation on which it necessarily builds and to which it must finally return, Shakespeare affirms his sense of the "truth"—and of its limitations—at which his pursuit of the dramatic illusion aims.

Appropriately, it is left to Caesar—master of the "real" world and its spokesman—to sum up our sense of the tragedy when he responds to the image of the dead Egyptian queen who has just evaded his design for her on her mortal—or "immortal"—throne:

> she looks like sleep,
> As she would catch another Antony
> In her strong toil of grace.
>
> (2. 344–46)

His words, spoken by one to whom the dignified public gesture comes naturally (he is, after all, to a supreme degree the public man), amount to a salute directed to the private and imaginative order of life, gathering into a complex interweaving of metaphors[12] the effect that Cleopatra's tragedy has made upon us. For Antony, the fascination of his Egyptian queen was a "toil," a snare that enticed him insidiously from the fulfillment of his Roman vocation and from affirmation of the personality that, in the real order of things, depended upon that vocation; but it was also, as re-created in his (and our) responding imagination, a "toil of grace," in which—at certain moments of supreme commitment—a sense of fitness, of human potentialities envisaged and momentarily achieved, has imposed itself in a creative action.

The entire development of the play, as it holds a living balance between the imaginative and the real—or better, perhaps, between the imaginatively and the the tangibly real—tends to this conclusion. The balancing of the generosity that Antony's folly sometimes seems to imply against Caesar's successful, necessary, but limiting practicality: the gradual ascent of the love imagery from earth and "slime" to "fire and air," are seen at the last to be one great process that tends to death as its completion. For death, which often in Shakespeare—in some of the most eloquent of the sonnets[13] and in the tragedies—seemed to offer incontrovertible evidence of the subjection of the most cherished human values to time's dissolving action, now becomes an instrument of release, the necessary condition of an experience that, though dependent on the temporal dimension that limits all human experience in the act of bringing it into being, is by virtue of its value and intensity incommensurate with it: that is, "immortal." As human beings immersed in the temporal process and limited to temporal perception, we value what we fear to lose: indeed, without the fear, it seems that the value could hardly exist.[14] The emotions of the central pair in this play have been built on foundations of "dungy earth," on "Nilus' slime." Upon these foundations, following a compulsion inherent in human nature—for, as another poet has put it, "man is in love, and loves what vanishes"[15]— they raised their fugitive intensities of creative transformation; but just as "earth" and "slime" can be quickened into "fire" and "air," so time itself, in which this tragedy of waste and shame was nurtured, became—within the always precarious limits of human achievement—an element in the creation of that "immortality" that, however intermittently or evanescently, the human imagination pursues as a condition of its being.

NOTES

1. For examples of these contrary readings, see G. Wilson Knight's essays in *The Imperial Theme* (Oxford: Clarendon Press, 1931) and the study of the play by John F. Danby published in *Poets on Fortune's Hill* (London: Faber & Faber, 1952).

2. I assume that we have moved far from the old idea of the unschooled "swan of Avon."

3. The word appears prominently in such early comedies as *The Comedy of Errors, The Two Gentlemen of Verona,* and *A Midsummer Night's Dream.*

4. The question, perhaps, has something dubious about it. We remember that Lear too asked his daughters to declare to him the *quantity* of their love for him, with disastrous results.

5. See 2. 3. 33–38.

6. We are reminded of Falstaff's catechism of "honor" in *Henry IV, I,* 5. 1. 127–29.

7. See *Julius Caesar,* 4. 3. 218–24, and—to different ends—Prospero's speech in *The Tempest,* 1. 2. 180–84.

8. T. S. Eliot, *Burnt Norton,* I.

9. *Romeo and Juliet* also concerns two characters who die separately: but these deaths, though not coincident in time, unite the pair in a single place and involve them in a common emotion.

10. Some editions read "the dug" for "the dung," and this alternative can be defended.

11. See L. G. Salingar's interesting discussion of this passage in *A Guide to English Literature,* Vol. II (Harmondsworth, Middlesex: Penguin Books, 1955), pp. 98–101.

12. See T. S. Eliot's comment on the passage in his essay on *Dante,* reprinted in *Selected Essays* (London: Faber & Faber, 1932), p. 230.

13. See, for example, Sonnet 64.

14. That is why such pictures of "heaven" as that offered by Milton in Books III and IV of *Paradise Lost* are so uniformly uninspiring.

15. W. B. Yeats, "Nineteen Hundred and Nineteen."

Shakespeare's Dramatic Illusion in *The Tempest*

INTERPRETATIONS of *The Tempest* have long been influenced—one might almost say bedeviled—by the notion
of Shakespeare's "last play." Critics have tended to look for
and variously find to their satisfaction a final statement,
the summing-up of a lifetime's work and preoccupation.
The argument on which these conclusions are based is
perhaps something less than entirely convincing. It is far
from certain that *The Tempest* was Shakespeare's last play
or that after writing it he abandoned the stage completely
to return to Stratford. *Henry VIII* is likely to be his work,
either entirely or in collaboration with John Fletcher; and
there are reasons, plausible if not conclusive, to believe
that he may have had a hand in *The Two Noble Kinsmen.*[1]
Given these probabilities, it seems at least rash to assume
that the epilogue to *The Tempest* represents a consciously
final gesture of farewell on the part of the dramatist to his
audience and his art.

Yet when this has been said, it remains true that *The
Tempest* does seem to occupy a unique place in the body of
Shakespeare's work. *Henry VIII* was probably at least in
part his (after all, the editors of the First Folio evidently
believed this to be the case); but if so, there is a sense of
slackness, of released tension, which can hardly fail to
strike us after the taut and concentrated achievements of

The Winter's Tale and *The Tempest;*[2] and, whatever may be the truth concerning *The Two Noble Kinsmen* (which is a retelling of Chaucer's *Knight's Tale* of Palamon and Arcite), it is hard to believe that a considerable part of the play can be Shakespeare's work. What seems to emerge is a definite distancing on the author's part from his art, a conscious withdrawal and possibly a gradual handing-over to a successor; and if this is a true impression, the position of *The Tempest,* though less unequivocally final than has sometimes been assumed, retains its significance as Shakespeare's last fully committed dramatic statement.

Such finality as the play has may concern the author's mature reflection on the nature and limitation of the dramatic illusion. Prospero, far from being the all-powerful magician-philosopher often envisaged, can be seen as the creator of an action over which he exercises such control as he has with notable difficulty and stress. There is meaning, perhaps, in the fact that the plot of *The Tempest* seems to be—almost uniquely for Shakespeare—the dramatist's own invention. Its taut and economical concentration—the containment, again so unusual for Shakespeare, within strict limits of time and place—makes of the play a consciously finished dramatic artifact of a kind calculated to raise questions concerning the nature of the spectacle offered and of the kind of validity to be ascribed to the imaginative effort that brought it into being.

It should not be forgotten that the play is called *The Tempest* and that it opens with a storm at sea. As in other works by Shakespeare, the sea is associated with the larger forces of life, which men neither bring into being nor initiate but which—having once accepted them as given—they can aspire, within limits, to shape to ends of their own. The early scenes of *Twelfth Night,* which deal with the shipwreck that brings Viola to the coast of Illyria to initiate her search for her lost brother, come to mind in this connection. Viola, making her first appearance in the play immediately after we have heard Orsino's beautiful but self-absorbed meditation on his unrequited love and been told of Olivia's impossible determination to keep her brother's dead love "fresh/ And lasting in her sad remembrance" (*Twelfth Night* 1. 1. 32–33), hears the captain of her lost vessel stress the resourcefulness of her brother, who, "most provident in peril," bound himself "to a strong mast, that lived upon the sea" (1. 2. 14). Expressing her will to believe that her brother is not dead—"Perchance he is not drowned" (2. 5)—she shows herself ready to place her trust in her own resources, assuming the disguise that will take her through unexpected and sometimes disconcerting situations to fulfillment of a kind that neither she, nor we as spectators, can foresee for her but that emerges as the natural response to her commitment. It is the nature of Shakespearean comedy to build upon the element of the incongruous in every human life, to show its characters as taken out of and beyond themselves by the unpredictable processes of life, and to bring those of them who are ready to recognize this necessary aspect of their human condition to the happiness that their faith, and their readiness to accept the risk that it involves, has placed within their reach.

Some of these considerations apply to Prospero's action as *The Tempest* opens. The storm witnessed by Miranda and the object of her innocent concern has been a creation of his "art," indeed, but the coincidence with the voyage to Tunis of his former enemies is the work of "bountiful Fortune" (1. 2. 178), presenting him with an occasion that he can either turn to the ends of his creative art or forever relinquish:

> By my prescience
> I find my zenith doth depend upon
> A most auspicious star, whose influence
> If now I court not, but omit, my fortunes
> Will ever after droop.[3]

(1. 2. 180–84)

The relation to the dramatist's art seems clear. The materials of his action, including the characters whose stage lives he molds—or aspires to mold—into a consistent imaginative pattern, are in an important sense *given,* cast up on the shore of his predisposed awareness, to be used as his imagination dictates. The control exercised by a playwright over the characters he has brought into being is at best precarious and is likely to become more so when the art in question is as powerful as Shakespeare's. In such cases the characters and situations originally envisaged tend to assume an autonomous life of their own, which often threatens to break through the limits of the original conception. To the dramatist this danger presents itself as a challenge, in responding to which he affirms the creative power of his art. Coming together at an "auspicious" time when he is imaginatively disposed to receive them, the characters and situations present themselves, compellingly and disturbingly, for his action upon them to become the material for a play: material that he must be ready to grasp and shape to his ends before it is carried away on the tides of life and escapes his controlling action.

Prospero, then, rather than the "godlike" figure sometimes proposed, can be seen on this reading as the author of his own "play," taking up his "characters" and fitting them, for as long as his power over them lasts, into a pattern governed by laws of his own creation. What this implies, what is the relation of the pattern so created to what we may choose to call "reality," is a principal theme of the play. The island, on this view, is the stage on which the pattern is to be worked out. Like other locations of this kind in Shakespeare—one thinks of the Forest of Arden in *As You Like It,* which is less a "place" than the sum of a set of converging attitudes in the minds of the characters who are exposed to it and to whose words the evocation of it is entrusted—its presentation on a bare stage[4] allows for it to be seen under as many different aspects as there are eyes to behold it. To the benevolent Utopian eyes of Gonzalo, the island presents itself as the setting for an Arcadian anarchy founded on the spontaneous following of natural instinct: a community with "no sovereignty" where

> All things in common nature should produce
> Without sweat or endeavor.
>
> (2. 1. 154–55)

untainted by competition or the shadow of ambition. To the "realists" Sebastian and Antonio, on the other hand, the unreality of Gonzalo's dream is apparent. Where Gonzalo's fellow courtier Adrian sees "subtle, tender, and delicate temperance," air that breathes "most sweetly" (1. 42–47),[5] *they* see only the exhalation of "rotten lungs" and perceive only the total absence of "means to live" (1. 48–51). Their comments, "realistically" cynical in tone, are evidently the projection of their own preconceptions; but they do point to *real* problems. It seems that the sources of unhappiness and stress among men are to be excluded from the ideal, "unfallen" commonwealth imagined by Gonzalo; but with them will go most of the distinctive qualities by which, in the *real* world, men and women achieve the full measure of their civilized natures. The "ideal" society of Gonzalo's dream is founded upon a benevolent amorality that leaves place for every kind of "weed"—the "nettle-seed," "docks," and "mallows" (1. 140) of which the courtly cynics speak—to take possession of a "virgin" soil. The fact that men like Antonio and Sebastian exist goes to prove that *some* cultivation of the human terrain is necessary.[6] The state of "primitive" nature posited by Gonzalo's musings on an impossible restoration of the "golden age"[7]—the classical equivalent of the Garden of Eden, the lost paradise of Christian myth—is one that men and women must, in the reality of their "fallen" nature, outgrow to achieve some measure of their true, their distinctively human potentiality:[8] the problem is not whether this will happen—in the very nature of things, it *must*—but whether the development is to be toward "good" in the shape of some acceptable moral and human standard leading to the free development of human potentialities, or toward the anarchy of unlimited personal appetites.

At this point it is well to remember that when Prospero came to the island he found it inhabited: inhabited, very notably, by Caliban. Half man and half beast and—since Prospero's arrival—uneasily aware of being neither, Caliban represents an ultimate comment on Gonzalo's benevolent theorizings. His is the *real* state of nature, and in his relation to his new master—who, at the close, recognizes that "this thing of darkness" (5. 1. 275) is, even in an intimate sense, "his"—the connection between "nature" and the civil, moral state is expressly considered. Finding him on the island—he was there before Prospero and thinks of himself as its rightful inhabitant—Prospero used his power to attempt to incorporate him into the new, "civilized" order of moral realities: there are evidently echoes here of the kind of speculation developed by Montaigne in his essay *Des Cannibales* and of the contemporary controversies concerning the nature and justification of European colonization in the New World and of its relation to theories concerning the "noble savage" associated with such defenders of the indigenous inhabitants as the Spanish Dominican Bartolomé de las Casas.[9]

Caliban at once admits Prospero's "civilizing" intentions and turns his admission into a formidable indictment of the process that began by flattering him and finally became his tyrant:

> When thou cam'st first,
> Thou strok'st me and made much of me; would'st give me
> Water with berries in't; and teach me how
> To name the bigger light, and how the less,
> That burn by day and night; and then I loved thee
> And showed thee all the qualities o' th' isle,
> The fresh springs, brine-pits, barren place and fertile
> Cursed be I that did so! All the charms
> Of Sycorax—toads, beetles, bats, light on you!

For I am all the subjects that you have,
Which first was mine own king.

(1. 2. 332–42)

From this denunciation we may learn more than one important thing. In the first place, Caliban's poetry was given
him, at least in part, by Prospero. The instinctive appreciation was, if we will, his own, but the gift of expressing it,
essentially social and civilizing in kind, came to him from
his master. Indeed, it is not clear that the native gift can be
separated from, or is conceivable in the absence of, the
means to give it expression. Can there *be* poetry without
words to express it in or an audience to communicate it to?
This is the old question, to which Shakespeare in one form
or another insistently returns and to which he had only
recently addressed himself in the pastoral scene of *The
Winter's Tale:* man as the "artful" creature (in both senses
of the word) and art as the completion of nature, art as the
distinctive expression of human nature.

There is no suggestion in *The Tempest* that his possession
of "magic" power affords Prospero any simple or final
answer to the problems raised by his intrusion on the island. Caliban complains that he has been made a prisoner,
who was formerly "his own king." Given his point of view
he is clearly in the right; but equally, the very fact of Prospero's arrival introduced on the island a fresh reality from
which there could be no retreat, only a going forward—
difficult but indispensable—into a new balance. It is the
nature of "Utopias" to be "nowhere,"[10] to represent permanent human aspirations while remaining always unrealized. At the moment of realization they cease, fatally
and unavoidably, to be Utopias. Prospero's retort to Caliban's protest shows the problem in all its intractable nature:

I have used thee
(Filth as thou art) with humane care, and loged thee
In mine own cell till thou didst seek to violate

The honor of my child.

(2. 2. 345–48)

"Filth as thou art": the urgency of the phrase proceeds from one who is at least as much a deeply disturbed man facing an obstinately unmanageable situation as a benevolent "magician" in control of the threads of his contrivance. Caliban, whose services are indispensable to Prospero, whose animal nature is a true part of the human reality and as such is not to be pushed aside or submerged under abstract assertions of rational "spirituality," remains recalcitrant to all the considerations of moral discipline and societal restraint which that design was intended to further; and so, when he was given the measure of "liberty" that a "reasonable" conception of life requires and asked to accept incorporation into the new reality of life on the island, he used it to attack Prospero's dearest possession in the person of his daughter.

"Natural" anarchism, then, of the kind proposed by Gonzalo is evidently no answer to the new situation brought about by Prospero's contrivances and indeed by the very fact of his forced intrusion on the island scene. Nor, for that matter, is Caliban's desire to be "free" to return to his former condition. Meeting the newcomers Stephano and Trinculo and being disposed to see in these sorry specimens of a supposedly "civilized" order a means of freeing himself from bondage, he is seduced—when the new reality thrusts itself upon him—by the "celestial" liquor that Stephano offers him and expresses his willingness to serve the drunkard as a "god":

> That's a brave god and bears celestial liquor.
> I'll kneel to him.

(2. 2. 115–16)

There is a sad contrast, germane to the play's deeper intentions, between this sorry creature and the Caliban who, in the very act of leading his newfound associates against

Prospero, can at a later stage waste upon them his perception of the natural beauty of his island home:

> Be not afeard: the isle is full of noises,
> Sounds and sweet airs that give delight and hurt not.
> Sometimes a thousand twangling instruments
> Will hum about mine ears; and sometimes voices
> That, if I then had waked after long sleep,
> Will make me sleep again; and then, in dreaming,
> The clouds methought would open and show riches
> Ready to drop upon me, that, when I waked,
> I cried to dream again.
>
> (3. 2. 132–40)

The poignancy of the speech rests largely on the evocation of a "dream," on the bitterness of awakening, and—above all—on the impossibility of returning to it. Evidently Caliban has lost his paradise and mourns his inability to reenter it. All that remains in its place is the fierce, pathetic desire to free himself from the harsh service to which he finds himself subjected. "I'll bear no more sticks, and follow thee" (2. 2. 159), he says to Stephano, saluting him with a parody of worship—for the instinct to worship, however misdirected, is strong in him—as "thou wondrous man."[11] In the event, he goes out drunk, crying "Freedom, hey-day" (2. 181), to follow his new, bottle-bearing "god": reduced in reality to a servitude more degrading than any to which he had been previously subjected.

Such then is the situation on the island-stage as Prospero assembles his 'cast' of characters—composed of intruders from what we are to see, in terms of the play, as the "real" world—in order to subject them to the judging and reconciling action he has in mind. This will be accomplished through the agency of Ariel, who was also on the island when he arrived but for whom his coming represented, as it did not for Caliban, a liberation. Prospero's "play" is to have in Miranda a "spectator" for whose benefit it will be enacted: a "spectator" on the stage who will also, in the course of it, become herself an "agent" in her father's project. His first move, after rousing the storm, is to incorporate the past into the present by exploring for his daughter's benefit the events that have led to the present situation. The passage of time, which had been in *The Winter's Tale* an essential element in the action, even to the extent of being personified by an actor,[12] is now recalled from the vantage point of the present and in the process is rendered subsidiary to the reconciling purpose. As Prospero, in the course of his long opening exposition, penetrates for Miranda the veil that has so far shrouded from her knowledge "the dark backward and abysm of time" (1. 2. 50), he brings her to awareness of the knot of mingled motives that constitutes the behavior of human beings in society. As he says to her, in response to her compassionate reaction to the fate of the beings whom she has just seen exposed to the action of the elements on Alonso's foundering ship:

> There's no harm done. . . .
> No harm.
> I have done nothing but in care of thee,
> Of thee my dear one, thee my daughter, who
> Art ignorant of what thou art, nought knowing
> Of whence I am; nor that I am more better
> Than Prospero, master of a full poor cell,
> And thy no greater father.
>
> (1. 2. 16–22)

These words, almost the first spoken by Prospero, give us a lead into the intentions that have moved him to set up his "play." The stages by which Miranda is to be led to emerge into the world of "experience" from the "innocent" dream that has so far constituted her island life will correspond to the development that, by bringing together her father and his former enemies, aims at restoring them—or those of them who, when put to the test, will prove to be capable of "redemption"—to a full participation in civilized life. In this process Miranda herself, by her relation to Ferdinand, will have a central part. Dream and reality, sentimental idealization and mature judgment, are to be integrated—in accordance with Prospero's creative plan—into the successive stages of a harmonizing action.

The realization of this plan involves dealing with the reality of evil as the play conceives it. Remembering earlier plays, we are not surprised to find, as we follow Prospero's story of the events that led to his expulsion from Milan, that the evil which he is now ready to confront has two aspects—personal and social—that stand in close connection. By casting Prospero with his infant daughter on the open sea, Antonio transgressed both against the Duke of Milan and against his own brother. The terms of the transgression are familiar from previous plays. We recall Duke Senior and Duke Frederick from *As You Like It;* also, in another order, Edgar and Edmund in *King Lear.* By his action Antonio struck both at the foundations of social order concentrated, for Renaissance thought, upon the person of a ruler, and at the primary unity of the family: with the effect, in each case, of overthrowing what is assumed to be the positive, life-giving order of things. The two crimes are in fact one and represent that descent into chaos prompted by personal selfishness that is, in the Shakespearean outlook of the great plays, the supreme cause of tragedy. By living "retired" from the world—rather like Duke Vincentio before him in *Measure for Measure*[13]—and by delegating his authority to another, Prospero in some measure brought about his own exile; and only now, after exposure to the tempestuous seas and confinement to "a most desolate isle" (3. 3. 80), a place unsuited for human habitation, is he ready to assume with authority his vocation as judge and reconciler.

This vocation, however, will be exercised by Prospero not in the real world beyond the island but within the limits of his imaginative action. It is to pass "judgment" as a prelude to reconciliation that he has assembled his cast of characters: the event will show whether, and if so, to what extent this particular action is viable. Once there the vari-

ous characters in his play are to be confronted, through
the operations of Ariel at the author's bidding, with the
reality of their respective responsibilities. It is interesting
to note that Ariel is another original inhabitant of the island, found there by Prospero and held by him under a
certain rigidity of control. His first appearance in the play
(1. 2. 242ff.) shows him "moody," resentful in the delay at
granting him the "liberty" he has been promised; and his
master is not backward in reminding him of the "torment"
to which he was subjected by the witch Sycorax and in
threatening him, not without a certain insistence (2. 294–
96), with a return to his former imprisonment. It seems
that the execution of Prospero's purposes involves an element of constraint, the subjection of the free-ranging
imagination, for the length of time that the creation of the
dramatic illusion requires and during which it has to be
held together, to the strict necessities of his art. To bring
the pattern into being and to affirm its permanence
against the tendency of all human efforts to fall apart, to
dissolve into the surrounding chaos, is to accept the existence of necessary boundaries and to impose upon what
naturally aspires to be "free," unlimited and unrestricted,
the "order" that can only be a product of accepted limitation. At the last (5. 1. 316–18), Ariel is granted the freedom he has craved from the start; but this can only be
granted him when Prospero's project has been completed
and at the price, which sooner or later imposes itself upon
every artistic creation, of recognizing the element of im-
permanence involved in the making of this illusion and of
renouncing the "enchantment" of his contrivance.

The responsibilities of the characters so assembled turn
out to be various in degree and kind. Alonso, king of Na-
ples, comes out of the test positively. Having, as he be-
lieves, lost his son in retribution for his earlier "sin," he
refuses to accept comfort; the inconsolable quality of his
grief shows him to be morally sensitive and so to be capable of receiving what is here, as in so many other Shake-

spearean actions, the healing visitation of sleep. Antonio and Sebastian, on the other hand, remain obstinately and unabashedly awake:

> SEBASTIAN: I find not
>   Myself disposed to sleep.
> ANTONIO: Nor I: my spirits are nimble.
>   (2. 4. 195–96)

Cynics of the familiar Shakespearean type, they—and especially Antonio—pride themselves, with the unprejudiced "modernity" of vision that reflects their possession of Machiavellian *virtú*, on the dispassionate exercise of reason.

Taken in itself, the cynicism displayed by Antonio and Sebastian in their comments on Gonzalo's "Utopian" dream does not seem of great moment. It may even be a salutory comment on the element of unreality that the dream fostered. It becomes, however, the prelude to greater crimes. As soon as Alonso succumbs to his inclination to sleep, Prospero's "nimble"-spirited enemy feels himself once more moved by the desire for power:

>   methinks I see it in thy face,
> What thou shouldst be. Th' occasion speaks thee, and
> My strong imagination sees a crown
> Dropping upon thy head.
>   (2. 1. 200–203)

This strikes a note familiar in earlier plays. Lady Macbeth, after crowning her husband in her thoughts, played in the murder of Duncan very much the part played by Antonio in the plot to dispose of Alonso. His motive, like that of Iago and Edmund, is a peculiarly self-sufficient conception of fortune:

>   Noble Sebastian,
> Thou let'st thy fortune sleep—die, rather; wink'st
> Whiles thou art waking.
>   (1. 209–11)

The new twist thus given to the prevailing sleep image is deeply characteristic of the speaker. To act is to be awake, to seize the chance for self-assertion that fortune has offered; to hesitate when the opportunity presents itself is to "wink," to sleep beneath the appearance of watchfulness. This is the "philosophy" that formerly led Antonio to play the chief part in his brother's banishment and that now, energetically communicated to Sebastian, leads his weaker associate to contemplate a similar betrayal of Alonso.

The nature of Antonio's domination over Sebastian is most clearly revealed in his reply to the latter's tentative expression of doubt: "But for your conscience?" The very word, as indicating any reality, is meaningless to him:

> Ay, sir, where lies that? If 'twere a kibe,
> 'Twould put me to my slipper; but I feel not
> This deity in my bosom. Twenty consciences
> That stand 'twixt me and Milan, candied be they
> And melt, ere they molest!
>
> (2. 1. 270–74)

The opening image, with its comparison of conscience to a purely physical inconvenience, is pure Iago. So is the sneering reference to "deity," a word that can mean nothing to Antonio but a sentimental illusion intervening between a man and the furthering of those selfish ends in which alone he feels his manhood. The rejection of sentimental unreality is driven home by the reference, common in Shakespeare and everywhere expressive of loathing, to "candied" and "melt":[14] the stomach of the practical man of action is turned by these finicky attempts to restrict his progress. The speech continues in the same strain:

> Here lies your brother,
> No better than the earth he lies upon,
> If he were that which now he's like—that's dead;
> Whom I, with this obedient steel (three inches of it)
> Can lay to bed for ever; whiles you, doing thus,
> To the perpetual wink for aye might put

This ancient morsel, this Sir Prudence, who
Should not upbraid our course. For all the rest,
They'll take suggestion as a cat laps milk;
They'll tell the clock to any business that
We say befits the hour.

                                        (1. 274–84)

Antonio's words are the reflection of an intense destructive energy, to which the intelligence is bound in faithful service. Behind them lies a deep-seated pessimism, the conviction that a dead man is "no better than the earth he lies upon" and that only three inches of "obedient" steel lie between his victim and extinction. If conscience is no more than a "kibe," an inconvenient "deity" that a moment's reasoning can put to "sleep," then the murder of a man who stands between him and power is the most natural thing in the world: so natural that he can discuss that man's death in terms of putting him "to bed for ever." As for Gonzalo and those who still feel conscience as a living thing, they are brushed aside in the contemptuous "ancient morsel," "Sir Prudence," and in the brilliant, scornful comparison implicit in "They'll take suggestion as a cat laps milk." The whole thing, given the will, the determination to act, is simplicity itself.

It is important, perhaps, to grasp exactly what is involved at this point: important for an understanding not only of *The Tempest*, but of the entire body of Shakespeare's work. No one should be tempted to neglect the plausibility, even the attractiveness, of the great "villains" in the plays. Richard III, the first of them and in a sense the origin of them all, stands out in his play as witty, intelligent, and consistently entertaining; qualities that do not prevent him from eliminating not only an ineffective king who stands between him and the crown, but all the variously selfish, brutish, and stupid rivals who bar his progress toward his goal. Iago, however mysteriously malevolent he may stand revealed at the end of *Othello*, is universally, even obsessively perceived as "honest." In appearance he is—we may reasonably think—more like "every man" in the unassuming garb of a noncommissioned officer than the "devil" whose cloven hooves his victim finally—but only finally—thinks he perceives.[15] Perhaps, indeed, to be like "every man," to harbor within himself in a state of "chemical purity" the desire—which exists, however unrecognized, in each one of us—to see superior things brought down to our own level and destroyed in the process, is an important part of the "devil's" nature. Edmund in *King Lear* builds his actions on a reasonable "philosophy" of "nature," thoroughly "modern" and unprejudiced, free of the astrological superstitions harbored by his old-fashioned and initially cynical parent.[16] If we had heard Edmund—so fashionable, well-presented, and "proper," in spite of his bastardizing—giving witty expression to these "with it" opinions at a social gathering, we might have seen in him a personable young man, well-informed, open-minded, attractively amusing—only to be shocked later to learn that these pleasing qualities bore fruit in the exile of his brother, his father's blinding, and the hanging of Cordelia. Antonio, belonging to a different kind of play, is by comparison less of a "character," more of a mouthpiece for the philosophy, the attitude to life, on which the actions of all of them are based: but his comments and actions, which express what most men in some measure and at certain times have been capable of thinking, represent a challenge to Prospero's purposes, which it remains to be seen if he can succeed in subduing to his design.

Such then is the material—much of it evidently refractory, barely answerable to his purpose—that Prospero proposes to weave into the pattern of his "play." How successful he will be remains uncertain and is a fact that need not surprise us if we recall certain precedents from earlier comedies. Shylock, in *The Merchant of Venice,* was initially conceived, no doubt, on conventional lines, as the outcast from society, the usurer, the enemy of Christian "truth," whose expected and merited discomfiture would constitute "the dram of evil"[17] required in a comedy and lead to the triumphant vindication of comic harmonies by Portia and Bassanio in the "poetic" world of Belmont and merchant adventure on the Rialto. That is no more than the audience would have expected and that is what at the end of the play they finally got; but Shylock's presence and his departure from the action surely tinge with uneasiness our intelligent acceptance of the resolution. Similarly, Malvolio at the end of *Twelfth Night* rejects the offered reconciliation and goes out, a prisoner of his own invincible self-image, crying "I'll be revenged on the whole pack of you!"[18]

These observations seem to throw light, not only on Shakespeare's conceptions but on the operation of the greatest art, one of the effects of which is—as a later poet has put it—to rouse us to "a new and shocking valuation/ Of all that we have been."[19] The characters and situations envisaged by a great writer are liable, in the process of their development, to move beyond the original intention of their creator, assuming a life of their own beyond that initially projected; and, if the writer is as great as Shakespeare, he is liable to allow them to follow the laws of their own being even at the risk of imperiling the symmetry of his original purpose. Only God—one supposes—can be thought of as in complete control of his creation, and Prospero, in spite of what has at times been said of him, has no claim to be God. The action of *The Tempest* confirms this precarious reality. By the time we have reached the central turning point of the action, two plots—one contrived by Antonio with the connivance of Sebastian against Alonso, and a second planned, as a kind of grotesque parody upon it, by Stephano, Trinculo, and Caliban against Prospero himself—have been launched, and the original seclusion of the island has been most effectively shattered. That is how it must be: no man is an island to himself or can realistically aspire to live in isolated suspension from the pressure of real, time-conditioned existence.

Prospero, however—who is, let us again remember, in the position of a playwright aspiring to control his action—

proposes to draw its threads to a harmonizing conclusion. At a central point in his contrivance, with his cast assembled for the purpose, he puts into the mouth of an Ariel disconcertingly transformed into the threatening guise of a harpy a speech, addressed to them all, which is intended to mark a turning point in the development:

> You are three men of sin, whom destiny—
> That hath to instrument this lower world
> And what is in't—the never-surfeited sea
> Hath caused to belch up you, and on this island,
> Where man doth not inhabit, you 'mongst men
> Being most unfit to live, . . .
> But remember
> (For that's my business to you) that you three
> From Milan did supplant good Prospero;
> Exposed unto the sea, which hath requit it,
> Him and his innocent child; for which foul deed
> The pow'rs, delaying, not forgetting, have
> Incensed the seas and shores, yea, all the creatures,
> Against your peace. Thee of thy son, Alonso,
> They have bereft; and do pronounce by me
> Ling'ring perdition (worse than any death
> Can be at once) shall step by step attend
> You and your ways; whose wraths to guard you from,
> Which here, in this most desolate isle, else falls
> Upon your heads, is nothing but heart's sorrow
> And a clear life ensuing.
>
> (3. 3. 53–58; 68–82)

Here, if anywhere, is the heart of the "play" that Prospero has brought into being on his island stage and to which he now proposes a resolution. Ariel addresses the characters assembled round the shadow of a banquet, which is at once removed from them because they are not yet worthy to partake of what is here, as elsewhere in Shakespeare,[20] a "sacrament" of sociability, of restored and restoring concord. He appears to them in a sinister, even a monstruous form, remote from his usual "gentle" appearance, perhaps to answer to the distorted aspect under which "justice" appears to the unreconciled and the unrepentant. "I and my fellows," he says, "are ministers of Fate." The implication is that the events we are witnessing—which, we remember yet again, constitute a "play," a proposed pattern of reconciliation—have a dimension that can be called "providential," a meaning in relation to some conception of justice conceived as operative and valid.

This insertion into the action of a "providential" dimension raises problems that are fundamental, not only for *The Tempest* but for our understanding of Shakespeare's art. Much of the symbolism increasingly displayed in his later works—in *The Winter's Tale,* for example—has "providential" undertones in which we shall not, if we are wise, seek to find evidence for directly personal conviction of whatever kind; but nowhere is destiny so directly asserted or conceded so much power (in terms of the "play") in the working out of human affairs. "Destiny," affirms Ariel, "hath to instrument this lower world." There *is*—he seems to be saying—a plan, a purpose to be discerned in things. Something *is* indeed working itself out—through the agency of the sea, which originally brought the cast of Prospero's action together at an appropriate time on the island stage—to a conclusion that we can think of, if we so choose, as "purposeful." "Delaying, not forgetting," this Destiny, like some more omniscient playwright, watches over the whole action to bring the characters concerned in it to judgment. For this end, the various actors—objects, as we have seen, of a favorable imaginative conjunction—have been brought together on "this most desolate isle," "where man doth not inhabit." "Desolate," surely, because the work of purgation to be accomplished implies a certain asceticism; but "desolate" also because it is not a place where men are to live fully human lives—after the final reconciliation it will be left by all save those whose attitudes debar them from playing their part in the "brave new world" (5. 1. 183), at once social and spiritualized, to which the fulfillment of their nature calls them—but one on which they may achieve a measure of understanding in the process of accepting the "judgment" passed upon them. Like other similar *loca* in Shakespeare—places as different as the Forest of Arden in *As You Like It* and the storm-battered heath of *King Lear*—the island is less a defined locality than the sum of a series of converging or contrasted attitudes adopted toward it by the various characters. It serves both to bring them together and to confront them with the measure of their respective responsibilities. For it is in the nature of uncontrolled self-affirmation, as the great tragedies have variously shown it, to lead to self-destruction; and Prospero's action, with its insistence upon the need for repentance and amendment, is conceived by him as nothing less than a counterpoise to this tragic process of ruin.

The last stage of the play can be seen as bringing this process to its conclusion in the act of questioning, or at least qualifying, its final validity. With Ferdinand and Miranda united under the eye of Prospero—it is significant that they are "discovered" at their game of chess by his drawing of a curtain, making of the "discovery," as it were, an action within an action, further distanced from the main proceedings on stage—Alonso and his companions are ready to be drawn into the final, harmonizing pattern. In preparation for their incorporation, they have already entered, spellbound, to be restored to the full use of their human, daylight reason. To the notes of music (always, in later Shakespeare, expressive of harmony attained), Prospero's cast of characters is restored to what his "action" conceives as the true sense of their human lives:

> The charm dissolves apace;
> And as the morning steals upon the night,
> Melting the darkness, so do their rising senses
> Begin to chase the ignorant fumes that mantle
> Their clearer reason. . . .
>   Their understanding
> Begins to swell, and the approaching tide

> Will shortly fill the reasonable shore,
> That now lies foul and muddy.
>
> (5. 1. 64–68; 79–82)

These lines convey, we may feel, something very like the resolution that Prospero had in mind in setting his "action" in motion. The entry, thus envisaged, into a new or restored life is symbolized in the final stages by a typically Shakespearean coincidence of blessing and forgiveness, the gesture by which fathers and children, separated by time and the results of passion, are restored to an awareness of their unifying and life-giving "bond."

Once again, this action has many antecedents in Shakespeare's later plays in which it tends to assume the force of a central and healing symbol. Cordelia, restored to Lear after an almost intolerable separation, asks her father as he awakes from a restoring sleep to "hold your hands in benediction o'er me" (*King Lear* 4. 7. 58), and tells him, in anticipation of his answering gesture of reparation, that he "must not kneel": and Lear, a little later, accepting the prospect of an imprisonment imposed upon him by a world that is for him no longer tangible or real, says to the daughter whom he has found again:

> When thou dost ask me blessing, I'll kneel down
> And ask of thee forgiveness.
>
> (5. 1. 10–11)

Similarly Pericles, restored to Marina, from whom he has been separated by actions of sin and by the process of time, breaks his self-imposed silence to welcome her to his arms in restoration of the most intimate of bonds:

> O, come hither,
> Thou that begetst him that did thee beget.
>
> (*Pericles* 5. 3. 76–77)

When, as the play closes, he is further recognized by the wife whom he believed lost:

O, my lord,
Are you not Pericles? Like him you spake;
Like him you are. Did you not name a tempest,
A birth, and death?

(5. 3. 30–33)

his greeting brings together loss and recovery, birth and
death,[21] as it leads to his daughter's rapt gesture of incorporation into the living unity she believed to be forever
lost:

MARINA: My heart
           Leaps to be gone into my mother's bosom.
                            (Kneels to Thaisa)
PERICLES: Look who kneels here! Flesh of thy flesh,
           Thaisa!
           Thy burden at the sea, and call'd Marina
           For she was yielded there.

(5. 3. 43–47)

Similarly, in *The Winter's Tale,* "our Perdita," "found"
again, is exhorted by the faithful Paulina to "kneel/ And
pray your mother's blessing" (5. 3. 119–20), and receives
from a parent "miraculously" restored to life a prayer addressed to the play's gods invoking the gift of their graces
upon her daughter's head.

With these parallels in mind, the sense of a similar conclusion in *The Tempest* falls naturally into place. Ferdinand
kneels to receive his father's blessing and is joined to
Miranda. In her father's presence, in the words of Alonso,
and in her rapt comment as she contemplates the prospect
of entry into a new life, the intuition of a reconciled, "redeemed" state is given full expression:

ALONSO: Now all the blessings
           Of a glad father compass thee about! . . .
MIRANDA: O, wonder!
           How many goodly creatures are there here!
           How beauteous mankind is! O brave new
           world

That has such people in't!

(5. 1. 180–85)

Although her father is quick to qualify his daughter's enthusiasm—as he has tended to do throughout—with the detachment of his comment," 'Tis new to thee," the sense of this is apparent. The vision of a new humanity, glimpsed by Miranda in her intuitive innocence at the outset[22] and now deepened to our understanding by the trials to which Prospero has put her, reaches at this point its full expression. This is the world of *wonder* with which Shakespearean comedy has been so consistently concerned:[23] a world endowed with the sense of life at each moment potentially new in its offered possibilities, surprising and evocative beyond the greatest mortal expectations. To live, in terms of these plays, is to be capable of wonder, receptive to each moment of experience as new, unpredictable, and transforming. Entry into this world depends upon the gift of that special grace with which these late plays are so amply penetrated and which the characters of Prospero's play are now offered. Moved by this awareness, Ferdinand responds to his father's gesture by recognizing that a bride has been given him by a design of "immortal providence" (5. 1. 189) and that he has received from his new father-in-law nothing less than a "second life" (1. 195), restored and graciously enhanced.

In that life those of his fellows who have shown openness to life, a receptive disposition in its regard, naturally participate. As the children are finally joined, the two fathers are also brought together in the familiar Shakespearean fashion, Alonso craving pardon for past sin and Prospero granting forgiveness, both under the blessing of a divine grace:

ALONSO: O, how oddly will it sound that I
            Must ask my child forgiveness!
PROSPERO: There, sir, stop.
            Let us not burden our remembrance with

A heaviness that's gone.

GONZALO: I have inly wept,
Or should have spoke ere this. Look down,
    you gods,
And on this couple drop a blessed crown!
For it is you that have chalked forth the
    way
Which brought us hither.

                                        (1. 197–204)

In the light of previous plays once more, this is not hard to interpret. Alonso, like Lear and like Leontes in *The Winter's Tale,* has come through repentance—by which, in Shakespeare, is implied an understanding of what is humanly *real*—to see his errors, recognizing them as part of his humanity, and to be ready to ask his own child forgiveness. Prospero too has been taught by his "nobler reason," affirmed against his equally human "fury," to understand that

                    The rare action is
    In virtue than in vengeance.

                                        (1. 28–29)

Fortified by this awareness, he is ready to indicate that the time has come to throw off the burden of past memories, including that of the "high wrongs" (1. 25) to which he has been subjected, and to look forward to a harmony that long and often bitter experience has gained for all his characters and, as he may hope, for himself.

Responding to this development, the faithful Gonzalo invokes the gods to "crown" this newborn vision with a symbol of royalty: the gods—who, or whatever they may be, for we must surely refrain from tying them too closely to any specific set of beliefs—who, acting through Prospero, have unwound the plot and brought it to a harmonious conclusion. The "crown" bestowed is a sign of the "second," the redeemed and "reasonable" life that has been given to the characters through their experiences on the island:

> in one voyage
> Did Claribel her husband find at Tunis,
> And Ferdinand her brother found a wife
> Where he himself was lost; Prospero his dukedom
> In a poor isle; and all of us ourselves
> When no man was his own.
>
> (1. 208–13)

The words so spoken evidently carry a level of meaning beyond that which plot summary requires. At this point, the entire action—the loss no less than the finding, the separations no less than the reunions—has grown into a closely woven texture of mutually supporting elements in which the substance of Prospero's "dramatic" intention is movingly conveyed.

Germane as it surely is, however, this cannot be the last word. Prospero's "play" need not coincide at every point with Shakespeare's. As though to underline the element of illusion in his contriving, and almost immediately after Ariel's speech of judgment, he brings into being an explicitly dramatic entertainment—an action, as it were, within an action—summoning into being out of "thin air" a set of vaguely classical deities to celebrate the betrothal of Ferdinand and Miranda in appropriate terms of life, gracious fertility, and harvest fulfillment. It is not, by the standards to which Shakespeare has accustomed us, a very impressive "play," and the elaborate, somewhat painstaking verse in which it is conveyed stands out, as it was surely intended to do, from the ease and fluency of what surrounds it. The point, however, lies principally in what follows. As soon as the "masque" has ended, to what the stage direction calls "a strange, hollow, and confused noise" (in other words, to sounds that suggest in some degree the sinister and the unforeseen), and after the actors have "heavily vanished," the real world (as the play conceives it) returns to possess Prospero's thoughts with an unmistakable urgency:

> I had forgot that foul conspiracy
> Of the beast Caliban and his confederates
> Against my life.
>
> (4. 1. 139–41)

He has, indeed, good reason to be preoccupied. Stephano and Trinculo may not be very formidable enemies, but Caliban—who is not to be deflected from his purpose by the sight of trumpery garments on a clothesline (1. 223)—has every intention of driving a large nail through his skull. In any event, the recall to actuality moves Prospero to a deep uneasiness, which is not lost upon those around him. Ferdinand refers to "some passion" that moves him "strongly," and Miranda comments that

> .   Never till this day
> Saw I him touched with anger so distempered.
>
> (1. 144–45)

This is the Prospero who, far from being a benevolent magician with semi-divine attributes, has expressed himself repeatedly as an impatient, even testy old man grappling with the problems represented by Caliban, exercising over Ariel an uneasy control that borders at times on tyranny, and moved to lecture incautious youth on the need to keep its natural passions under strict, even harsh constraint.[24]

What follows are the words on the "insubstantial pageant" that every one remembers but that not everyone perhaps has read in their context. We are to keep in mind that the "spirits" that have "melted" into "thin air" are Prospero's "actors" and that "this insubstantial pageant faded" is—whatever else it may turn out to be—in the first instance the spectacle he has just brought into being and the validity of which, as an imaginative projection of the "real," he is now, however obscurely, being moved to question. Beyond this, the words, far from being uttered in Olympian detachment as an impressive statement of the *Vida es Sueño* theme,[25] reflect the anxious mood of an aging man burdened with the weight of his responsibility,[26] conscious of the limitations of his "magic" in the face of the mysterious and always ungraspable "reality" that so insistently breaks into and dissolves the imaginative harmonies it has brought so painstakingly into being. The last words of the speech are loaded with a sense of emotional burden:

> Sir, I am vexed.
> Bear with my weakness: my old brain is troubled.
> Be not disturbed with my infirmity.
> If you be pleased, retire into my cell
> And there repose. A turn or two I'll walk
> To still my beating mind.
>
> (4. 1. 158–63)

What, we may well ask, is happening at this point? How is the actor who is embodying the role on stage to convey his sense of Prospero's meaning? It is, of course, impossible to be sure, easy to project into the words elements of our own creation; but the answer may be something like this. Perhaps Shakespeare, in the person of his creation, is asking himself, and asking us to consider with him, certain questions concerning the nature and the limitations of the dramatic illusion, with particular reference to the drama of fulfillment and reconciliation that is being enacted on the stage. As he reflects on these matters, still through the person of Prospero, he makes his character consider the action that he has brought into being—both the "masque" within the play, which is Prospero's immediate concern, and the entire process to which it belongs—and, as a result, raise certain questions.

They are questions, we may think, with which Shakespeare's dramatic life has in one form or another been consistently engaged. What part does the creative imagination play in the lives of men and women? To what extent do its creations correspond to what we may call, perhaps begging a large question, "reality"? And is this "reality" something brought into being by the strength of our imaginative commitment or something that can be said— but again in what sense?—to be really, "objectively" (as we so inadequately say) *there?* Shakespeare, in other words, is—if there is any truth in this argument—looking back on a lifetime dedicated to the writing of plays and confronting his achievement, asking himself what this effort may finally *mean.* Man, he may be saying, is distinguished from the rest of the creation by the ability and the need to give a shape to his sense of his existence, to project it into formal patterns expressive of his sense of fitness, of what we call "beauty." By so doing, he is giving expression to the human need to feel that the patterns so created answer to something *real* in the nature of things, that life *has* a shape, a form that we may be unable to perceive—or, if we do perceive it, to hold—in any adequate or lasting way, but that we are compelled to think of as *true,* as corresponding in some measure to the nature of things.

It ought to be stressed, in any event, that these considerations are advanced as questions and are not offered in any way as answers. Perhaps what the play finally "says"—if the inadequate and even misleading word may be forgiven, for strictly speaking, a play "says" nothing that can be abstracted as a "message" to the audience: a play *is* what it "says" and "says" what it is—is that man is a creature who has the faculty and feels the need to ask questions; that the questions he asks are such as to provoke necessarily provisional answers, and that each answer leads of its very nature, to further questions. A question leads to an answer, which in turn raises two more questions: these lead again to two answers and four questions and so on without a possible end, in time, to the process. This perhaps is not a depressing conclusion but is simply rather a recognition of what it means to be human. At the end of the play, Prospero, having set aside his "magic," is about to return to Milan, to the "real" world—as Shakespeare's comedies invariably conceive it—of human interaction and human responsibility. He is returning, however, not so much, it seems, to exercise benevolent rule there—this may be the task that shortly will fall to a younger generation—or even to indulge in intellectual speculation of the kind that in earlier life led to his deposition, so much as to consider the prospect of his own human end: "Every third thought shall be my grave" (5. 1. 302).

Even at this point we can hardly fail to feel that the reconciling action that he proposed to himself in setting up his "play" has certain limits. Already in earlier comedies we have come to expect that someone is going to be left out or at least remain marginal when the moment comes to round off the comic pattern in a dance of married harmonies. Jaques, in *As You Like It,* expresses himself as being "for other than for dancing measures" (5. 4. 186–87), and Malvolio leaves *Twelfth Night* crying out his determination to seek revenge for what he sees as the indignities so unjustly heaped upon him (5. 1. 367). Now Prospero's reconciling mood does not seem to extend very far towards the brother who remains very much what he has always been, notably unresponsive, and whom he addresses for the last time in terms of no very noticeable benevolence:

> you, most wicked sir, whom to call brother
> Would even infect my mouth.
>
> (5. 1. 130–31)

Not surely a very reconciling or brotherly comment, but one that we need to incorporate as best we may into our sense of what has been achieved in this final stage of the play.

In all this, and in the closing Epilogue in which Prospero, stepping forward on the now-empty stage to address his last word to the spectators, seems to be recognizing that the dramatic illusion is the product of a marriage between an author's creative imagination and the response of each member of the audience, the implication seems to be that a play has *no* single meaning of the kind that can be abstracted from the action or proposed for approval or dissent in terms of its final and exclusive validity. In other words, what we are left with is *As You Like It, Twelfth Night, or What You Will,* or even perhaps *Much Ado about Nothing.* The possibility involved in these earlier titles has at least to be considered in relation to this later effort. It does not necessarily point to cynicism or even to a destructive degree of skepticism. The effort was worth making, if only because it was required of the author by his deepest sense of his humanity, but having made it and imparted to his audience in the theater the satisfaction that comes from a pattern consistently followed through to its conclusion, it may be as well to recognize that it partakes of the incomplete and provisional nature of all that is human.

The last word, accordingly, seems to rest with a refusal to push affirmation beyond the limits that experience imposes. It may be that in Ariel's great speech affirming Destiny something was said that differs, by its firmness of assertion and gravity of emphasis, from anything previously stated or implied in the dramatist's work. It may be that Shakespeare has chosen at this point to raise more explicitly than elsewhere the question of the reality, the "truth," of that conception of a destinal order to which so much in his earlier writing seems to posit, but which he is invariably careful not to affirm as "real" outside the order of dramatic fiction. If this is so, the question raised is *not* followed in the play by a categorical answer. The important thing, perhaps, in this connection is what Shakespeare chose *not* to do. He did not go on to write his personal version of a morality play, though certain plays already written—*Macbeth,* perhaps, and to a very different end, the unfinished experiment, as it may have been, of *Timon of Athens*—seem to point somewhat in that direction: nor did he conceive the English equivalent of an *Autosacramental* of the kind written fifty years later and in the context of a very different tradition by Calderón de la Barca. He chose to do neither of these things and chose, no doubt, for what are likely to have seemed to him good reasons. It may be that he finally refused to contemplate or to accept as true to his experience, the kind of play that the affirmative statements in Ariel's speech, taken to be literally true, might have implied: that he chose, in the last resort, to remain true to a vision that has indeed its "wonders," but wonders humanly conceived and sharing in the limitation of all that is human. For in the words spoken by Theseus at the end of *A Midsummer Night's Dream* in relation to another and even more "human" entertainment: "The best in this kind are but shadows; and the worst are no worse, if imagination amend them" (5. 1. 209–10).

NOTES

1. The argument in favor of Shakespeare's authorship has been most fully stated by Paul Bertram in *Shakespeare and "The Two Noble Kinsmen"* (1965). Most scholars have been unwilling to accept in its entirety the position there advanced.

2. For a contrary view of *Henry VIII,* see G. Wilson Knight's *The Crown of Life* (Oxford: Clarendon Press: 1947), where great importance is attached to the play in the author's interpretation of the Shakespearean pattern.

3. For the statement of a similar idea in *Julius Caesar,* see Brutus's speech at 4. 3. 218–24.

4. Shakespeare is in fact likely to have written the play for the theater at Blackfriars, which offered less of a "bare stage" than the Globe; but the habit of the "bare stage" persists and conditions the dramatist's sense of his art.

5. Gonzalo's words remind us of the exchange between Duncan and Banquo as they pause on the threshold of Macbeth's castle at Inverness (*Macbeth* 1. 6. 1–10).

6. For similar issues approached from a rather different point of view, see the dialogue between Perdita and Polixenes on the process of "grafting" in *The Winter's Tale* 4. 4. 85–103.

7. For an eloquent statement of the "golden age" theme, see *Don Quijote* 1. 11.

8. Once again, it is useful to turn to *The Winter's Tale* and compare the speech of Polixenes on his boyhood friendship with Leontes (1. 2. 62–75).

9. The numerous polemical works of Las Casas (1474–1560) in defense of the indigenous populations of the New World greatly influenced attempts, largely ineffectual, by the Spanish authorities to regulate the conduct of the European explorers. They were widely read in Europe and contributed to "ideal" literary interpretations of the life of the peoples discussed.

10. This idea is reflected in the title that Samuel Butler gave to his novel *Erewhon.*

11. Caliban's use of the word can be seen as bearing on its repeated use by Miranda to describe her "innocent" sense of the newcomers on her island home. See 1. 2. 6–7 and 5. 1. 181–84.

12. *The Winter's Tale* 4. 1.

13. *Measure for Measure* 1. 3. 19–39.

14. For use of these same words in close conjunction see *Antony and Cleopatra* 4. 10. 20–23.

15. *Othello* 5. 2. 286.

16. Edmund declares his "philosophy" in his opening soliloquy at 1. 2. 1–22, the first words of which are an appeal to Nature as his goddess.

17. *Hamlet* 1. 4. 36.

18. *Twelfth Night* 5. 1. 367.

19. T. S. Eliot, *East Coker,* II.

20. Compare, for example, the banquet in the Forest of Arden interrupted by Orlando (*As You Like It,* 2. 7) and the contrast, in *Macbeth,* between the reports of Duncan presiding over his feast of generosity at Inverness on the night of his murder (1. 1.; 2. 1) and Macbeth's failure as king to take his place at the head of his own table in the company of his thanes (3. 4).

21.

> O, come, be buried
> A second time within these arms!
>
> (*Pericles* 5. 3. 43–44)

22. See note 11 above.

23. For an expression of the sense of "wonder" as an important element in Shakespearean comedy, see Sebastian's speech in *Twelfth Night* 4. 1. 1–4.

24. Compare 4. 1. 14–23.

25. Calderon's most famous play can be dated to 1634 or 1635.

26. There is, of course, no intention of implying here any parallel of a "biographical" nature with unknown circumstances in Shakespeare's life.

Index